In The Three Sisters Garden

Written by
JoAnne Dennee
with
Jack Peduzzi and Julia Hand

Illustrated by
Carolyn Peduzzi

KENDALL/HUNT PUBLISHING COMPANY
4050 Westmark Drive Dubuque, Iowa 52002

Authors: JoAnne Dennee with Jack Peduzzi and Julia Hand

Editor: Jack Peduzzi

Illustrator: Carolyn Peduzzi

Book Design: Carolyn Peduzzi

Many of the designations used by manufacturers and sellers to distinguish their products are claimed as trademarks. Where those designations appear in this book and Food Works was aware of a trademark claim, the designations have been printed in initial capital letters.

Neither the Publisher nor the Author shall be liable for any damage or injury which may be caused or sustained as a result of the conduct of any of the activities in this book, from not specifically following instructions or conducting the activities without proper supervision, or from ignoring the cautions contained in the text.

We are grateful to the following people for their permission to reprint or adapt their work: pg. 178, "Deep Deep", author unknown, from *Children's Songs for a Friendly Planet* by Evelyn Weiss, Children's Creative Response to Conflict Resolution, Nyach, NY, © 1986; pg. 46, illustration, Carolyn Peduzzi; all other stories, poems and songs are original work of the authors or Native American legends retold through the oral tradition.

Food Works at Two Rivers Center
64 Main Street
Montpelier, VT 05602
(802) 223-1515
E-mail: info@tworiverscenter.org
Web: www.tworiverscenter.org

Library of Congress Catalog Card Number: 96-77315

ISBN 0-7872-2175-9

Printed in Canada
10 9 8 7 6 5 4 3 2

Printed on recycled paper

Common Roots
A Framework For Integrated Living Curriculum
Social Studies
creative arts
language arts
math
gardening
Community Service
health \ nutrition
Science \ ecology

In The Three Sisters Garden

TABLE OF CONTENTS

Journey One: First Farmers and Gardeners

Fall ❧

Winter ❧

Spring ❧

Summer ❧

Journey Two: Farmers and Gardeners of the Longhouse

Fall ❧

Winter ❧

Spring ❧

Summer ❧

Preface

For us at Food Works, and for literally hundreds of children, teachers, parents and community members, this Common Roots™ Guidebook represents far more than a collection of hands-on environmental activities for the young learner. For all of us, this Guide is a roadmap for placing schools back at the center of communities - by providing students with opportunities to address critical concerns in their neighborhoods, towns, surrounding countryside and larger world.

Food Works grew out of our community work attempting to unravel the spiral of hunger, poverty and ecological collapse locally and globally, from rural Vermont to urban centers.

Through this work, we discovered that the very ways we learn about the endangered world both reflect and recreate that world. In elementary school, for example, we learned to divide up the world into neat categories - Math, Science, Social Studies and so forth. We then applied those same tools in adulthood to divide up the world— Politics, Economics, Environment, etc.— which has led to a patchwork of temporary band-aids rather than sustainable solutions to these endemic problems.

In trying to create a world that nourishes all forms of life, we must from the earliest ages teach ourselves to see the world as an interconnected whole of which we are an integral part. We at Food Works believe the purpose of schooling should be to nurture the natural curiosity, imagination and dreams of all children, in order to re-create a world capable of responding to the diverse spectrum of intellectual, emotional, creative and nutritional needs of all its inhabitants.

Common Roots provides the practical skills enabling our children to more holistically understand and explore the inter-relationships between the natural and human world. Therefore, we at Food Works have dedicated our work to transform the role and responsibility of our schools in order to identify and respond to the food and ecological concerns of our communities in order to create a healthy future.

Joseph Kiefer

Executive Director

Acknowledgements

The *Common Roots*™ framework as a vehicle for re-inventing schools would not have been possible without the desire and enthusiasm of the many teachers, parents and children to change the way we look at the role of our schools.

The Rumney School was the first to offer us a school to pioneer the development of the *Common Roots* framework that included the K-6 Historic Theme Gardens.

The Barnet School hosted our first *Common Roots* graduate course which taught us the critical importance of each teacher owning his or her unique journey for integrated learning. This collaborative relationship continues to grow and bear fruit.

Additionally, we would like to thank all of our new schools and the unique way they have adopted *Common Roots* to meet their needs.

Unquestionably, none of this would have been possible without the dedication and vision of the Food Works collaborative team. The rich insights and personal teaching experiences of JoAnne Dennee, Julia Hand, Carolyn Peduzzi, Elisheva Kaufman, Jack Peduzzi, Joseph Kiefer, and Martin Kemple have inspired the genesis of *Common Roots.*

The guidance and support of our Board of Directors has been instrumental in sustaining the *Common Roots* vision. Their collective wisdom is a constant source of inspiration and direction.

Most importantly, we would like to acknowledge the many family and foundation funders whose generous support has enabled us to realize our common dream. By believing in our vision and continuing to support this evolving work, this group of friends has become part of our growing Food Works family.

Above all, listening to the voices of children has taught us the timely need to provide meaningful opportunities for them to create a better world.

A WORD ABOUT
COMMON ROOTS
A GUIDE TO AN INTEGRATED, LIVING CURRICULUM

Welcome to the Common Roots Guidebooks, a collection of hands-on seasonal projects and activities for the curious child.

The Common Roots Guidebooks have been designed for teachers, parents and community members to create a living curriculum for children which integrates the human and ecological roots of their own community. These K-6 Guidebooks offer hands-on learning activities and projects for children to discover the past, explore the present and build their common future. These adventures are developmentally designed along a 7 year journey that help tell the story of each child's community, from its very first inhabitants (1-2) to its local heritage (3-4) to a look to the future (5-6), thereby creating a living curriculum of meaningful activities.

These Guidebooks integrate traditional subjects into each of the projects and activities that build upon each other as the child moves from Kindergarten through Sixth Grade. Social Studies is an integral part of the historic theme gardens - the hub of the Common Roots learning process for each grade level. The Applied Scientific Method is part of every activity. Children marvel at fermentation processes as they bake bread; track the life cycle of seeds; observe the effects of weather, fertilizer, insects and worms in their own gardens; and investigate and analyze sources of local water for pollution. Language arts are acquired as children write garden journals, read recipes or create a community ecology-action newsletter. Math skills are developed through designing a garden, measuring cooking ingredients and graphing changes in ecosystems. Art, music, dance and physical activity are also integrated into the activities to allow children to celebrate seasons and the cultures they are learning about.

Common Roots is an inquiry-based journey for children, guided by their teachers and parents and accompanied by their elders and neighbors. The meaningful hands-on projects and activities nurture children's natural curiosity by providing the opportunity for each child to express their creativity and knowledge in order to answer their own questions. This student-centered approach engages students in the process of learning rather than providing textbook answers to rigid curriculums.

Common Roots provides children with real-life opportunities to

develop problem solving skills to research, document and help preserve their fragile environment and disappearing heritage - building a better world for tomorrow. The projects and activities climax at the 6th Grade level, but the journey exploring our natural and human world is lifelong.

Put on your pack and come along with us!

In The Three Sisters Garden

Introduction to a Caretaker's Journey in Food, Ecology and Community

Who - or what - are the Three Sisters?

Sisters Corn, Squash, and Bean are both an ancient and a contemporary Native agricultural tradition. The Three Sisters provided - and continue to provide - more than the gift of food for Native American communities. They are the basis for an "agri-culture," a way of living rich with gardening technology, stories, ceremonies and other traditions. Indeed, the Iroquois name for the Three Sisters means "life support."

In The Three Sisters Garden attempts to keep these lifeways alive through teachings, stories, ceremonies, and activities. But although the activities in *In The Three Sisters Garden* have been modeled on the Abenaki and Iroquois nations of the Northeast, you can easily substitute the cultures, traditions, and skills of the Native Americans who live in your own local region.

Inquiry-based learning lies at the heart of *In The Three Sisters Garden*. Who are the Native Americans in your area? What are the agrarian roots of your community, both Native and European? What arts, music, theater, dance, and foods nourish your community? What family and neighborhood values enrich your life? Who are your community elders and what are their stories?

As young gardeners strive to answer these questions, they develop a sense of their own "agri-culture." By examining - or recreating - their "common roots," they begin to understand the nature of their relationship to their community. Children who understand and respect their own roots insure their community's survival. Equally important, by bringing that vision of the future forward, they celebrate and honor the lives of all of Earth's beings.

In *In The Three Sisters Garden*, Three Sisters gardeners learn how to be "caretakers of the Earth" by using Earth-friendly gardening principles - rustic tools and hands-on, hearts-on gardening techniques. In this way, they gain wisdom directly through experience. The passing on of such wisdom has a positive impact on future generations.

Today's generations of farmers and gardeners are faced with serious ecological and agricultural questions. How they answer those questions will determine the fate of future generations. By drawing on the ancient wisdoms of the land and its peoples, by drawing on the historic roots of their own neighborhoods, by practicing an agriculture of renewal, one that is in harmony with the Earth, young gardeners will learn how to live in today's complex world and insure a better tomorrow.

May today's young gardeners be inspired by the words of the Iroquois confederacy:

"In our every deliberation, we must consider the impact of our decisions on the next seven generations."

Food, Ecology, Community - The Three Sisters

Why Food?

Just look around at a garden with children working in it! They are munching on snap beans, nibbling spinach, and breathing "dragon breath" after eating scallion greens. Sowing, tending, and harvesting food is the most successful way to promote good eating and caretaking habits.

In *In The Three Sisters Garden,* **Health, nutrition, and self-reliance activities** create a personal journey wherein a child explores his only permanent home - his body! Wise food choices are easier to make when children eat home-grown vegetables. Activities in the guidebook demonstrate that food is more than just something to feed the body: food is understood to be part of the larger circle of life because it makes important contributions to one's sense of well-being. This fact is demonstrated in Earth-friendly organic gardening practices. It is further celebrated in the taste of cornbread made from home-ground corn - you savor a corn taste so alive that you also taste the rain, earth, and wind! Food also nourishes one's well-being when it is shared with family, friends, and neighbors. The full circle of life is celebrated in the gardener's caretaking partnership with her garden.

The Three Sisters - Sisters Corn, Squash and Bean - are an excellent choice for low-maintenance summer crops. They prosper even when children are on vacation. Little can deter the Three Sisters from upholding their promise of an autumn harvest!

However, **you need not grow your own food to do many of the activities in this Guidebook**. The Three Sisters are diet staples, and thus are readily available at markets, farm stands and co-ops. Children wishing to share a Three Sisters journey can "adopt" a local farmer or gardener. Small container gardens or indoor gardens can be as much a home to the Three Sisters as a large outdoor garden. All that is required is a little imagination!

Why Ecology?

The word "ecology" is derived from the German *ökologie,* which in turn comes from the Greek *oikos.* Ecology's roots mean *home.* The study of ecology helps us to understand our "sense of place," and teaches us how to care for it - whether the "place" is our body, our family dwelling, our backyard or neighborhood. In *In The Three Sisters Garden,* a "sense of place" is first experienced in our only permanent house - our body. Connections are then made between our bodies and our families, our families and the neighborhood, the neighborhood and the natural world.

The journey is enhanced by the ecology found in each child's backyard - the wonders of the garden, the promise of the harvest, wildflowers growing on a lawn, the magnificence of an autumn day. The garden ecology journey expands as it explores relationships between garden neighbors - seed and soil, plant and animal, earth and sky.

Caretaking the garden, as well as one's human and natural neighbors, strengthens and supports a child's innate respect for the Earth and her creatures. Deeper connections to the larger world of the "Earth Garden" form as a child matures. A loving relationship with the Earth drives a child to ask (and seek the answers to) questions concerning the complex issues of caretaking the planet Earth and her peoples.

Why Community?

A caretaker's journey would not be complete without examining one's relationship to the community. In *In The Three Sisters Garden,* caretakers are invited to discover and build upon their sense of place in the human and natural community. Step by step, children are invited to experience the fabric of living history in their family and neighborhood. They might pursue these discoveries through the making of traditional gardening tools, or by meeting and interviewing the elders of their neighborhood, or by practicing Three Sisters gardening with their Native neighbors.

All of these real-life discoveries lead to a respect for the unique and diverse fabric of humanity. Children are empowered to celebrate the multi-cultural fabric of humanity by undertaking projects that serve their community. Community service projects stretch the possibilities of education, allowing it to embrace the lives of the entire community - human and natural.

Finding Your Way through the Two Seasonal Journeys of *In The Three Sisters Garden:*

"First Farmers and Gardeners" and "Farmers and Gardeners of the Longhouse"

Two distinct, year-long journeys through the Three Sisters garden offer an array of activities designed to engage the child in the miracle of growing food. The first journey, "First Farmers and Gardeners," explores the Three Sisters garden through the lives of a contemporary Native American family. The second journey, "Farmers and Gardeners of the Longhouse," explores the Three Sisters garden through the medium of a traditional Native American community. Each is a unique journey through the four seasons, in which Sister Corn, Sister Bean, and Sister Squash guide children along a path of adventures, discoveries, and ideas.

Three Sisters gardeners learn about the history of corn - the gift of Native people to the world. They discover the role that corn plays in family and neighborhood communities. They learn how to grow corn and preserve seeds. They learn how to grind and make their own corn-bread and Three Sisters soups. Through storytelling and arts, they celebrate their diverse and common roots.

Similar activities revolve around Sisters Bean and Squash.

Beginning in **Autumn**, Three Sisters gardeners journey to a time when the first farmers and gardeners lived in harmony with their local ecology. Using the Northeast nations of the Abenaki and the Iroquois as models, they uncover seasonal rhythms in the autumn harvest of their own neighborhood. Pursuing various inquiries about caring for the Earth, they come to understand the cycles of the garden, as well as the cycles of the seasonal landscape. Intertwining themes - the land's ability to produce food, the preservation of the harvest, expressions of gratitude for the harvest, the preparation of the fall garden, and an awareness of the seasonal landscape - provide numerous experiences for Three Sisters gardeners to caretake the self, the neighborhood, and the Earth.

During the **Winter**, Three Sisters gardeners search for ways to keep the spirit of life ever present, a practice that reflects Native American traditions. Storytelling, arts and harvest feasts give gardeners opportunities to build on existing foundations, yet challenge them to create new traditions which reflect their local environment. The Indoor Garden

Center enables today's gardeners to grow vegetables during the cold winter months, insuring quality foods all year long. Strengthening community ties is an easily achieved goal during the "Sweeten up the Winter Blues" community breakfast, which revolves around one of Mother Nature's gifts - maple syrup. Saving harvest seeds and respecting their life force offers everyone an opportunity to reflect on her own inner life force. What gifts - perhaps hidden inside a young gardener - can someday be brought into full bloom to benefit your neighborhood?

Spring creates renewed enthusiasm in the Three Sisters gardeners. The changes and promise within a tiny seed are witnessed firsthand as the children care for tender seedlings germinated indoors. This gives them an opportunity to experience the interdependence of all living things - and makes the long winter wait worth the struggle! These integrated activities help children feel more fully the ways in which their family, neighbors, and the Earth care for them. Additionally, the activities foster self-reliance and a sense of self-worth.

Summer, for every Three Sisters gardener, revolves around the joy of watching the garden grow grow grow - unfolding like a dream. The summer garden also creates an opportunity for games and playing, which brings the entire family and neighborhood together in a spirit of community in the Three Sisters garden.

Each season's activities revolve around questions, and then follow through with discoveries that lead to the answers. The activities are presented in such a way that one question leads to another. Additionally, each activity contains a section entitled "Want To Do More?", which guides the child to a deeper understanding of the world he or she is exploring. For the child who wishes to explore even further, another set of activities follows. Entitled "Even More Curious?", these activities include reading suggested books or arranging meetings with people who can elaborate upon the subject through their own life experiences.

In a traditional classroom setting, subjects such as Math, English, Science or Art are pursued individually. But in *In The Three Sisters Garden,* subjects are entwined in the activities rather than being treated separately. In this way, nature itself becomes the teacher of science, history, art, writing, music, and health. Sometimes a particular subject is highlighted in an activity - such as "Math, Nature's Way", a section which appears regularly throughout the guidebook. The child receives an education that is relevant and engaging - and makes sense. The Project Web on the following page illustrates this concept of integrated learning.

The delightful pen-and-ink illustrations that accompany each story invite children to color or paint them. Or, after you have read a story let the child draw his or her own imaginative illustrations.

An Inquiry Approach to Integrated Learning

PROJECT WEB

SOCIAL STUDIES

Iroquois Indian Nation
history of corn
Native American Foods

SCIENCE/ECOLOGY

plant identification
plant biology
garden ecosystem
insect identification
weather patterns
effects of moonlight
effects of sunlight
earth's rotation

LANGUAGE ARTS

harvest songs
Native American stories
poetry
write and tell stories
journal entries

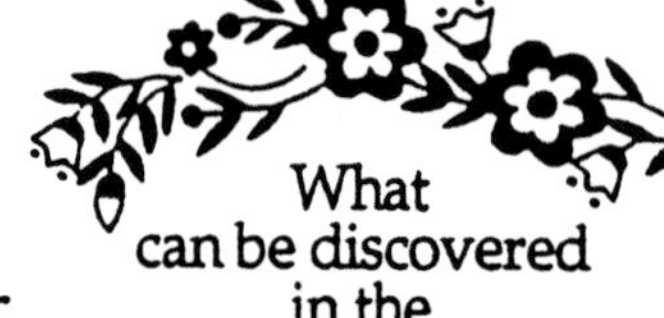

What can be discovered in the THREE SISTERS GARDEN?

MATH

average yield of crops
volume, weight of seeds and produce
graphing
charting
symmetry
recipes

CREATIVE ARTS

harvest mural
make cookbook
draw plants
dibble and possession sticks
journal drawings and paintings
costume making
puppets
plays

COMMUNITY SERVICE

donate soup
corn gifts
cookbook gifts
share harvest
displays, exhibits
Gifting Garden Ceremony
Three Sisters Harvest Celebration

GARDENING

design
preparation
compost
fertilizer
pH
cover crops
seed storage
germinate seeds
mulch
maintenance

NUTRITION/HEALTH

Food Groups
cooking
food preservation
drying vegetables

Presenting a Cultural Journey Without Bias

In The Three Sisters Garden contains a variety of Native stories, guided journeys, and activities. Some teachings are rendered through the voices of elders, who recall a time when they were young gardeners. Some ancient stories are so new they might have been written only yesterday. The illustrations often depict a setting which no longer exists - it is important that young and old learners understand this. Native peoples have changed, just as our grandparents have changed since their childhood.

It is important to note that what has not changed among most Native peoples is an attitude of "caretaker mind." This attitude of respect, care, and generosity has been passed on by elders from one generation to another. That which has been "passed on" is something that develops and lives deep inside a person. It is a means of sustaining life for those who follow. A "caretaker mind" is much more than an outer appearance - an association with buffaloes, beads, or feathered headdresses. A true "caretaker mind" challenges the stereotype of "wild Indians," which is still often perpetuated today.

The teachings from Native cultures that are presented in *In the Three Sisters Garden* support the development of a "caretaker mind." This journey is a celebration of diversity, gratitude, commitment, and respect for all cultural roots.

How to Work with Native American Stories

"Remember only this one thing," said Badger. "The stories people tell have a way of taking care of them. If stories come to you, care for them. And learn to give them away when needed. Sometimes a person needs a story more than food to stay alive. That is why we put these stories in each other's memory. This is how people care for themselves."

from Crow and Weasel by Barry Lopez

Stories are gifts that have been passed along by generations of "story-carriers." In *In The Three Sisters Garden*, you will find stories from many Native traditions. Stories shared through oral tradition seem to "live" inside the story-carrier, as well as in the listener. You may notice a difference in the way learners receive living stories, as compared with stories read from a book. When someone takes in a story deeply, it affects the storyteller as well. This gift from your listeners should provide the encouragement you need to tell more stories.

But how do you begin working with stories, and how can you gain confidence in your storytelling abilities? Some stories will speak to you; others will not. Choose a story that touches you - a story can deliver its true meaning only when its truth is held in the heart of the teller. Use your own words or mold the story in your memory, creating images to help you weave it all together. When you feel comfortable, retell it. In keeping with the traditions of the Native storytellers, retell Native American stories between the first and last frost.

When no story exists for your purpose, create your own. Start with simple, short stories. Over a period of several weeks, you may feel ready to embellish the basic tale as you go along, weaving a story that has no beginning and no end. Yet each separate story you tell should be related to an earlier tale. Characters and landscapes come and go with the season of the story.

You can further the importance of this ancient craft by creating storytellers among your listeners. Throughout *In The Three Sisters Garden,* we suggest that you ask children to retell a story. Retelling a story is a living language experience, as well as a memory-strengthening activity. When practiced on a regular basis, it builds confidence in the young teller's ability to speak in public. This practice builds more than language or listening or memory skills. It provides an opportunity for children to "carry" a story and feel it "living" deep inside themselves. Wisdom is carried and shared through storytelling. So gather the children around, and tell a story of long ago. . . .

A Note about the Stories Retold in *In The Three Sisters Garden*

It was our wish in *In The Three Sisters Garden* to include solely traditional Native American stories about the Three Sisters. However, modern restraints (copyright laws) limit the stories we are able to retell.

Stories guide us along life's path, and a story that has been told and retold many times over the years has garnered a richness and polish that holds a special meaning for each teller and listener. Inspired by this tradition, our authors have created stories that reflect the spirit of Native American tales and legends. Wherever these stories appear in *In The Three Sisters Garden,* our authorship is indicated to distinguish them from authentic stories and legends. Although our stories are newly created, the wisdom each contains is time-honored.

Journey One

FIRST FARMERS AND GARDENERS

The sun is shining. The soil is moist. The breeze whispers memories of long ago. The Three Sisters are calling you. . . .

AUTUMN

In The Three Sisters Garden

Journey One: "First Farmers and Gardeners"

Fall ❧

"AMA HEYA AND THE THREE SISTERS"

The Three Sisters' history stretches a long way back in time, to the days when the earliest inhabitants of North America discovered the magic of corn, squash, and beans. For thousands of years, one garden after another provided food and a way of life for the peoples of this continent. One generation after another of Sisters Corn, Squash, and Bean passed its seeds down to the next generation. This magic continues today.

❧ Ama Heya is a living Cherokee woman whose ancestors were originally from Georgia. Over the years her ancestors moved north, but they never forgot the old ways. Ama Heya learned the old ways from them during her childhood. Her stories demonstrate that Native American culture is very much alive today - and will be alive for many tomorrows. For tomorrow is linked to today, today is linked to yesterday, and yesterday is linked to tomorrow. The world turns round and round, and time passes on, but we are all connected through the retelling of old stories and the creation of new ones.

When Ama Heya was a young girl she lived in Brooklyn. To get away from her pesky brothers - Kenny, John, and her twin Darryl - she passed the hours beneath the large, high porch in the back of their city apartment, imagining that she lived in a castle in a far-off land. Ama Heya had just enough space beneath the porch to grow some flowers, and she tended the ones around her "fortress" with great care. Growing things came naturally to her, for Ama Heya was descended from a long line of women who knew the ways of the Earth. Like those women, Ama Heya had a green thumb.

Each evening before supper, Ama Heya strolled out her city door to her mother's "quick-pick garden." She was grateful for the gift of beans and greens that complemented her family's dinner, and told the green children so.

"Gali ili ga," she whispered as she harvested them.

Inside the house, Ama Heya helped her mother with the

cooking. She was such a spindly-legged youngster that some people thought she was not fond of eating. But this was not true. She loved the Caribbean foods - rice and beans - that her father's family was accustomed to eating. As she stirred the bean pot on the stove, she listened to her grandmother Nana - her father's mother - who spoke longingly about picking juicy oranges, coconuts, or avocados from the lush trees on the tropical Caribbean island where she grew up. Ama Heya was entranced by these stories. But as she stirred the pot she found her thoughts drifting to her mother's side of the family, to her great-grandmother who lived on an island not far from Brooklyn. . . .

Ama Heya had spent all six of her summers with her great-grandmother. The original inhabitants of the area called the island "Sawanakka", which means "people of the long land". Today most people call the island "Long Island". Few of them are aware of the ancient name in the Mohican language. Nor do they know that the village of Wyandanch, where Ama Heya's great-grandmother lived, is named after a great Indian chief.

But Ama Heya knew these names of yesteryear. For Gram - as she called her great-grandmother - passed along the old ways by inviting Ama Heya into her Three Sisters garden, where Sister Corn, Sister Squash, and Sister Bean flourished. Watching her great-grandmother move through the garden, Ama Heya was as entranced as a child staring at fireflies. Gram put a lot of love into everything she did. To Ama Heya's eyes, it seemed that magic burst forth wherever her great-grandmother's fingers touched the earth.

Indeed, the very first time Ama Heya went into the garden she watched curiously as Gram pressed a seed into the dark soil. Soon - in less time than it took to finish a dream! - a green child burst into the light. Ama Heya wondered whether the magic was hidden in the dark soil or in the seed. From that point on, she watched with keen interest, hoping to understand this great mystery.

Ama Heya was delighted by the mounds of potatoes

hilled up to their necks in rich blankets of soil. All her great-grandmother had to do was to bury a shriveled-up chunk of potato - and in a few days the green children sprang up! Ama Heya wondered if there was something about the love Gram put into the gentle hilling of the circular mounds that made her want Gram's potatoes more than fresh-baked cookies!

Cloud-white asparagus also flourished in her great-grand- mother's garden. The asparagus grew like spears, pointing straight up to the Sky World.

All the plant-children her great-grandmother tended seemed very old and wise. Gram treated them like friends from times long ago. Ama Heya was sure that the plant-children spilled out their stories whenever her great-grandmother worked beside them. Often, Ama Heya found herself leaning closer in an attempt to hear what they were whispering.

Her favorite garden companions, though, were her Three Sisters - Corn, Bean, and Squash. No matter what her great-grandmother planted each summer, the garden revolved around these three crops. Ama Heya loved to watch Sister Corn grow straight and tall. She wished she had a real sister to curl up with, as Sister Bean curled around Sister Corn. And she loved the way Sister Squash spread her leafy blanket over the entire garden. Year after year, Ama Heya and her Three Sisters passed the time catching up on stories - real and pretend. Spending the summer moons alone with her Three Sisters was exactly what Ama Heya needed. After all, three real-life brothers sometimes wore out a small, young girl!

Ama Heya loved the meals her great-grandmother cooked from the summer garden. Roasted sweet corn dripping with butter was one of her favorite treats. She also looked forward to the bowls of steamy, delicious corn porridge Gram concocted at breakfast. And her great-grandmother made lots of jars of her favorite plum jam.

At night as she lay in bed Ama Heya could almost hear the gardens growing below her window. At these times her family in Brooklyn seemed so far away. But even as her time in the countryside grew short, Ama Heya was content, for she knew that each summer she would be able to visit Gram - and her Three Sisters.

First Farmers and Gardeners: Land of the Dawn People

The Abenaki are called the People of the Dawn because they were the first Native Americans to greet the sun as it rose over the eastern shores of this continent. The Abenaki nation stretches from as far south as northern Massachusetts, north through Maine and up into Canada, and west to Lake Champlain. Long before the first settlers arrived the Abenaki, primarily hunters and gatherers, were also farmers and gardeners. The Three Sisters gardener can learn a lot from the Abenaki.

❧ Traditionally, the Abenaki made their homes along rivers and lakes. Hundreds of years ago, when the earliest European settlers reached the "new world," the Abenaki were the first to greet them on the Massachusetts coast.

Although the Abenaki nation is spread out over a large territory, the tribes are united by their Algonkian language and strong ancestral ties with the land they continue to inhabit. Today, Lake Champlain and the St. Lawrence River valley are still home to the Abenaki.

The Abenaki have always grown corn, squash and bean, but in the early days these crops were not reliable food sources because killing frosts often ended the growing season before harvest time. The Abenaki had to depend upon wild foods and game, especially the abundant fish in the lakes and rivers, to supplement their garden food. But as time passed and ways of life changed, corn, squash, and bean - called The Three Sisters by the Iroquois - continue to be important to the People of Dawn.

The Abenaki year is divided into seasons whose rhythmical patterns follow the cycle of the moon. The story on the next page, written by our authors, describes many of the subsistence activities the Abenaki undertook in the wheel of the year.

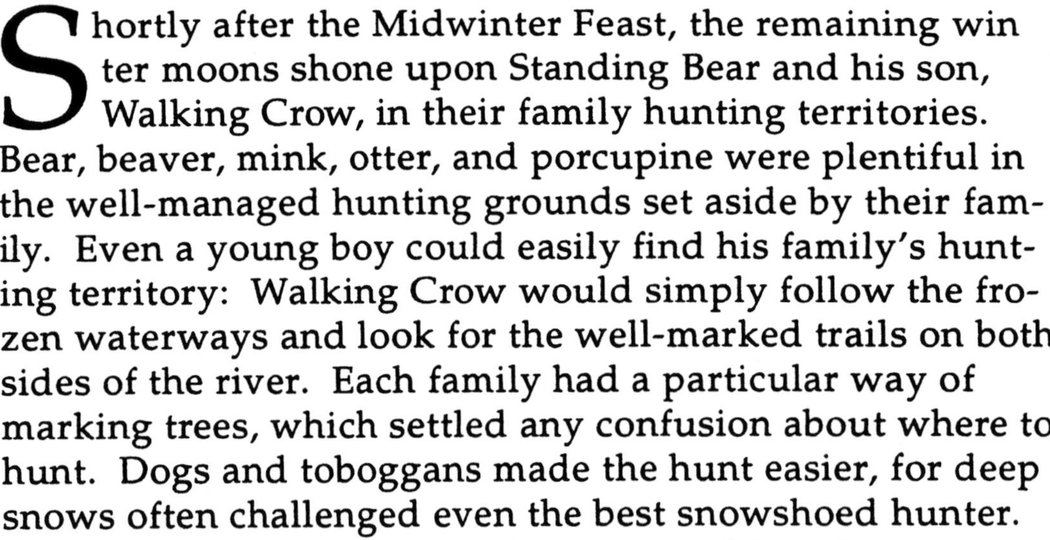

"The Rhythm of the Seasons"

Shortly after the Midwinter Feast, the remaining winter moons shone upon Standing Bear and his son, Walking Crow, in their family hunting territories. Bear, beaver, mink, otter, and porcupine were plentiful in the well-managed hunting grounds set aside by their family. Even a young boy could easily find his family's hunting territory: Walking Crow would simply follow the frozen waterways and look for the well-marked trails on both sides of the river. Each family had a particular way of marking trees, which settled any confusion about where to hunt. Dogs and toboggans made the hunt easier, for deep snows often challenged even the best snowshoed hunter.

The women and elders who were unable to hunt remained at the winter camp. Sitting around the fire in bark-covered houses, Walking Crow's mother crafted clothing and household tools. Elm bark containers, called "quick-baskets" because they were so easy to make, were created for gathering maple sap. Moose and deer hides from the autumn hunt were cut and sewn for clothing and moccasins. In addition to painting the hides with colorful dyes, porcupine quills added beauty to the garments and showed off her creative and skillful handwork.

When the spring sap began to flow, Walking Crow's mother joined the other women and brought in the maple harvest. Leak-proof bark containers caught the sweet waters dripping from the slashed trees. The women heated stones, which they added to the maple sap, causing it to evaporate. Soon only a sticky, thick syrup was left.

As Walking Crow's mother gathered groundnuts and spring greens during the maple harvest, her songs filled the woodlands. The syrup, greens, and groundnuts seasoned the fowl and fish brought in by Standing Bear.

Planting season began during the late spring moon at the end of April or in May. Walking Crow's mother tended the Three Sisters in the fertile floodlands. Standing Bear planted and tended the ceremonial tobacco, which was farmed separately from the food crops.

During the spring and summer moons Standing Bear was busy fishing on the waterways, while Walking Crow's mother tended crops. She gathered fruits and berries, and used them to season the flatbreads and stews she cooked.

Walking Crow's sister joined his mother and elders, foraging for the medicinal herbs that flourished during the summer moons.

During the warm days and nights, Standing Bear's mother found plenty of time to make pottery. At the Green Corn Ceremony, she gave thanks for the late summer foods through a sampling of green corn and beans. The main harvest, of course, did not take place until the harvest moon.

An Abenaki family harvested other foods in addition to the Three Sisters during the autumn moons. While Walking Crow's mother dried, preserved and stored the crops, Standing Bear and Walking Crow again prepared for the hunt. They scoured the waterways in their canoe in search of moose, whose hides were at their best this time of year. A plentiful kill would mean new garments for the winter hunting season, which lay just a few moons ahead. Deer were stalked by land in the hunting territories set aside for their family. Each year, only a portion of their family hunting territory was used. This practice insured plentiful game. The success of the hunt depended on the skill of the individual hunter, young or old. Knowing that game was the main food source of his family, Standing Bear and Walking Crow took their responsibility seriously. And each expressed his thanks to the Great Spirit for Ndakinna, "our land."

❧ The Dawn People, or Abenaki, still live according to the rhythms of the seasons. They continue to fish along the waterways and grow corn, squash, and beans. Sadly, the right of the Abenaki to access their ancient territories and waterways for fishing and hunting is in dispute today.

❧ **What do you think has changed and what remains the**

same in the Abenaki's seasonal tasks today? For example, snowmobiles have replaced toboggans, and rubber boots are worn in place of moose hide boots. Can you draw pictures of the seasonal tasks described in the previous story, and then draw pictures of the changes in those tasks that occur today?

❧ **Have you ever thought that some of the names of places and things that you use are unusual?** Many Native words from different nations are part of our English language today, such as woodchuck, moose, potluck, toboggan, squash, wigwam, papoose and chipmunk. Do any waterways or towns where you live have Abenaki or Native names?
The Abenaki name for corn is "skamon". Bean is "adbakwa", and squash is "wassawas." Can you find out what other Native American names are for the Three Sisters?

❧ **Draw the seasonal, rhythmical patterns of your family's life that help fulfill your needs.** What is your relationship with the Earth in these tasks?

Want To Do More?

❧ Throughout the year, notice the hands-on, seasonal subsistence activities you and your family perform, such as gardening, sugaring, hunting, or getting your sled or skis ready. Draw these seasonal activities in a journal.

❧ Read stories about Abenaki family life in *The Faithful Hunter* by Joseph Bruchac.

Even More Curious?

Imagine a child in an Abenaki family long ago.

Dawn lived with her family - grandmother, grandfather, parents, brothers, and sisters - in a rectangular house with a rounded roof. One to four families, all blood relatives of her mother or father, lived in this dwelling. The shelter was covered with bark from the beautiful birch

trees surrounding her homeland. Her family had to work well together to survive. She shared the tasks of gathering food, preparing meals, making and repairing clothing, and caring for and protecting the family.

Uncles, aunts, and cousins related to her parents might live close by, but her nearest neighbors - and her friends - lived many miles away. Her immediate family was part of a larger family group, called a band. Perhaps her ancestors farmed the very first corn of the Abenaki people.

Now, imagine an Abenaki child today.

Danielle lives with her parents and goes to school in Swanton, Vermont. After school, she returns home with a friend. They ride their bikes to the edge of the neighborhood, where they stop, jump off, and race one another to their favorite wild place in the berry brambles. Some late raspberries cling to the branches. They gratefully harvest the fruits of Indian Summer (called the Summer of Mankind by the Abenaki), savoring the melt-in-your mouth flavor of summer's end.

Dawn remembers to pick a handful of raspberry leaves for her grandmother, who will dry the leaves and brew them as a raspberry tonic for women. Dawn always listens and watches when her grandmother prepares herbs. When she becomes a woman she wants to be wise like her grandmother.

Excited about her gift of raspberry leaves, Dawn jumps on her bike and pedals to her grandmother's house. Waving good-bye to her friend, she goes to the back of the house where her grandmother is tending the garden.

"*Quai,*" her grandmother says in greeting.

"*Quai,*" says Dawn. "I brought you some raspberry leaves, but I am afraid we ate all the fruit ourselves! I wish I had thought to save some for you, Grandmother."

"The leaves and your visit are your gift to me, Granddaughter. Later I shall prepare the leaves for drying and you can help me. But now let's go see how much the pumpkins have grown since your last visit."

❧ How have the Abenaki changed over the generations? In much the same way that your grandparents have changed! Once they, too, were just children growing up.

❧ The Abenaki language has not changed. **"Quai"** still means hello. **"Adio"** still means good-bye. Though Abenaki is spoken less often than English, many Abenaki children are learning - and continue to speak - their ancestral language.

Meet Sister Corn

Have you ever wondered how so many colorful Indian corns came into existence? This life-giving grain has sustained the Native peoples for thousands of years. Each nation is a caretaker of its own seed. Nations pass this gift along to their own future generations, to neighboring nations, and to the world. The different kinds of seeds produce different colors of corn - as beautiful as a rainbow!

> ☛ ***Note:*** *The corn referred to in In The Three Sisters Garden is Indian corn (drying corn) or popcorn. These corns can be preserved through the Winter, and later ground or popped into delicious food. (Sweet corn may be planted in your garden as well but, like snap beans, this variety of corn is meant to be eaten as soon as it is ripe.)*

Creating a Mood

❧ Display different examples of Indian corn, such as Hopi Blue Corn, Hopi Turquoise Corn, Hopi Amethyst Corn, Black Aztec Corn, Red Corn, Mandan Rainbow Corn, Yellow Seneca Corn, and so on. Farm stands or specialty food markets often carry these "exotic" varieties of corn. The vision of so many different kinds of corn sets a wonderful stage for the following story.

Ask the listeners to sit in a circle. Then dim the lights and relate the story the Grandmothers tell of a time long ago.

The Grandmothers say that every nation has its own story about the gift of corn. These stories are as colorful as the rainbow, and carry with them a promise that only the rainbow can foretell. The "Rainbow Corn Maidens" is a Pueblo story retold by Phil Lucas of the Four Worlds Development Project.

"The Rainbow Corn Maidens"

Long ago, there were fewer people on the Earth. Their only food was grass and wild, seed-bearing plants, and they were often hungry. Raising their voices to the Great Mystery, the people made offerings of their most colorful and finest seeds. They asked for new foods to satisfy their hunger.

In answer to their prayers, six beautiful Rainbow Maidens - each representing a color of the rainbow - appeared in the Sky World. Red, Orange, Yellow, Green, Blue and Purple Maidens, lovely and brilliant as the sky, danced upon the Earth where the people stood. Where they danced, corn grew.

Yellow Corn Maiden said to the gathering, "We have come to teach you how to plant. Ask permission of the Earth before scratching her skin with a tool. Then scratch the hard ground with a sharp stick, and make a well to receive the seed. Be grateful as you bury the seed in the red blanket of soil, which will mother it. The rains will bring ample water, which will collect in the well and free the life inside the seed. Do this planting with great respect."

The people did as they were instructed by the Rainbow Maidens. An abundant harvest bore fruit that year. A young flute player gave thanks to the Maidens, asking, "What might you like in return for this great gift?"

"It gives us great joy to see the people happy. That is all we need. But you can play your flute for us."

Flute Player was honored to play for the Rainbow Maidens. His song rose into the sky and throughout the village.

The harvest lasted for some time. But eventually the people became lazy. This disturbed Flute Player, who said, "Why don't you care for the gift of corn? You must stop lying around and take care of what we have been given."

The people complained. "The Rainbow Maidens simply danced - they left all the work for the people! We are tired of this."

Then Orange Corn Maiden descended from the Sky World. She spoke to each of the people, but was ignored or laughed at by them. Finally the Rainbow Maiden left, discouraged by the people's laziness.

For a while longer the corn remained plentiful and the harvests bountiful. Because of this, the people grew lazier and lazier. They threw the corn to the dogs and did not share what remained with their relatives. Soon only a few corn kernels remained. The people planted them, but nothing grew.

Before long, the people were forced to eat wild grass again. A council of elders gathered to discuss what had happened. "Our actions brought this hunger," one of them said. "We must send for the Rainbow Maidens and ask their forgiveness."

So they sent three messengers - Eagle, Hawk, and Raven - to find the Rainbow Maidens. Eagle and Hawk unsuccessfully searched the skies, flying in all the directions of the compass. But clever Raven managed to find the Bringer of the Dawn, and explained about the people's great sorrow.

Bringer of the Dawn said, "You must look to your Flute Player. Only his music can create healing and call back the Rainbow Maidens."

Flute Player's music filled the morning air. Through the mist came the Rainbow Maidens - Red, Orange, Yellow, Green, Blue, and Purple - dancing to the music of his flute. The people begged the Rainbow Maidens' forgiveness.

As the Rainbow Maidens danced, they again instructed the people. "From now on one man from the village will play the flute, and all the village maidens shall dance in our place. Do this every year. In this way the harvest will be blessed by the Rainbow Maidens."

Then the Rainbow Maidens returned to the Sky World. The people felt a deep gratitude. They also reached a new understanding: people who receive gifts must act responsibly. After that, the people never forgot to be thankful for the corn and to show respect for the Rainbow Maidens' gift.

To this day the Zuni people still bless the harvest. And the Flute Player's music continues to rise to the Sky World. And the young maidens dance with hearts full of gratitude and deep respect for all the Rainbow Maidens' gifts. *Ho!*

❧ The Rainbow Maidens brought several gifts to the people - corn seed, planting instructions, forgiveness, and ceremonies. Perhaps this story will inspire you to design your own traditions for your harvest ceremony this Fall.

Look at the colorful diversity of corns displayed. What names would you give each variety? Learn to identify as many kinds of corns as you can.

Want To Do More?

❧ **Create a story about the different colored corns.** Some people say there are six colors of Corn Sisters. According to the Zuni, the oldest sister is Yellow Corn. She comes from the North and symbolizes Winter. Blue Corn of the West is the next oldest. She represents the Waters of Life. Sister Red Corn of the South embodies the spirit of Summer. White Corn, or Lightning, bears gifts from the East. Speckled Corn embodies the cloudy Sky World. And the youngest sister, Black Corn, represents the womb of the Earth Mother.

❧ **Ask the Native people in your community how corn was given to their elders.** What color corn was given? How did these ancient farmers and gardeners exchange corn? Which corns do these people raise today?

❧ **Give a rainbow ear of corn and a story to a gardening friend.** Retell the "Rainbow Corn Maidens" story - or any other story you have created or discovered about the first corn.

Even More Curious?

❧ In Mexico, highly sophisticated farmers - such as the Aztecs - cleared and burned fields and created very complex irrigation systems for their gardens. These fine farmers passed their Black Aztec Corn to nations living north of them. Today, over 7,000 years later, we still enjoy the corn that these first farmers and gardeners found growing wild! Corn knows no national boundaries.

Can you trace on a globe the route and distance corn traveled from Mexico to North America?

❧ The emphasis on gardening coincided with the development of non-nomadic settlements. This was the beginning of "agri-culture." For example, the Wampanoag people tell how Raven carried the first seeds of corn to their people. To this day they never chase Raven from their garden fields. The Cherokee speak of Selu, the Corn Goddess, who brought her life-sustaining gift to yet another Algonkian nation. The Hopi, ancient desert gardeners, still pass on the Hopi Blue Corn traditions. There is a rainbow of stories to gather and share!

What are the cultural traditions and heritage of corn where you live? Share this knowledge with your friends and family.

❧ **Which food crops were gifts of the first farmers and gardeners of this land?** Cultivated crops were developed from plants growing in the wild by three great nations of South and Central America: the Incas of Peru, renowned for irrigation and terracing; the Mayans of Southern Mexico, who were famous for their fertile jungle farming; and the Aztecs of Central Mexico, who cleared and burned fields. These early cultures domesticated and hybridized over 150 kinds of plants, including six varieties of corn and five species of beans! Squash was first cultivated over 8,000 years ago, corn over 7,000 years ago, and beans over 4,000 years ago. Half of the world's food crops were cultivated by Native Americans <u>before</u> Columbus landed. In fact, the potato, which many people believe originated in Ireland, was first cultivated by the Incas. From Peru it traveled overland to North American Natives long before the Irish brought potatoes to America.

MEET SISTER BEAN

Find out who's who in the world of Sister Bean. There are as many kinds and colors of beans as there are of corn.

> ☛ ***Note:*** *The beans referred to in In The Three Sisters Garden are soup (dry) beans. These beans may be stored through the Winter to be cooked into delicious soups and stews. (Summer snap beans may be planted in your garden as well but, like sweet corn, these varieties are meant to be eaten as soon as they are ripe.*

❧ The Iroquois believe the cornstalk bean to be the oldest bean. However, there are countless other varieties of beans in existence today. Interestingly, the root of the word for "bean" among the Hidatsu people of Minnesota is "ama." "Ama" means sister. The Hidatsu cultivate Amacahici (red bean), Amacacipica (white bean) and many other colorful Sister Beans.

❧ **Display bowls of colorful beans** originating from a variety of Native gardens. Include Anasazi beans, lima beans, scarlet runner beans, white soup beans, kidney beans, turtle beans, and pinto beans in your display. How many can you name? For beans whose names are unknown, have a "naming party" before researching the true name.

Choose a single variety of beans. Can you find two beans in it that are exactly alike?

❧ **Everybody loves soup,** and soup made from beans is especially hearty and tasty. You can make Sister Bean Bottled Soup gifts by combining a variety of common ingredients. Here is an especially delicious recipe!

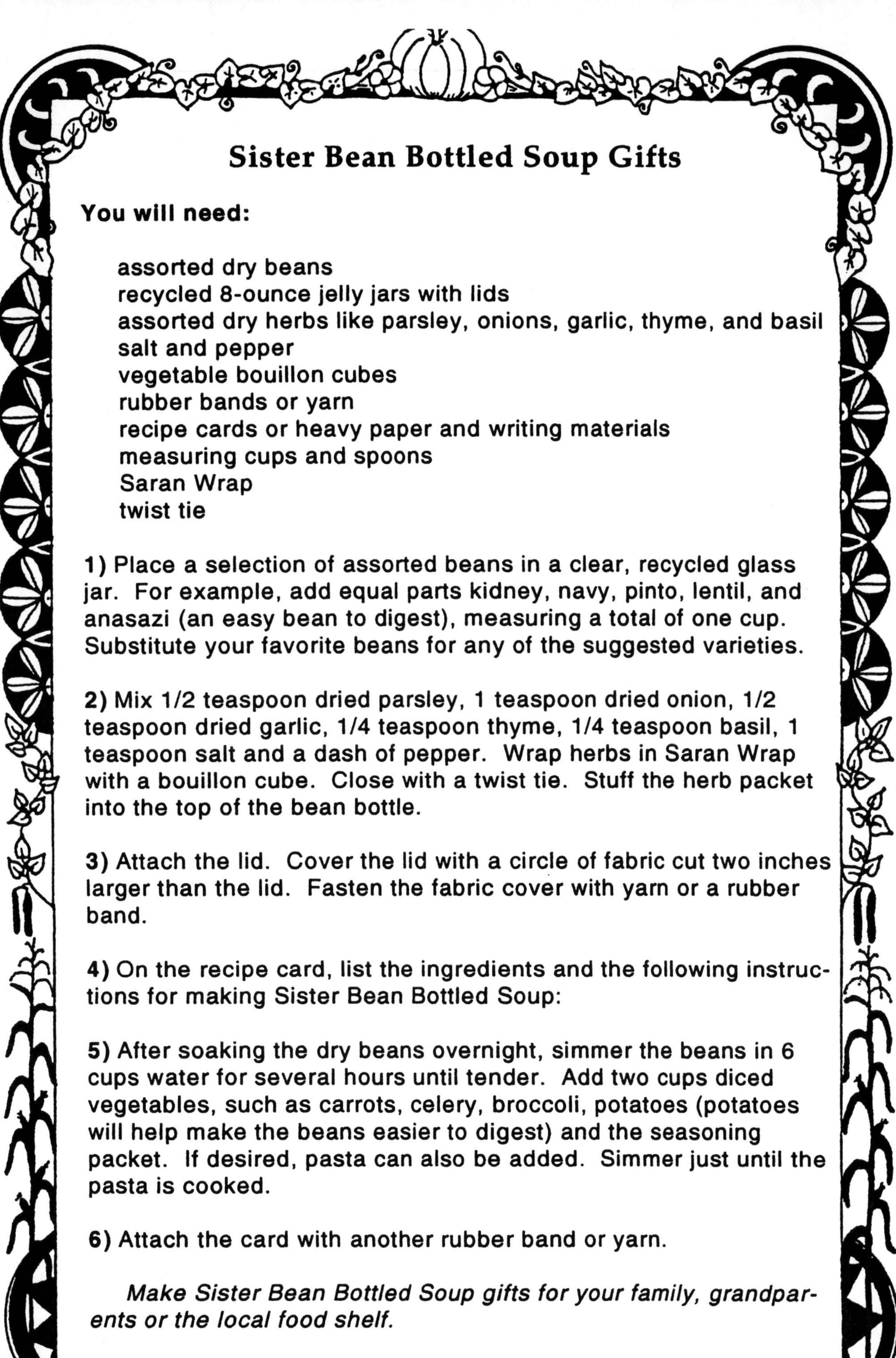

Sister Bean Bottled Soup Gifts

You will need:

assorted dry beans
recycled 8-ounce jelly jars with lids
assorted dry herbs like parsley, onions, garlic, thyme, and basil
salt and pepper
vegetable bouillon cubes
rubber bands or yarn
recipe cards or heavy paper and writing materials
measuring cups and spoons
Saran Wrap
twist tie

1) Place a selection of assorted beans in a clear, recycled glass jar. For example, add equal parts kidney, navy, pinto, lentil, and anasazi (an easy bean to digest), measuring a total of one cup. Substitute your favorite beans for any of the suggested varieties.

2) Mix 1/2 teaspoon dried parsley, 1 teaspoon dried onion, 1/2 teaspoon dried garlic, 1/4 teaspoon thyme, 1/4 teaspoon basil, 1 teaspoon salt and a dash of pepper. Wrap herbs in Saran Wrap with a bouillon cube. Close with a twist tie. Stuff the herb packet into the top of the bean bottle.

3) Attach the lid. Cover the lid with a circle of fabric cut two inches larger than the lid. Fasten the fabric cover with yarn or a rubber band.

4) On the recipe card, list the ingredients and the following instructions for making Sister Bean Bottled Soup:

5) After soaking the dry beans overnight, simmer the beans in 6 cups water for several hours until tender. Add two cups diced vegetables, such as carrots, celery, broccoli, potatoes (potatoes will help make the beans easier to digest) and the seasoning packet. If desired, pasta can also be added. Simmer just until the pasta is cooked.

6) Attach the card with another rubber band or yarn.

Make Sister Bean Bottled Soup gifts for your family, grandparents or the local food shelf.

Want To Do More?

❧ Write a story about the first bean.

Even More Curious?

❧ Look for wild bean relatives growing on your lawn or in wild places in your neighborhood. The pod signifies family membership in the legume (or bean) family.

❧ On a map or globe, locate the origins of bean varieties.

Meet Sister Squash

Believe it or not, there are as many varieties of squash as there are of corn and beans!

> ☛***Note:*** *The squashes referred to in In The Three Sisters Garden are winter squashes. These squashes may be stored well into the Winter for a delicious meal to warm up a cold day. Summer squash may be planted in your garden as well but, like sweet corn and snap beans, summer squash should be eaten as soon as it is ripe.*

❧ **Sister Squash gets her name from the Algonkian word for squash, "askuta," which means "sister". She is considered to be the eldest of the Three Sisters.**

- Invite your friends to hold a contest. The challenge is to collect as many different kinds of squash as possible. Make a display of different varieties of Sister Squash. How many can you name? How many have you tasted?

- **Cook as many recipes as possible and have a Sister Squash bake-off!** Don't forget, maple syrup performs magic in any baked squash dish - for even the most reluctant squash lover!

- **Make Sister Squash lanterns from a variety of squashes.** Carve out interesting shapes, animal faces or scenes - in the same way you would carve a jack-o'-lantern! Illuminate your squash with a candle and sit around and tell stories in the dark.

Want To Do More?

❧ Can you illustrate a story about the first squash? If you don't know a story, make one up!

GROWING WITH YOUR THREE SISTERS: A GUIDED JOURNEY

Re-experience the summer growing season with the Three Sisters by embarking on a guided journey.

Creating the Mood

❧ Visit a Three Sisters garden, a friend's garden, or a corn or pumpkin field at a neighbor's farm. Or visit the Three Sisters in your imagination. Divide into groups of Three Sisters and Brothers to act out this guided journey. Sit in a circle, each Sister or Brother representing the seeds of corn, beans, or squash.

"A Three Sisters Guided Journey"

Many moons ago, a Three Sisters garden was planted here. Imagine that you are one of the Three Sisters growing in this garden during the summertime. Close your eyes. Curl up like a seed lying beneath your Mother, the Earth. Feel her damp, moist soil covering you like a protective blanket. It is dark yet calm below the ground. Your friends the worms join you. The warmth of sunbeams reach down into this dark chamber. Feel the soil growing warm around you. Feel the raindrops falling on the ground above. They filter down, softening the soil and awakening you.

(Sister or Brother Corn are the first seeds to rise.)

Deep in your dark earth chamber,
Whispering winds tumbled and called.
Move into the light, grow strong and bright.
Spread your roots deep in your home.
Anchor yourself, the earth gives you health.
Stretch your stalk to the sky.
Green leaves unfurl, toward the Earth they curl.
Stretching down, leaves reach for their Mother.

(Sister or Brother Corn, stand tall, arms reaching toward the
th. Look down to see Sister Bean beginning to grow.)

The raindrops have soaked your heavy seed coat.
You soften,
Roots search and take hold.
From under the earth, a stem pushes up dirt.
You move toward the warmth of the sun.
Uncurl your bean head, wide green leaves spread,
Reach and open to take in the sun.
Upward by day, you spiral and sway.
You wind, you hug your way 'round.
Dance 'round Corn, another Sister is to be born -
To see her you must look way down.

(Sister or Brother Bean, rise, and twine
ound and around Corn. Corn and Bean
nd together now. They watch Sister or
other Squash reach for the light of day.)

Strong roots spread deep, but Squash
does not sleep.
Two huge leaves appear in the light,
Then a vine rambles 'round, rapidly
covering the ground.
A golden face grows day by day -
Looking up through your leaves,
Corn and Bean you do please.
You shelter the earth 'round their
roots.

Prickly leaves spread far soon, chasing greedy raccoon -
To the compost pile late in the night!

(Sister or Brother Squash, move from a sitting position and lie down across the ground around Corn and Bean's feet.)

Now Sisters Three in the garden you be,
Life given from above and below.
Together as one, you grow with the sun -
waiting for the harvest moon.

- JoAnne Dennee

Want To Do More?

❧ What do you notice about the Three Sisters' behavior in the garden?

❧ Are there times when you feel like one of the Three Sisters? Which one, and why?

❧ Can you find other plants or crops that grow as a team like the Three Sisters?

❧ If you plan a trip to a neighborhood garden or farm, consider combining your trip with the activity on the next page: "Planning Your First Three Sisters Garden."

Planning Your First Three Sisters Garden

Your first Three Sisters garden is an exciting adventure into the mysteries of plants, insects, earth, and sky. By starting out with a simple plan, you can achieve the sweet taste of success - which means corn, beans, and squash - and not bite off more than you can chew!

❧ Visit a friend who has a garden of corn, beans, or squash plants. This experience will help you to determine what questions you need to ask before starting a garden of your own. Write down all your questions. Ask your gardening friend or farmer to tell you about his very first garden. What did he learn? Consult with your garden friend about your ideas. Ask him some of the questions you have written down.

❧ Though very different from one another, the Three Sisters have a special way of getting along. Here are some hints for starting your own garden:

Three Sisters Garden Hints:

Hint #1: Sister Squash spreads out her vines and thick leaves like a blanket. The vines crowd out the light and prevent other plants, such as weeds, from growing. This is a helpful hint for beginning your garden.

Hint #2: Can you believe that **Sister Bean** actually feeds food to the soil, food that Sister Corn needs? Beans replace the important nutrients - especially nitrogen - that Sister Corn soaks up. How cooperative these two sisters are! You can mimic Sister Bean's efforts.

Hint #3: Any gardener who has grown corn will tell you that **Sister Corn** is a hungry feeder. She demands lots of nutrients from the garden soil. Humans are similar to Sister Corn in the demands they make on their garden. Start out with a moderate-sized garden plot filled with nutrient-rich soil. This will provide a lot of food for Sister Corn.

Plan to spend an hour a day tending your garden. Watch the Three Sisters grow - and wonder about the magic of it all!

Are you ready to start your garden plot?

❧ **Sister Squash's behavior serves as a reminder to remove any grass or wild plants growing at your garden site.** Dig out the wild plant roots with a hoe, a digging fork, or a spade, and put them in the compost pile. Any worms you find should be gently returned to the garden. These are the hidden tillers of the soil - and are great allies of the successful gardener! Lots of worms indicate a healthy soil.

❧ **Autumn is a wonderful opportunity to look at mature root systems.** Remove plant material after a rain, when the garden soil is dry enough to work in yet moist enough to release roots easily. Plant roots are amazing extensions of what you see growing above the ground. They are as individual in appearance as the plants growing all around you, and are worth examining.

❧ **Do you dream of growing bushels of popcorn, the largest Jack-o-Lantern, the tallest bean vine, or beautiful sunflowers?** If so, Sister Corn serves as a reminder that the first gift to your garden should be a good feeding. In the Fall, perform a simple soil pH and soil nutrient analysis. Your county Cooperative Extension Service will recommend how much organic fertilizer, lime, or organic material to add to your garden during the Fall. Giving to your garden before receiving from it creates a special connection between you and the Earth.

The Three Sisters benefit from working together, and so will you. Get together with your gardening partners and compile a list of important ideas to think about.

Consider these ideas when starting your first garden:

1) Planting your garden in the shape of a circle reflects nature's - and the garden's - cycle.

2) Traditionally, the Three Sisters are planted together in a mound or hill in the garden. Each mound is about three feet in diameter and holds four corn seeds, two bean seeds in the center, and one pumpkin seed along the edge. Each mound is approximately three feet from the other Three Sisters mounds. Three feet between mounds is ample space for paths and for accommodating a wheel-barrow or wheelchair. It is not necessary to create these mounds until after the Spring tilling, but be sure to consider these spacing needs when planning your garden.

3) How many mounds of Three Sisters can you care for? For school gardens, begin with one mound per trio of Three Sisters and Brothers gardeners. Home gardeners can handle more mounds. Remember that weekly garden care during the summer months is necessary for a successful garden. Consider how much time you can devote to this adventure, and plan the number of mounds accordingly.

4) A wigwam in your Three Sisters garden creates a setting that reflects the lifestyle of the first farmers and gardeners. In the Northeast, wigwams were designed as temporary shelters for sea-sonal camps. Wigwams are conical, tipi-shaped structures covered with bark. They are similar in appearance to the Plains tipis, which were covered with hides. Build a wigwam in the center of your garden. The wigwam poles will support climbing vines which will cover the poles much as bark used to do. Gardeners will love to sit in the cool, shady interior.

5) Be sure to leave enough room for other adventures in your Three Sisters garden. Make a fence of tall sunflowers, a bench or a sitting area, a compost pile or a scarecrow.

6) To determine how large an area you need for your garden, add up the amount of space needed for growing, the area needed for walking paths and fences, and the amount of space necessary for other structures or crops.

7) Begin your garden in early Autumn. Remove the grass and start a compost pile. Fertilize the soil, adding lime and a cover crop, as necessary. For hints on how to begin a successful compost pile, see the Fall activity "And the Circle Goes Round: Compost" on page 94.

Three Sisters, Three Garden Designs!

You can celebrate the Three Sisters, whether you have lots of fertile, sunny space for a garden, or simply a corner in an urban neighborhood. The garden can be large or small - it's up to you! Whatever you decide upon, one of the following plans will provide you with ideas to dream about between now and Spring.

❧ Three Sisters Garden in the Round

Break ground for a new garden, or use part of an existing one. Inscribe a large, circular growing space for your Three Sisters. The circle will serve as a reminder of the power and beauty of natural cycles within the garden, as well as of the cycle of life itself. Divide the garden into four sections by creating walkways three feet wide, each path heading in one of the four directions. These paths should easily accommodate a garden cart or wheelchair. Mark the paths with stones that have been removed from the garden.

Establish mounds in each of the four sections. Plant all Three Sisters in each mound. Build a wigwam at the center of the garden where the pathways meet. A lush wigwam cover of trellised beans will provide living shelter throughout the Summer!

Garden in the Round

❧ Three Sisters in a Barrel

If you have limited space, an oak barrel makes a nice compact container garden for the Three Sisters. Put the barrel in a location where it will receive at least six hours of direct sunlight daily. Make drainage holes in the barrel, or line it with two inches of gravel. Add soil, compost, peat, and organic fertilizer.

Plant four popcorn seeds and several bush beans. A Jack-Be-Little Pumpkin planted near the edge of the barrel will look nice as its vine trails over the edge of the oak container. Miniature flowers - such as Miniature Zinnias, Dwarf Marigolds, or Calendula - planted around the barrel make a showy, decorative, colorful ring. Or, plant one miniature sunflower at the back of the barrel. The butterflies and birds will love it!

Three Sisters in a Barrel

❧ Three Sisters Mound or Raised-Bed Trellis Garden

If you have a garden nook the size of a postage stamp, you can still create a Three Sisters garden. Inscribe a half-moon mound approximately three to four feet across, and three to four feet wide. Install a trellis against the back wall of the half-moon bed. The trellis will be home to Sister Pole Bean and Sister Jack-Be-Little Pumpkin. Plant popcorn in the middle of the bed.

A six-inch wall made of stones will nicely outline the half-moon raised bed. Add soil, compost, and peat until flush with the top of the stone wall. Plant some flowers or herbs around the half-moon stone wall as companions for the Three Sisters.

Three Sisters Trellis Garden

Building Community: Games in the Spirit of the Three Sisters

After preliminary decisions and plans for the garden have been made, it is time to take a rest. While Mother Earth does her work in the garden, Three Sisters gardeners can strengthen their team-building skills and community spirit by playing cooperative games.

Three Sisters and Brothers Challenges

Form trios of Three Sisters and Brothers and try these cooperative games:

❧ **Chair Carry** a sister or brother gardener to a specific destination. Two gardeners form a chair by facing each other with their arms crossed at the wrists and their hands securely clasped. The third gardener sits upon this "arm chair" and is carried to a destination.

❧ **Six-legged Walks** require three pairs of legs tied together. The person in the middle has each leg tied to one of her partners' legs. Gardeners try to reach a destination together, or try to perform specific tasks. Find ways to move rhythmically and comfortably together.

❧ In a **Caterpillar Walk,** three gardeners lie down on their stomachs in a line with their hands touching the feet of the gardener in front of them. Gripping the ankles of the person in front, try to creep like a caterpillar. Set a certain distance as a goal, and try to get there with the "segments" intact.

❧ **Stand Up!** Threesomes sit "back to back" on the ground, crosslegged. Link arms at your elbows and try to stand up together!

❧ Lap Circle Game

The Lap Circle Game is a group challenge! Gardeners standing front to back in a tight circle attempt to sit on the lap of the gardener behind them - until everyone in the entire circle is sitting on someone's lap!

When there are great differences in height among the players, it helps to have the group line up in order of size before forming the circle that starts the game. (This can be suggested at the beginning of the game, or allow the players to discover the idea themselves after evaluating the success of their attempts.) The players stand in a circle, shoulders touching, then all turn left, so that everyone is facing the same direction. To form a tighter circle, everyone takes one step inward. On a given signal, each person tries to slowly squat down on the lap of the person behind him. When all are sitting supported by the group, raise both arms outward and give a cheer!

❧ The Workers of Jobe

This challenging game was taught to us from Medicine Story, a Wampanoag man who played it during his childhood. After reading the following directions, you might have a better appreciation of the oral traditions passed down in Native American communities!

All you need is a circle of friends, a stick, a pencil, or a corncob. Then recite the following chant:

The **work'**ers of **Jobe'**
Are **play'**ing kats kin **yah'**
Put' it, **take'** it
Let' the jumble **ah'**
And the **war'**riors and the **work'**ers
They go **zig'**gy **zig'**gy **zag'**
And the **war'**riors and the **work'**ers
They go **zig'**gy **zig'**gy **zag'**!

To play "Workers of Jobe", everyone sits in a circle. Each person places a stick (or a pencil or a corn cob) on the floor in front of her. While singing the chant, each member of the group passes her stick in a clockwise rhythm.

But first, the group should practice passing the stick in a rhythmic way without chanting. The player should pick up the stick in front of her, then plunk it down in front of the neighbor on her left; reach for the stick in front of her (which has just been passed by the neighbor on her right), plunk it down in front of the neighbor on her left - and so on. The emphasis of the plunking stick creates the rhythm, and should be the only sound heard as the group practices.

Next, the group should practice the chant without passing the stick. Notice that each line contains accented words (in bold). Have the group read the chant aloud, putting a special emphasis on the accented words. To gain a proper appreciation for this rhythm, the members of the group should simulate passing a stick to the neighbor on their left during the chant. The accent or emphasis occurs when they pretend to plunk the stick down in front of their neighbor. Look at the last word in the second line of the chant, and the first word in the third line, and you will see why acting out the rhythm is important. Since both **yah'** and **put'** are emphasized, the players will have to take a breath between the two words. This breath is taken when they are reaching for the imaginary stick in front of them.

The exciting part of the game occurs near the end of the chant when the stick reverses direction for a moment before resuming its usual journey round the circle. When the group sings **zig**'gy **zig**'gy **zag**', everyone will fake passing the stick. Pretend to pass it to your left on the first **zig**'gy. Bring it back in front of you on the second **zig**'gy. Pass it for real on **zag**'.

After everyone has learned the rhythm, pick up your sticks and begin passing them for real while chanting!

This game is great fun. As you improve, speed up the rhythm. See how many rounds you can build up during the year!

❧ Trust Walks

Trust Walks build a caring community of Three Sister gardeners by showing them how to work in pairs. A blindfolded partner is guided on a walk to explore the meadow, forest, garden or a nearby tree. On a dull, rainy day, play the game inside.

Gardeners pair up. Decide who will be blindfolded and who will be the guide. The guide should consider what actions are helpful in caring for a blindfolded friend. What actions might not be helpful, or might even be harmful? The seeing partner looks for a special place or object to visit. She will not tell the blindfolded partner where they are going.

Carefully, step by step, the blindfolded partner is guided to the chosen place. When the guide reaches the special object or place, she invites the blindfolded partner to use his sense of smell, taste, touch, and hearing to discover where he is. When the blindfolded partner has had sufficient time to explore, he is guided home by the seeing partner.

At the trail's end, the blindfold is removed. The challenge is for the blindfolded partner to return to the place or natural object just explored. Guides may accompany their blindfolded partner on the search, possibly giving clues like "hot" or "cold."

Trust Friends now exchange roles. After both partners finish, they can share experiences of how they felt while being led on the Trust Walk.

What actions build trust? Which actions challenge trust? What does it mean to be a guide? How does it feel to depend upon one another?

❧ Knots

With the exception of one person, who is the Doctor, all the gardeners stand in a circle facing the center. The Doctor stands away from the group. The gardeners reach their hands into the center of the circle, where each grips the hand of two different players. When all have joined hands in a great tangle, the group calls out, "Doctor, Doctor, come here quick. Help us get out of this fix!" The Doctor comes to untangle them by twisting, turning and looping the players, but he is not allowed to disconnect their hands.

Want To Do More?

❧ Discuss the ways in which the cooperative group games worked, did not work, or could work better. Strengthen small group cooperation, enhance problem-solving skills, and build a sense of community by playing cooperative games regularly. Invent your own community-building games!

Three Sisters Harvest Hints

Can you tell when it is time to harvest? The Three Sisters display helpful harvest hints.

❧ Do you know Sister Corn's, Sister Bean's, and Sister Squash's most important job? As parent plants, they return their seeds to the earth so another generation may grow. For Sisters Corn, Bean, and Squash, harvest time comes when their seeds are fully developed and mature.

Both raccoons and gardeners depend on the Three Sisters to sustain them. Who will harvest the food? It depends on who is the first to notice that the crop is ripe! Most people believe that the harvest is ready when the vegetables are bursting with color, aroma and flavor. Before food ripens, people often say it is "green." Can you remember a time when you tasted something that was green?

❧ Raccoon and gardener both watch for **clues** from the Three Sisters to determine when the corn, bean, and squash harvest is ready.

Sister Corn's silk turns brown when the kernels hidden inside the husks have passed beyond the soft, milky stage. The brown, silky strands are like a flag which announces that corn-grinding time is near. As the first frost approaches, these kernels become still harder and dryer. Eventually they become as hard as the ornamental Indian maize on display at the farm stand.

To determine if the grinding corn is ready for harvest, probe the inner kernels by gently squeezing the husks. Compare these kernels to those on a cob of last year's Indian Corn. Each hardened kernel of Sister Corn protects the soft inner germ. When the kernels are completely dry, you can grind fresh cornmeal.

Popcorn ears, though smaller than dry meal corn, also display dark brown strands of silk when ripe. These tiny kernels feel hard when you squeeze them. Popcorn ears must be left on the stalk until the husks are brown and dried. If you think raccoons may beat you to the harvest, wait as long as you dare, then bring the nearly mature corn indoors and let it dry for a month. Plan a delicious popcorn feast to celebrate the harvest.

Sister Bean dangles her plentiful pods in the wind. The pods signal the harvest by rattling their dry shell cases. Pick the dry pods from the vines just before frost. Open the treasure boxes and you will discover shiny, colorful seeds inside.

Sister Squash nearly shouts about her gifts! As the carpet of prickly, umbrella-like leaves dies back, she reveals the brilliant and plentiful fruits that you nursed during Summer. She announces herself with true autumn colors. Thump on each mature shell to see if it sings its "harvest song." Hollow sounds sing of readiness. Dull, heavy sounds signal immaturity. If a freezing frost threatens to arrive before harvest, simply cover your fruits with a tarp or cloth at night.

A GARDEN HARVEST CELEBRATION

Whether you have an established Three Sisters garden, are just starting one, or have no garden at all, you can celebrate harvest time. After all, the fruits of a farmer's labor are readily visible in Autumn, and the harvest is something to celebrate! The ways of celebrating the abundance and beauty of the harvest are limited only by your imagination. Do as indigenous people around the world have done for generations - plan a Garden Harvest Celebration Day!

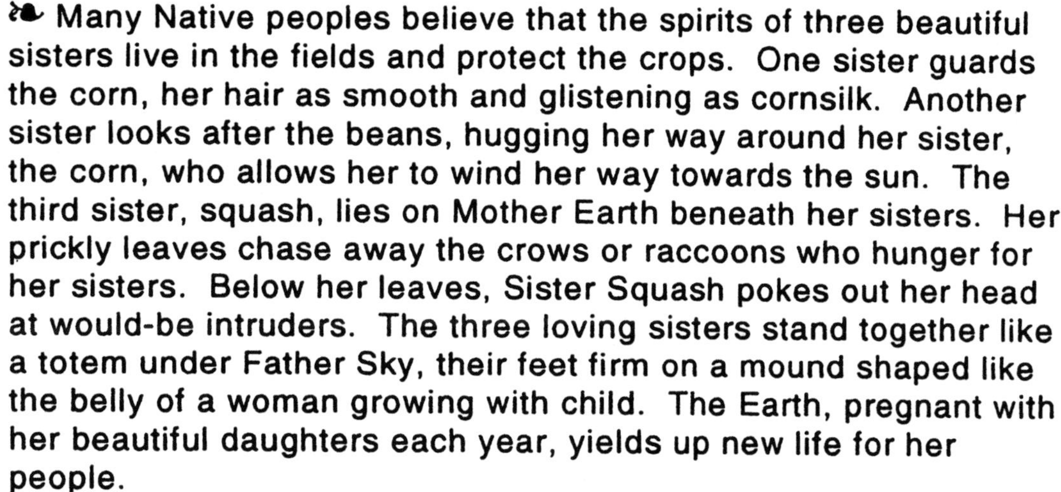

❧ Many Native peoples believe that the spirits of three beautiful sisters live in the fields and protect the crops. One sister guards the corn, her hair as smooth and glistening as cornsilk. Another sister looks after the beans, hugging her way around her sister, the corn, who allows her to wind her way towards the sun. The third sister, squash, lies on Mother Earth beneath her sisters. Her prickly leaves chase away the crows or raccoons who hunger for her sisters. Below her leaves, Sister Squash pokes out her head at would-be intruders. The three loving sisters stand together like a totem under Father Sky, their feet firm on a mound shaped like the belly of a woman growing with child. The Earth, pregnant with her beautiful daughters each year, yields up new life for her people.

❧ The following legend of O-na-tah is a story from the Seneca Nation written by Arthur C. Parker. This story can set the theme for your Harvest Celebration Day, and is a wonderful way to share the history of corn with your guests. This story concerns the Great Mother Earth's love for O-na-tah, the bringer of life-giving grain to the Native peoples. Tell it around the garden.

"The Legend of O-na-tah"

Some time ago, O-na-tah, Spirit of the Corn, had two companions: Sister Bean and Sister Squash. The three stood together in one hill, their spirits entwined. They were called De-o-ha-ko.

O-na-tah, Spirit of the Corn, had silky hair and a soft

Courtesy of New York State Museum, Albany, NY.

O-na-tah: Spirit of the Corn

green cloak of husks. Spirit of the Squash was crowned with golden, vessel-shaped blossoms. Spirit of the Bean was dressed in the leaves of its winding vine. In the summer breeze, her velvety bean pods swooped and swayed.

One day, O-na-tah wandered off in search of the dew left by Grandmother Moon. While she was away, the Dark One came to blight the fields. Spirit of the Squash and Spirit of the Bean fled far from home. O-na-tah was captured by the Dark One and taken deep beneath the Earth. There she wept, longing for her home and companions. But a searching sun ray found her and guided her back to the fields.

Upon her return, O-na-tah vowed to the Sun that she would never leave her fields again. And she kept her promise - she never abandons her fields until the maize is ripe.

In the Spring, O-na-tah's crows flock as she welcomes the planting season to the land. When the sun shines too brightly and causes the maize stalks to bend low, O-na-tah folds the husks to shade the jewel-like grains from the strong rays. And when the corn's tassels plume, O-na-tah crowns the maize, life-giver for all the people.

To this day you will often see O-na-tah tending the corn alone, longing for her two companions and guarding against the return of the Dark One.

❧ This ancient story tells what can happen when gardeners plant a field with a single crop. The health of the crop may be threatened by blight, insects, or diseases. The Three Sisters, on the other hand, are companion crops that improve plant and soil health when they are planted together. The beans feed the corn, the corn provides a stable trellis for the beans, and the squash mulches the earth to prevent moisture loss and weed growth. The living mulch cools the roots of all Three Sisters. Together the Three Sisters are strong; alone they are weak.

❧ Create another paragraph for the story of O-na-tah, explaining why she prefers Spirit of the Squash and Spirit of the Bean - rather than other crops - as garden companions.

Planning a Harvest Day Celebration

❧ You can celebrate the harvest whether or not you have a garden. Harvest foods are available at the farmer's market, the co-op or the grocery store. When planning your harvest ceremony, include traditions that can be passed on from year to year. The story of the Rainbow Maidens might inspire you to research meaningful traditions.

Here are some suggestions to consider:

❧ **Pass along the teachings of Sisters Corn, Bean, and Squash.** Perhaps the Story of On-a-tah will become the traditional story repeated at every Harvest Day Celebration in your neighborhood. This will insure that the wisdom of the Three Sisters is shared every year with fellow gardeners!

❧ **Create a lovely, life-size Corn Spirit who will magically appear in your garden on harvest day!** Or prepare a costume and play the part of O-na-tah yourself, retelling her story to your harvest guests. Perhaps her two companions will appear in costume at the very moment you add the newest paragraph to O-na-tah's story!

❧ **Decorate your garden wickiup with autumn leaves and wildflowers.** Weave them into a living bean trellis that climbs the wickiup. Or build a harvest shelter near the Three Sisters garden and fill it with baskets of freshly harvested garden foods.

❧ **Dedicate a portion of your garden harvest as a "give away"** to a community elders' group or to your local food pantry, and post it with a sign. If you don't have a garden, or are just beginning your garden, then ask a garden stand or a market or farm to donate a variety of harvest foods as a "give away."

❧ **Prepare harvest foods for a potluck dinner.** Potlucks are a tradition derived from the Native "potlatch."

❧ **Pass around a "talking rock."** Each person holding the talking rock shares what she or he is thankful for during this harvest season.

Want To Do More?

✍ In your journal, draw De-o-ha-ko. (De-o-ha-ko is the Iroquois word for the Three Sisters.) From your journal drawing, design a Three Sisters totem. Here is one way to make a **Garden Spirit Totem of the Three Sisters:**

1) Lash two poles together to make a T-shaped pole for support.

2) Nail a small wooden platform on top of the T. This will support a pumpkin head.

3) Wrap the upright pole with cornstalks.

4) Place a carved or painted pumpkin "head" on the wooden platform.

5) Hang more cornstalks from the horizontal pole. If you wish, add muted, green gauze for a cloak, or dangle strips of cloth that will blow in the wind.

6) Adorn the totem with a bean pod necklace and a corn-bean-squash seed crown.

7) Add any other creative materials that bring the spirits of your Three Sisters to life.

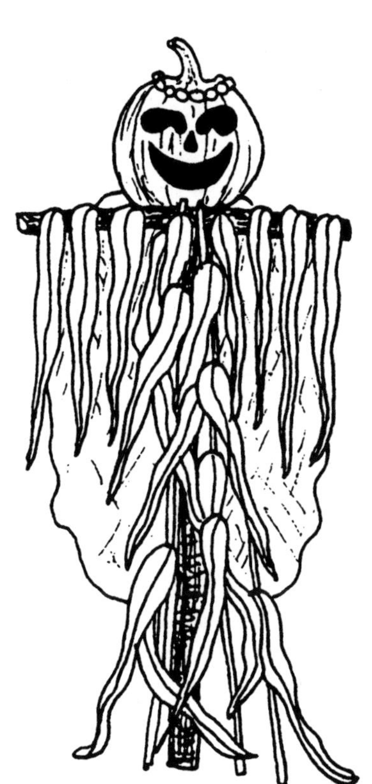

Put your totem in your garden or festival area as a welcome for your harvest day guests. Leave it there throughout the Winter!

Even More Curious?

❧ As noted earlier, the story of O-na-tah is a reminder of what can happen when a single crop is planted in a garden or field. Today, many farmers and gardeners still plant a single crop in a huge field. Many prefer this method, known as "mono-cropping," because it is easy. But although the method is easy, it is not wise. The frequent occurrence of blight and pestilence throughout the world teach us that only the power of a healthy Earth and wise planting techniques can bring forth the gifts of the land for generations to come.

❧ Find out more about the Three Sisters technique of "**interplanting**" several crops. Ask your gardening neighbors about plant and soil relationships that build strong food systems.

Three Sisters Harvest Center

Whether you have your own garden or are working in a friend's garden, Fall is harvest time. Create a festive harvest corner or central table to display harvest time with the Three Sisters.

Choose from the many following harvest display ideas:

❧ **Design life-size characters to represent the Three Sisters.** Make body tracings on cardboard or large brown paper. Use paint or pastels for harvest colors. To decorate Sister Corn, add golden yellow glitter crowns, corn silk, or a dried and pressed husk headdress. Sister Bean's regalia might include bean vine crowns or necklaces, dried pods, and dried bean necklaces. Create clothing made of dried, pressed bean leaves. Sister Squash will look great with a mosaic made of rows of pumpkin seeds, which can be fastened into a golden-orange headband. Surround the Three Sisters with freshly picked produce from your own garden or neighborhood farm!

❧ **Gather corn stalks from the garden or a neighborhood farm.** Tie the stalks in bundles to make corn shucks. Corn shucks work well as a decoration around overflowing harvest baskets. Show off your harvest with jars of popcorn kernels, cornmeal, applesauce, jam, sauerkraut, pickles, or dried beans!

❧ **Native American gardeners dried their corn braids on walls or hung them from rafters and drying racks. You can, too!** For easy braiding, moisten the corn husks. To braid the husks of individual corn cobs, divide the husks into three sections. Braid as usual. Or braid many corn cobs together in a fancy style, just as you would braid onions or make a French braid in a friend's hair.

To braid in a fancy style, begin braiding the husks of three ears of corn together. Ask a friend to add another corn cob to the left strand of the braid. The two husks on the left now become a single strand. Twist the braids for a bit, then ask a friend to add a corn cob to the right strand. Continue adding new corn cobs every few twists until you have a long stretch of corn cobs braided together. Finish by tying a moist corn husk or raffia knot at the end.

A month later your fancy braided meal corn will be fully dry and ready for grinding. However, it can remain hanging in beautiful braids until needed for a winter or spring recipe.

❧ **Popcorn ears can also be individually or French braided.** Or simply pull back the husks and allow the corn to dry. Remove the corn silk and put it in the compost or use it as hair on corn husk dolls. Popcorn will dry in a month. To determine whether it is ready for storing, remove a kernel from an

ear and test-pop it. If the kernel pops, store the entire cob in large glass jars. Or remove the kernels from the cob by rubbing two cobs together. Store the kernels in a glass jar. Proper storage will preserve the kernels' moisture, which causes them to pop. Display jars of popcorn in your Indoor Garden Harvest Center until you are ready to use them. Check popcorn jars monthly for moisture buildup or mold. If you find either, open the jar for a day to let excessive moisture escape, then close the jar tightly.

❧ **Display Jack-O-Lantern Pumpkins in your Indoor Garden Harvest Center.** Pumpkins require cool storage or they will mold. Store them away from direct sun or heat vents. Properly stored pumpkins should last until Halloween or even Thanksgiving. Pie pumpkins are stored in the same manner, but they can also be dehydrated, cooked, pureed, or frozen. After processing them, eat the pie pumpkins immediately. Or save them for a delicious meal on a cold winter's evening.

Harvest Math, Nature's Way

❧ At harvest time there are numerous opportunities for math - nature's way!

Weigh the smallest and largest pumpkins. Record the weight on each with a tag. Estimate the weight of the remaining squash or pumpkins without picking them up. Write down your estimates, then pick up the pumpkins and weigh them in your hands. Compare these weights with the weights of the largest and smallest pumpkins. Line up the pumpkins in the order of their estimated weights. Check your predictions by weighing all the pumpkins on a scale. Try to guess which pumpkin, or combination of pumpkins, weighs the same as you do! The only way to know for sure is to weigh yourself and the pumpkins.

Can you estimate the number of beans in a pod? Shell the beans, then count them. Can you count them in twos, fives, sixes, and tens?

Can you estimate the number of kernels of corn on one cob? Count loose kernels in sets of twos, fives, and tens to see how close you came to the estimated amount.

Compare your height to the height of a corn plant. Measure in inches, feet, hand height, or corncob lengths.

Measure the volume of whole dried kernels before grinding the corn. Then measure the volume of the ground corn meal. Compare the two volumes. Are they the same? Why do you think they are different?

Want To Do More?

❧ Measure the volume of dried kernels of popping corn, then pop the corn and compare that volume to the volume of dried kernels.

What happens when a moisture-filled kernel of popcorn heats to expansion? To learn more about this exciting process, read *The Popcorn Book* by Tomie de Paola.

SEEDS AND SEED CARRIERS

As soon as the harvest is in, a young farmer's thoughts must turn to next year's garden. This means thinking about seeds. Although community elders literally handed down the seeds of life to their great-grandchildren, today many people buy seeds from seed companies.

❧ But where did the first seeds come from?

According to an old Iroquois story, they were gifts from the earth and sky to the people of the world. The following story is an adaptation by our authors of the theme of this ancient tale.

"Nothing But Mud"

This story begins long, long ago, on a day when Muskrat placed a pawful of mud on Turtle's back and the land began to form.

That day, the Creator invited a multitude of creatures to make Turtle's back their home. Four-, six-, and eight-leggeds, as well as many winged creatures, eagerly climbed onto the solid earth. Since it was Autumn, they began to build nests, dig holes and search for dens. Unfortunately, everything had to be made out of mud. When the rains came, all their hard work was washed away. The animals quickly realized that this was a serious problem.

The animals assembled to discuss their situation. Everyone was hungry from the work they had been doing, so they decided to have a feast. But they soon discovered that there was nothing to eat! The land might be solid, yet there was no food on it, and nothing but mud with which to build their homes.

The animals summoned the Great Creator from the Shining Mountains, and voiced their concerns. Everyone was given a chance to speak. Many of the creatures were wistful, yearning for the food of their dreams. A few complained of their terrible hunger. Some of the more creative

CSP

and resourceful ones offered solutions.

"Oh," said Deer in her soft doe voice, "how I would love to nibble on tender green grass and the buds of young trees. I'm so hungry I would even eat tree bark! And I would love to take shelter beneath some trees - it's no fun lying on cold, damp soil. I would much prefer a bed of pine needles."

"And I," said the pudgy Caterpillar, clearing his throat so he could speak louder, "would like nothing more than to gorge myself with leaves. Then I could wrap myself in a milkweed leaf and go to sleep. That is what I dream of."

Bear's stomach growled so loudly he did not have to speak - the rumbling and gurgling spoke for him.

Jay squawked, screamed, and prattled, until finally Hawk swooped down and sat beside him, her eyes piercing and her talons sharp. "If you don't pipe down I'll eat <u>YOU</u>," she said. Subdued, Jay retreated to a lower branch.

The council went on all day, each creature making his needs known. Birds wanted grasses and sticks and soft stringy things for their nests. They asked for nuts and seeds and berries to eat. Squirrel and Chipmunk wanted leaves and grass for their dens, and nuts and seeds to store for winter. Raccoon wanted a hollow tree to live in, and anything and everything to eat.

After all the animals finished speaking, the Creator promised them that their desires for food and shelter would be taken care of. But first the animals must go to sleep, the Creator said. As the creatures settled down for a final night on the cold, damp earth, the Creator cast a deep slumber over them all.

And then - strange things began to fall slowly from the sky. Some of them were soft and fluffy, others had hard outer shells and were much larger. But everything fell so gently that the sleeping animals were not aware of the magic taking place around them. They dreamt of a life without mud. And as they dreamt, the magic falling from the sky took root and began to grow in the rich soil.

When the Creator had finished, the earth was transformed. It was lush green now, and carpeted with trees, flowers, shrubs, and bushes. The verdant plants were laden with marvelous things to eat - nuts, seeds, berries, fruit, mushrooms, tender shoots, and grasses. As the Creator stepped back to admire his work, a single gold leaf fell from one of the trees.

The Creator waved his hand - and the animals woke from their sleep. Delighted with their new habitat, the animals began making new homes and soft beds. They devoured the delicious food that had sprouted while they slept. They scurried, hopped, crawled, and flew about.

When the animals' hunger was satisfied and everyone was snug in his new home, the first snowflakes fell. Soon the land was covered with a warm white blanket, which protected the animals and plants from the bitter winter cold. On the ground beneath the snow were precious nuts, berries, and seeds. In the spring these seeds would sprout, and once again the earth would be carpeted with green and growing things.

And so the cycle of seeds and plants began on Turtle Island, where the soil absorbed the sun and rains and nourished the creatures of the earth. Ho!

✍ **Draw pictures of the creatures living on Turtle's back.** What special gift was given to these creatures? What special gifts do Native peoples give to the world?

❧ **Do you know anyone who carries the spirit of Turtle within them?** Seed Carriers bear a great responsibility upon their backs and in their hearts for the people of their community. They keep alive the community's hope by caring for the seeds that will ensure the community's future. They also "plant seeds of good cause and right relationship" in their community.

Choose Seed Carriers from among the gardeners who worked in this year's Three Sisters Garden. These are honorary positions because Seed Carriers are entrusted with the seeds that will be planted in next year's garden. The seeds themselves symbolize the community's hope for the future.

❧ **Interview elders who love to garden.** You might discover a Seed Carrier in your own family or neighborhood. Record and illustrate her story!

❧ **Observe the process of seed-making in your garden and on the land.** Record and illustrate this cycle in your journal.

Want To Do More?

Native Americans have passed down invaluable information to our society. Some of these things include agricultural wisdom, medicinals, and a "caretaker mind." What is a "caretaker mind"? A caretaker mind is an attitude of generosity and caring. Draw some pictures of yourself or your friends practicing "caretaker mind."

❧ **What special gifts have your grandparents handed down to you or your family?** Write a poem about these gifts and draw some pictures to accompany your poem.

Even More Curious?

❧ **Read about Seed Carriers.** Some good stories about Seed Carriers include *Johnny Appleseed, Miss Rumphius, The Legend of Bluebonnet, and Rising Fawn and The Fire Mystery.* (See the Bibliography.)

❧ Read Joseph Bruchac's "The Creation" in *The Wind Eagle and other Abenaki Stories.* This is the story of Sky Woman, and how she brought the first seeds to earth. You may find all of the stories in this book so inspiring you will wish to retell them in the years to come!

Caretaking Seeds: Seed-Saving Pouches

Caretaking seeds is a way of accepting responsibility for your time on the Earth. A Seed Carrier safeguards the Earth's gifts for the community. At harvest time, Seed Carriers prepare a special bundle for safeguarding seeds until the spring planting ceremonies.

A Seed-Carrying Pouch

You will need:

a 9 x 12 inch piece of felt, leather, or sturdy fabric
sharp scissors for cutting the fabric
a darning needle
heavy thread or yarn
optional: small beads that can be threaded onto the yarn or fabric

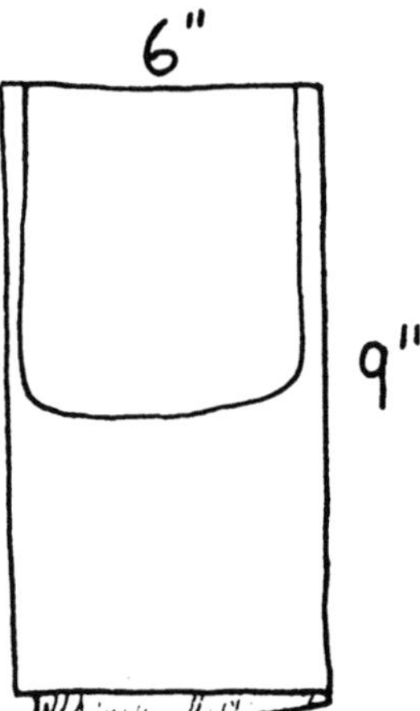

1) Fold the fabric in half so that it measures 6 x 9 inches. Draw a simple pouch shape on one half of the fabric.

2) Trace the same shape on the other side of the fabric. If you would like fringes on the pouch, leave some space at the bottom on one side of the fabric (see illustration).

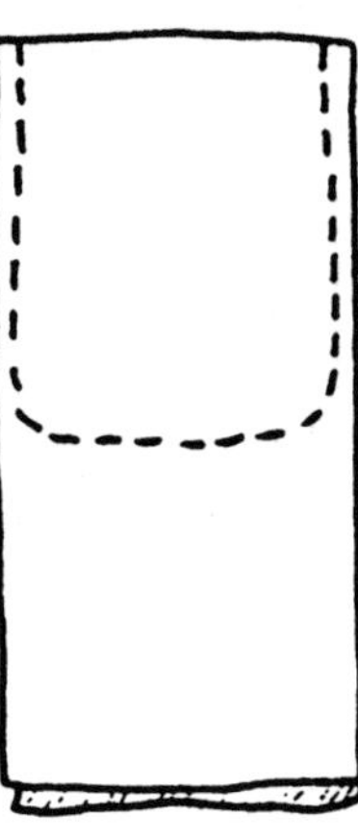

3) With heavy thread or yarn, sew together the two pouch pieces. Use running stitches close to the edge of the sides and bottom. These stitches should be visible on the finished pouch (in other words, do not turn the pouch inside out to hide the stitches). Do not stitch across the top of the pouch.

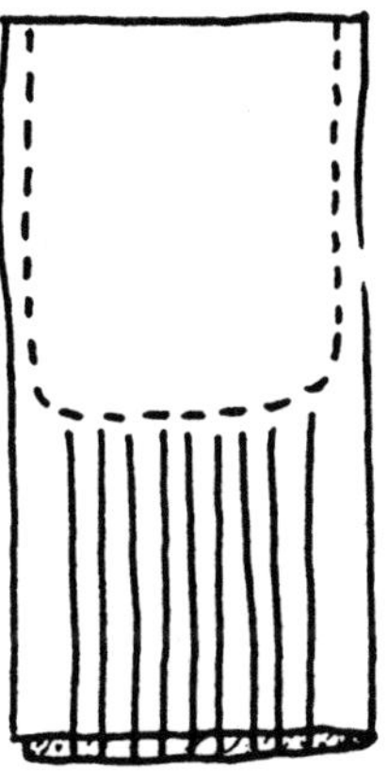

4) After sewing the two pouch pieces together, fringe the bottom (if desired) by cutting several slits into the excess fabric.

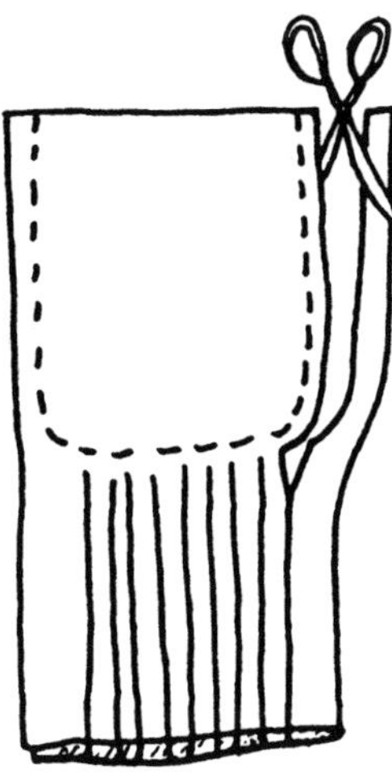

5) Cut out the pouch pattern along the folded edge. All the fringes will now dangle freely.

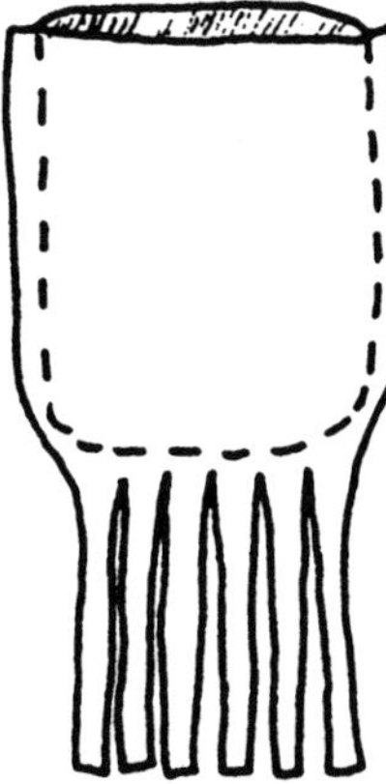

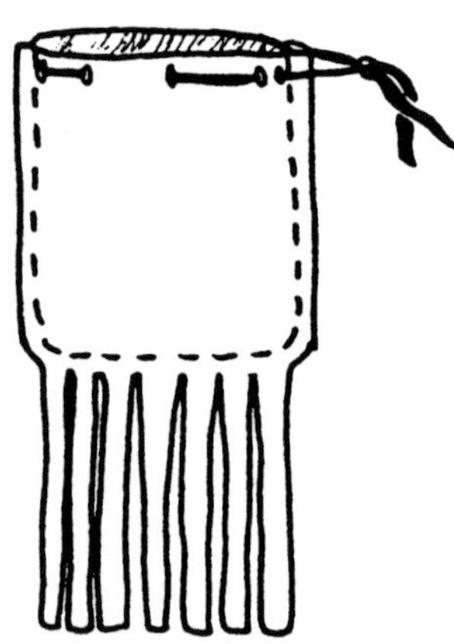

6) Using a long running stitch, thread a strong yarn drawstring through the top of the pouch.

7) If you decide to use leather for the drawstring, punch holes in the top of the pouch. Then thread a thin piece of leather drawstring through the drawstring holes.

8) After adding the drawstring to the top of the pouch, experiment with opening and closing the pouch to determine the proper length for the drawstring. Cut the drawstring at an appropriate length and tie a knot near the end.

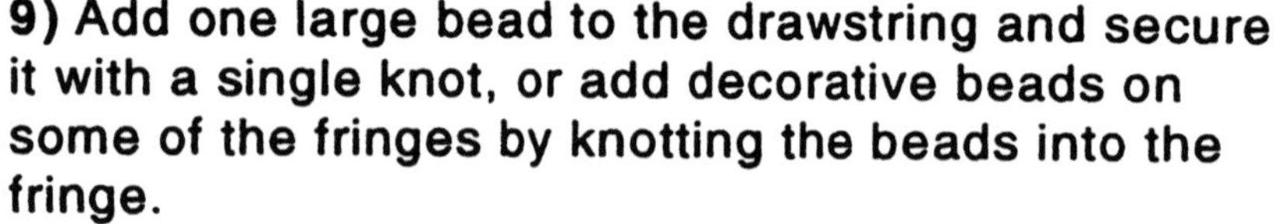

9) Add one large bead to the drawstring and secure it with a single knot, or add decorative beads on some of the fringes by knotting the beads into the fringe.

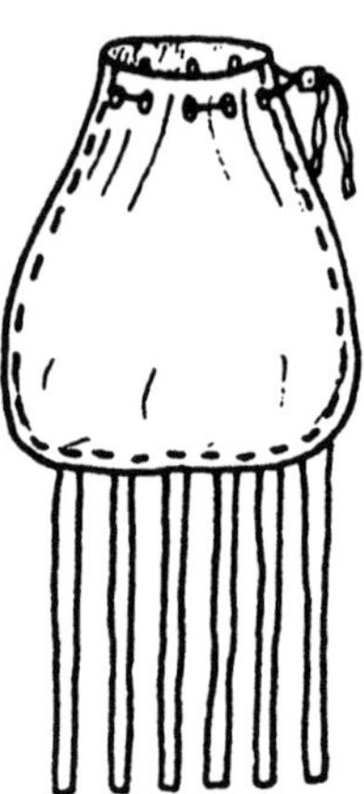

Want To Do More?

❧ Create a special place to keep the seed pouches or bundles. Good places might be on a nature table decorated with special objects, in a wooden box, or in a ceremonial basket.

❧ Seed Carriers can encourage their fellow gardeners to spread the "seeds of good cause" in their community throughout the year. May your seed be strong unto seven generations!

❧ During monthly checks of the bundles, indulge yourself with daydreams of the seeds bursting with the nourishment the people need to feed themselves in body and heart.

Three Sisters Seed Bank

Most people are familiar with saving money in a bank for a rainy day. But a seed bank saves seeds for a rainy day. Such banks will enable you to save seeds for upcoming generations. Imagine passing your seeds along to the seventh generation of Three Sisters gardeners!

Saving seeds is like saving a part of history - you can preserve the magic of life with your very own hands! When strong, healthy plants grow under your care in the garden, they provide an abundance of food at the harvest season. This crop carries with it a promise. The promise is contained within the seeds cradled inside the parent plant - the promise to create more food! All the seed requires is the proper care you give it.

Seeds pass on their strength and health to the next generation of plants. If they survived last year's drought or chilly weather, they will surely make it through this year's garden challenges. In a sense, these seeds have special adaptations that come from their unique growing experience. Only your seeds have this particular experience, and no seed company can offer you the same promise.

To start a seed bank. . . .

❧ **Save any variety of non-hybrid seed.** The varieties recommended for growing in your Three Sisters garden are heirloom seeds. Heirloom seeds are descendants of an ancient variety. None of them are a contemporary, laboratory hybrid. An heirloom seed will remain true to its parent plant and produce the same vegetables year after year, just as it has done for hundreds or thousands of years.

❧ **What seeds should you save?** Only the highest quality stock is best for a seed bank, so you should store seeds that display the best qualities of their parent plants. For example, look among your corn plants for those with the largest ears or the most beautiful color, or those having the healthiest, most pest-free, and productive growth.

❧ **If you save seeds from a hybrid vegetable, plant several as an experiment.** Hybrid seeds sometimes "revert." This means they may favor one of their parents over the other - just as one child might have her mother's blond hair, while her sibling has her father's dark hair. By planting hybrid seeds, you might discover some fascinating parent vegetables. This is especially fun when planting the seeds of hybrid squashes.

❧ **Check the health of your seed bank on a regular schedule - for example, on every new moon or on the first day of each month.** The future of your garden depends on it! Look for moisture and mold. If necessary, change your preservation methods.

❧ **Why plant heirlooms instead of hybrids?** Did you know that of all the food plants available to your grandparents, 97% no longer exist? Since Columbus arrived in the New World, 75% of the Native food plants have disappeared. These old varieties nourished generations, and were able to adapt to nature's changes for thousands of years! What do you suppose happened to them?

Heirloom seeds, having survived for hundreds of years or more, possess strength and endurance. Their ability to adapt to diverse growing seasons, pestilence, and other environmental factors is unsurpassed. For example, sunflowers - now domesticated wonders that soar above our heads in the garden - were once wildflowers that bloomed across the prairies of the Plains people. The Native people knew the importance of sunflower oil for cooking and nutrition, and planted the wild seeds in their own gardens. Sunflowers, heirlooms of the Plains people, now stand tall across the world, even in Soviet gardens!

Sunflower seeds and oil are included in the major food and bird-seed crops of the world.

When you plant an heirloom seed, think of the hands of the ancient farmers and gardeners who tucked the relatives of these seeds into the earth. These hands tended the crops, carefully selecting the most vital seed year after year. They even created a better quality crop by transferring pollen from one variety to another. Their efforts resulted in the fine, quality seeds available today. All this was accomplished long before contemporary scientific processes began hybridizing seed!

Hybrid plants, on the other hand, are new kinds of seeds - many of them are designed by seed companies. They combine different qualities of plants, too, but the seeds have not survived the same process and test of time as the heirlooms. Seed companies create hybrids for special commercial characteristics, such as toughness for shipping purposes, ripening qualities, and cosmetic appearances. They are especially concerned with seeds that will adapt to petrochemical agriculture. Hardly a home gardener's dream! The seed saved from hybrid plants will most likely revert to one of the original parent plants from which it was formulated. As a result, hybrid seeds must be purchased from a seed company every year. Home gardeners who depend upon them lack independent seed-saving options.

Want To Do More?

❧ What story, or memory, do you preserve when saving seeds? Is it the memory of a gigantic pumpkin you grew when you were five years old? Is it the memory of the pansy faces that smiled at you in your grandmother's garden? Help your seed's story survive by telling it to the members of your family!

❧ Visit a farmer in your community who saves seeds. You might be surprised to find large stashes of seeds banked in a barn! These seeds contain the history, or story, of food grown by generations of the farmer's family. What history - or "herstory" - do you think you will discover? Local garden club members who save seeds from their favorite garden plants have wonderful stories to share - as do Native gardeners.

❧ Abundant harvests of seeds can be dried and saved for gifts or trading. Design and illustrate your own seed packets. For a spring fundraiser, sell seed packets. Use the proceeds to purchase materials or tools for your Three Sisters garden. Or donate the funds to support a community garden.

Two Stones and the Gift of the Wolf

Have you ever thought that animals - and maybe plants too - seem to know how to live wisely and in harmony among each other? People can learn animal and plant wisdom just by watching their ways.

❧ The following story takes place at harvest time. It is a story created by our own authors about a young brave who, with the help of a silver-white wolf, cures his village of the "Not Taking Care" sickness.

"Wolf Medicine"

Once there was a village that was blessed with great health. Illness rarely invaded the neat cluster of well-maintained tipis. When it did, a tribal elder named Sings With The Wind, who was versed in the ways of earth medicine, quickly healed the sick.

The people's excellent health was attributed to their cleanliness. Wigwams were swept out each day. Blankets, rugs, and clothing were aired regularly. Fresh bedding, such as cattail fluff or balsam boughs, was changed often. People bathed in a nearby, swift-flowing stream. Leftover food was carefully buried, and dirty dishes were never allowed to attract flies. The people were especially careful to ask for the blessings of the great spirits who presided over their health. All of this took much hard work and careful planning.

Over time, however, the people grew lazy. Instead of carefully burying leftover food, the women began to throw it out of their tipis, where it collected in smelly piles. Mistrust spread through the village as the men began to close their hearts to each other. Everyone had known vibrant health for so long that the people failed to train a new healer, and when Sings With The Wind died there was no

one to take his place. The villagers took their well-being for granted, and forgot to honor the great spirits.

Although no physical illness manifested itself, a secret, ugly disease slowly crept over the village. It was known as the disease of "Not Taking Care." Everyone - except a young brave named Two Stones - was infected with it.

People in the village thought that Two Stones was strange. He often left the depressing village, with its cluster of dingy wigwams and rotting food piles, for days at a time. Sometimes he wandered for weeks in the woods and mountains that spread beyond the village. There he befriended the creatures, plants, and spirits that inhabited the wild lands. And when Sings With The Wind died, Two Stones mourned, for his people grew more slovenly than ever. He began to wonder if anything could be done to change their ways.

One day he came upon the home of an elderly grandmother, who lived alone high in the mountains. Her wigwam was as clean as the North Wind, and everything that surrounded it was neat and orderly. She had carefully piled stacks of wood near her fire. A soup simmered over the smoky fire, filling the air with its rich, wonderful scent. Two Stones knew he had never been here before, yet the setting seemed oddly familiar to him.

How was it possible he had never come across this place before?

As Two Stones approached her wigwam, he saw that the elderly grandmother was intently fitting an axe head to its handle. Two Stones was sure she had not heard him, so he greeted her from a respectful distance.

"Good afternoon, grandmother. What a beautiful home you have here!"

She looked up from her work, her eyes sparkling. At that moment Two Stones had the strange sensation that he knew her. The elderly grandmother greeted him as if she had been expecting him, calling him by his name, though they had never met.

"Two Stones - you have arrived at a good time! Come share a meal with me. I have made some soup from

plump orange squashes fresh from my garden!"

Two Stones was surprised, and a little afraid. But unlike the members of his village, who had black, closed hearts, his heart was open. And so he allowed himself to trust the hospitality of the elderly woman.

"What may I call you, grandmother?" Two Stones asked her as they went to the fire.

"My name is Shadows and Light," replied the elderly woman, ladling some savory-smelling soup into a carved, wooden bowl. "And over here," she said, motioning to a beautiful, silver-white wolf who mysteriously appeared, "is Moon On The Water." The wolf thumped his tail and licked Two Stones' hand in a friendly greeting before settling in the shade of a mountain ash.

The two humans sat on the soft earth and ate in companionable silence, listening to the sound of the wind in the trees and the ravens cawing in the distance.

After awhile Shadows and Light broke the silence. Looking into Two Stones' eyes, she said, "I can see that you are wondering how my wigwam suddenly appeared here. For you have come to this meadow many times, and basked in the warm sun, but never seen me. How do you think I got my name? Shadows and Light play tricks on the eyes. I have always been here! Trust the feeling in your heart, which tells you that you know me - that you have seen me before."

That night, asleep in Shadows and Light's home, Two Stones had an amazing dream. In it, he stood at the edge of the woods outside his village listening to a rustling sound. He was afraid because he thought it might be a wolf, come to destroy his village. His fear was prophetic, for a beautiful silver-white wolf emerged from the forest and made its way towards the village. Two Stones threw a rock at it, yet the wolf came on, undaunted. Oddly, the wolf did not harm the villagers. Instead it trotted proudly through the cluster of wigwams, its tail high and senses alert. Eventually the wolf retreated into the woods - but Two Stones knew it would return.

The next day, Two Stones awoke to find Light and

Shadows gone. That night, he camped in a lush, boulder-strewn meadow enclosed by firs. He chose a smooth rock for a bed and quickly fell asleep. Stars blazed above him, and soon the moon emerged from behind a great cliff.

Once again Two Stones dreamt about the silver-white wolf. This time the wolf sat down and sang as Two Stones slept in the meadow. The song was mournful and disturbing.

When Two Stones awoke the following morning, he sat for a long time in wonderment, as one does after a powerful dream. He decided to search for Shadows and Light, hoping she could help him understand the medicine in his dreams.

Two Stones arrived at her camp that evening as the Hay-Making Moon rose full and clear. As before, she had a steaming meal ready for him. In exchange, he handed her a gift of ripe berries from the valley.

After their meal, Two Stones told her about his dreams. Shadows and Lights stared seriously at him as she replied.

"The dreams are a message about the demise of your village, Two Stones," she said. "They are warnings. For too long your people have taken their health for granted, and now they are in great need of healing. Unless you bring wolf wisdom to your village, everyone will perish."

"Why do you speak of wolf wisdom?" Two Stones asked her.

"Wolves are known for their immaculate dens," she said, "as well as for their love and care for each other. Wolf medicine teaches us to pay attention, to take care of and respect all that surrounds us. Also," she added, "the dream indicates that it is time for you to take a new name - 'Walks With Wolf.' And my wolf friend here," she said, motioning to Moon On The Water, "shall be your new companion. He will help you to heal your people."

The next day, Walks With Wolf and his four-legged companion returned to the village. What Walks With Wolf saw made him very sad. Many people were dying.

He called the villagers to the central fire for a great healing. That night, everyone slept around the fire and

dreamt the same dream. In the dream, a great silver-white wolf - who happened to look very much like Moon On The Water - came to the fire and warned them about their slothful, uncaring behavior.

"Heed the words of Two Stones, who now calls himself Walks With Wolf, or I will devour everyone in the village. I come but once to give you this warning."

As dawn crept over the sleeping people, Walks With Wolf and his four-legged companion piled wood on the smoldering fire. Soon the blaze roared with healing power. The people awoke, ready to do whatever Walks With Wolf asked, for they were afraid. He told everyone to throw their soiled bedding and clothing onto the fire. Once this was done, the people collected fresh bedding from the forest and swept out their wigwams.

They worked from sunrise until moonset. On sunrise of the second day, their work was at last finished. Everyone was exhausted from the work - but invigorated from their efforts. What a pleasure it had been to work toward a common goal! They gazed around at their village. It was transformed into a neat, orderly, cared-for home. How wonderful everything looked! Smiling with long-forgotten pride, the villagers went into the forest to gather food for a celebration.

Walks With Wolf and Moon On The Water became revered as great healers, for they had cleansed the people of the "Not Taking Care" sickness. Once more the village sparkled with care and love. And after that, no one ever took his health for granted again.

❧ **How did Two Stones gain an understanding of the ways of animals?** How did Two Stones' love for these ways make him a great caretaker and a healer?

Want To Do More?

❧ **An observant gardener can learn the secret ways of plants and apply their wisdom to ensure a healthy garden.** Awareness is the first step in gaining true knowledge. You might enjoy reading *The Other Way to Listen* by Byrd Baylor. Through this story you, too, can discover how to hear a wildflower seed burst open, a rock sigh, or the Earth sing!

❧ **Try this Sit 'N' Watch Experience:** Sit quietly in the garden, on the lawn, or in another natural setting during different times of the day - at sunrise, in the morning dew, at high noon, during the cool of dusk, or under the moonlight. What do the plants and animals reveal to you about their moods, their gestures, their work?

❧ **Begin a partnership with your garden** or with a special place in nature. Mimic and apply some of the revealed "plant wisdom" when caring for your garden. You will become more aware of these wisdoms as you spend time in your Three Sisters garden during Spring and Summer.

And The Circle Goes Round: Compost

All things find purpose in the circle of life through the Earth's natural cycles. Nothing is wasted. Life moves round and round, renewing itself through people's and nature's creativity. Find your way around the circle - with compost.

❧ After Sisters Corn, Bean, and Squash provide crops for the family, the garden rests. Yet the garden does not simply lie empty, for the people's thankfulness has been planted deep in its soil.

❧ Long ago, Native gardeners watched to see if new life sprouted voluntarily from the garden the following Spring. If not, a new garden was planted elsewhere to let the earth replenish itself. Every few years the Native peoples moved their garden to a new area, where it was planted, tended, harvested, then allowed to rest again. This cycle of caring continued from year to year.

Today it may not seem practical to move a garden every year, yet this is an important lesson worth remembering. Some farmers still make good use of this wisdom. They allow a field to rest, or they plant a crop that feeds the soil. Ask a local farmer or gardener how she creates a circle of giving to and receiving from the Earth. Just as the Three Sisters care for one another, you can begin your own cycle of giving. If you do not want to move your garden, you must feed the soil to restore its health. Then it will have the nutrients necessary to grow healthy plants.

By building **compost**, your can make food for your Three Sisters garden. By Autumn's end, it may seem that everything of value was removed from your garden during harvest. What remains hardly resembles summer's lush vegetation. But are the remnants only rubble and refuse? If you allowed the garden to remain in this state for several years, you would see that the debris and seeds scattered upon the ground were beginning a process of renewal. As the debris began to decay, it would release organic matter into the soil, creating a perfect breeding ground in which seeds could sprout. This cycle of decay and renewal is a natural composting process.

❧ Make Your Own Compost!

Speed up the natural recycling process and experience nature's magical power firsthand! Build a 3' x 3' x 3' compost pile or heap. To prevent animals from scattering the compost, enclose the pile with chicken wire, wooden pallets, or fencing made from fallen tree limbs.

To make the compost pile:

1) The compost pile should be made in layers, the bottom layer consisting of "earthy" (brown), woody materials, such as corn stalks, straw, or dry leaves. This layer, which should be 3 to 6 inches deep, should lie directly on the earth.

2) The second layer - also 3 to 6 inches deep - should consist of "watery," or fresh green materials, such as kitchen scraps, weeds, grass clippings, and manure.

3) With a shovel, chop large pieces of corn stalk, bean vines and other plants into smaller pieces. Place this 3- to 6-inch deep layer on top of the fresh green materials.

4) Continue to layer the compost pile, alternating earthy and watery materials.

5) If the materials are very dry, sprinkle additional water on the pile. But do not drench it. Air circulation helps compost decompose.

6) If soaking rains occur where you live, cover the pile with a tarp. This will prevent an overabundance of water from disturbing the circulation of air. It is easy to tell when there is too much water in the compost pile. Just sniff! If the pile smells rotten, moldy, or sour, it is time to circulate the air by turning the pile and adding "earthy" materials.

The sun's warmth provides "fire" to keep the compost pile active. Tiny insects and invisible bacteria also help the compost pile decay.

7) Turn the pile every two or three weeks. This airing helps the materials decompose more quickly. If you do not turn the pile, it will take longer to make compost.

❧ **Do you have too many materials for a compost pile?** Build another 3' x 3' x 3' pile and begin the process again. The smaller your compost pile, the easier it will be to turn and manage it.

But remember, as Fall glides into Winter the weather will be too cold to create compost. Unless you live in a warm climate, you will have to wait until the sun's warmth returns next Spring and begin anew.

Want To Do More?

❧ **As you turn your compost pile, chant:**

Earth, Water,
Earth, Water,
Fire and Air,
Fire and Air.

Which ingredients in the compost pile represent the elements Earth, Water, Fire, and Air? How do they work together to make compost?

❧ **Make two different compost piles.** Use the turn and no-turn method. Compare the results.

❧ **Watch for changes in the compost pile throughout the season.** Tie a brightly colored twist-tie around a sturdy piece of plant stalk. Bury the stalk in the pile. Each time you turn the compost heap, try to uncover this plant sample. What do you see happening from week to week? Illustrate these changes in your nature journal.

❧ **What do you think compost looks like?** Can you estimate how long it might take for compost to form?

And The Circle Goes Round: Creative Arts

Harvest necklaces, Corncob dart game, Cornhusk masks and dolls

Is it possible to recycle all parts of the garden harvest? What plant materials can you use for art projects? The Three Sisters provide many of the materials needed to create beautiful harvest necklaces, cornhusk dolls and masks, and a challenging game of corncob darts.

Three Sisters Harvest Necklaces

Make Three Sisters harvest necklaces, using leftover corn, bean, and squash seeds.

1) Soak corn and bean seeds in water overnight to make them soft and easier to string.

2) Dye squash seeds with food coloring that portrays the colors of Autumn. Dry the dyed seeds overnight on a paper towel.

3) Make different patterns of seeds for your necklace, such as corn-bean-squash-bean. Or bean-corn-corn-squash-squash-corn-corn. Create your own special design!

4) Seeds can irritate the back of your neck or catch in your hair. To prevent this from happening, use felt or a leather neck band for the back half of the necklace. Cut the felt or leather into a 1-inch wide, 6- to 8-inch long piece.

5) Using a large-eyed sewing needle, thread a fish line or quilting thread through one end of the felt or leather neck band and knot it. Now string the seeds (arranged in your special design) by passing the needle and fish line through them. Caution: if the needle is too large, it could shatter the corn and bean seeds.

6) You can make the necklace any length, but before knotting the fish line to the other end of the neck band, be sure the necklace fits over your head.

Pass the Three Sisters legend along by giving a Three Sisters harvest necklace to a friend or family member!

Corncob Dart Game

1) To make a corncob dart, break a corncob in half. Discard the back half (the end that was attached to the cornhusk). Sharpen both ends of a stick in a pencil sharpener. Insert one end of the stick into the front (the narrow end) of the cob. Make holes in the back of the cob with a toothpick and add feathers to balance the dart.

2) The hoop can be made from a willow branch. Twist the branch into a circular shape. If the branch is brittle, soak it first in a stream or a sink. Hang the willow hoop from a tree. Test eye-to-hand coordination by tossing corn cob darts through the hoop. Can you or your friend make ten consecutive tosses of the dart through the hoop?

Cornhusk Masks

Cornhusk masks are fun for Halloween harvest celebrations!

1) Make the mask from pliable cardboard.
2) Cut eye and mouth spaces.
3) Remove husks from corncobs and braid the husks.
4) Cover the mask with the braids.
5) Add flat dried husks wherever a flourish may be needed.

Put on your cornhusk mask and see what a "corny" character you have become!

Cornhusk Dolls

Cornhusk dolls can be fashioned in the following way:

You will need:

ears of corn
heavy books or a flower press
scissors
one or two pipe cleaners
string or yarn
water
dye (optional)

1) Remove the husks from several ears of corn. Husks vary in color from white to green to burgundy, although green husks generally turn white after drying. White husks can be dyed with tea, food coloring, or Rit Dye. When assembling the doll, weave the colors into your own special design!

2) Save corn silk for hair (or substitute brown wool fleece).

3) Use a heavy book or a flower press to keep the husks pressed flat as they dry.

4) Soak the pressed husks in water to make them pliable.

5) To make the doll's head, fold a strip of husk lengthwise, then roll it. Insert a pipe cleaner into the rolled husk head. The pipe cleaner will serve as a neck, and will become the torso around which the doll's body is built.

6) Cover the head with a large piece of husk. Tie the husk at the neck (the pipe cleaner). Leave several inches of husk hanging below the neck. Later, this husk will become part of the shirt.

7) Use silk or wool fleece for the doll's hair. To make a headband, cut a thin strip of husk lengthwise. Secure the hair by tying the headband at the back of the head.

8) To make the pants or skirt, you will need six to eight husks. Tie them together with string at their tapered ends. Now hold the tied end in your fist so that the husks stand up straight. One by one, fold the husks down and fan them out in a circle around your fist. You now have a "skirt."

9) Still holding the husks in your fist, insert the pipe cleaner into the skirt. Secure the pipe cleaner to the husks by tying them with a string underneath the skirt.

10) To complete the skirt, trim the husks to an even length. This will help the doll to stand up by itself.

11) To make pants from the skirt, split the husks into two bunches. Hide the pipe cleaner in a leg. Tie the legs at the feet with string.

12) To add a shirt, place the center of a husk behind the doll's neck and drape the ends forward over the doll's shoulders. Cross the ends of the husk over the chest in an "x" pattern. Now bring the ends around and tie them at the waist in the back. Secure the shirt at the waist with string.

Cornhusk dolls are wonderful for puppet shows, for decorating a nature table, or as gifts.

Want To Do More?

❧ Can you design a circle dance or circle song with accompanying movements as an expression of the special cycles of your garden or other cycles in nature?

Now I Walk in Beauty

Now I walk in beauty.
Beauty is before me,
Beauty is behind me,
Above and below me.

-Hopi chant

Walk in a circle as you chant or sing this Hopi chant. Step mindfully, letting each foot fall gently as if representing the beauty that is felt when walking in harmony and peace. Reach both arms forward when you sing "beauty is before me." Gently arc your arms behind you as you sing "beauty is behind me." Reach both arms overhead, gesturing to the wonders in the sky, when you sing the word "above." Bring your hands down and turn your palms toward the Earth when you sing the words "below me."

For an extra challenge, divide into groups and sing the song in rounds. Each group should walk in opposite directions around a concentric circle while singing its round.

Squanto's Secret: A Guided Journey

The celebration of Thanksgiving reminds us to express gratitude for food and other life necessities. The holiday is associated with stories of the starving Pilgrim forefathers and foremothers. But let us not forget the story of Tisquantum, better known as Squanto, the Native gardener who shared his people's agricultural wisdom with these imperiled newcomers. The Native people's gift of corn became the staff of life for the starving Pilgrims.

❧ In this guided journey, imagine yourself to be a young Pilgrim barely surviving in the new land. . .

It is nearly Winter. The land is cold and hard and offers no food. Your family huddles inside your newly built log house, trying to keep warm. The fire is burning low, but you hesitate to add another log to it, for you have very little wood and the Winter is long. Your food supply is nearly gone. Little nourishment remains aside from the seeds you carried from your faraway home to this new land.

Wild plants greened the land throughout the Summer, but no one knew which were safe to eat and which were harmful. Everyone expected the harvest to fill the cupboards. But the European seeds planted that year were strangers to the new land and did not grow well. Harvest time came and went, and now there is little to show for it - only the meager bit of food left, your kind but hungry neighbors, and the seeds' promise to help you through another year.

At last Spring graces the land, inviting you and the other newcomers to sow your seeds in the moist soil. Weakened by the harsh Winter, you harness your remaining strength to open the hard ground and tuck some seeds into their earthen home. You plant a seed of hope - a hope that the starving times will end with this year's Autumn

harvest. You wait and wait for green sprouts to appear in the fields, but none burst forth. Just as all seems hopeless a stranger appears - a Native of this land. Everyone wonders who he is and why he has come.

The Native man's name is Squanto, and he wishes to share his people's agricultural wisdom with you. His hands work your fields as he teaches your family and neighbors about Sister Corn. Beneath a soft mound of earth, he places a fish as a gift for the land and the seed. In this same soil he places his people's corn seed. It will sway to songs of sky and earth, he says. It will renew your people, it will bring them life. His words convey thankfulness and hope, and are lifted by the winds.

Squanto works throughout the Summer with you and your neighbors, helping you tend the green cornfields outside your village gates. The green fields soon grow taller than the children who hide in the long rows. Eventually the tall, green stalks seem to swallow every deer, every elder who enters the fields. Everyone in the village daydreams of the time when the corn will be brought in, knowing that Squanto has saved them from another starving Winter.

❧ **Remember the gifts of Squanto and the Native people in your gardening practices, medicinal needs, and in other aspects of your daily life.** The Europeans Squanto saved had been farmers in their former homeland. They brought seeds from Europe to help establish a good life in America. However, they were not prepared for the New England landscape. They were accustomed to planting tiny seeds in long, plowed furrows, but that was impossible here because forests covered the land! Until huge tracts of woodlands were cleared, they would have to learn a new method of agriculture.

The Native people planted their seeds in small, mound-like gardens. First, they cleared a small tract of land by girdling the trees. Though it took many returns of the seasons to rid the fields of all the stumps and roots of the dead trees, the people's gardens flourished. This was due in part to Squanto's expertise. Each of the large, round seeds he planted in the mounds was hand-selected for its valuable life force, so that only the strongest, most productive plants took root. Squanto passed this knowledge on to the European settlers, instructing them to tend the mounds with careful attention.

To this day, Native gardens consist of mounds that fit easily among tree stumps. Each mound receives the personal attention of a gardener. Fish, crabmeal, and other nutrients are added directly to the mounds, concentrated in the place where they are most needed. Organic matter from last year's plants is also turned into the mounds - again, this concentrates enrichments where they do the most good. When the Three Sisters are planted in one mound, a diverse but natural environment is created. Diversity is the song of life because it deters insects and helps maintain the balance of nature. Mound planting also prevents water runoff and soil erosion in hilly terrains. This practice is used widely today on large hillside farms. It seems that Squanto helped more than just the first settlers of New England!

Want To Do More?

❧ **In the spirit of Squanto, preserve seeds and design seed packets.** With each seed packet include seed-storing recommendations and a brief story about Squanto's wisdom or your Three Sisters garden.

✍ **Illustrate a garden guide using Squanto's gardening techniques**. Pass it along to a gardening neighbor.

❧ **In a share circle**, tell about a time when someone helped you out of a hopeless situation.

❧ **You might enjoy reading chapter books** about Squanto, such as *Squanto: The Pilgrim Adventure* by Kate Jassem.

Even More Curious?

❧ Squanto was a Pawtuxet man living in the area we now call Massachusetts. Can you find out more about this Native nation?

❧ **Develop a gardening partnership or pen pal relationship** with someone from your local Native community and exchange gardening information. How do Native people in your community work with their Three Sisters?

❧ In ancient times, Native gardeners understood that "corn travels." When two different types of corn were planted in adjoining fields, the women noticed that some of the ears would develop a new strain. Native gardeners deduced that pollen from corn tassels travels by wind to the silk of a developing ear of corn. They called this phenomenon "traveling corn."

Like today's plant-breeding scientists, they realized they could enhance their community's horticultural needs by growing only the best quality corn, so they began to let the wind transfer pollen from one plant variety to another. As a result, our corns today range in color from white to red to purple! Also, today's farmers can select the best corn for their growing season by choosing from varieties that mature from within sixty to one hundred days. Now we have suitable grains for every purpose - dent corn, sweet corn, flour corn, flint corn, and popcorn!

❧ **Do your own "traveling corn" experiments** and see what you can develop! Be sure to write to the "Three Sisters," at Food Works, 64 Main Street, Montpelier, VT 05602, and let us know what you discover!

Three Sisters Cookbook

Make an easy-to-use cookbook of your favorite recipes. Include crafts for corn, squash, and beans. Cookbooks make a nice gift at Thanksgiving.

❧ Design a cookbook cover with illustrations of Sister Corn, Sister Bean, and Sister Squash. You might want to include the following recipes:

- **Cornmeal.** Hang grinding corn and let it dry on the cob for one month. Remove the kernels with your thumb. Grind them with a mortar and pestle or vegetable grinder. Store the cornmeal in glass jars until you are ready to use it in your favorite cornmeal recipe. (For more information about grinding corn and cornmeal, turn to page 144 in "Winter Corn and Corn Grinding.")

- **Sumac Lemonade.** Pick red, fuzzy Sumac fruits. Grind them with a mortar and pestle. Place fruits in hot water and steep for 15 minutes. Strain, then add ice and a sweetener, such as maple syrup or honey.

- **Roasted Pumpkin Seeds.** Remove seeds from a pumpkin. Rinse off the pulp. Place the clean seeds on a cookie sheet and add a little tamari or salt. Broil each side of the seeds for three to five minutes.

- **Beans.** Dry beans. Soak them overnight. Cook them for several hours in a pot of water or soup stock. Add them to stew or soup recipes.

- **Popcorn Buttered with Sunflower Seeds and Nutritional Yeast.** Dry popcorn on the cob. Remove the kernels with a flick of your thumb. Pop them in a popcorn popper. Sprinkle with melted butter, sunflower seeds, and nutritional yeast.

❧ Here is an easy, imaginative way to enter the preceding recipes into your cookbook. Notice that each recipe consists of four separate instructions. Using a format of one recipe per page, divide each page into four boxes. In each of the four boxes, illustrate one of the four-part instructions. Design decorative page borders using small corn or pumpkin stencils. Dip a sponge in paint, then dab the paint inside the stenciled area.

❧ **Include additional delicious Three Sisters recipes** - corn muffins, pumpkin bread, vegetable bean soup or other tasty treats. Don't forget to illustrate your Three Sisters recipes! To assemble your Three Sisters Cookbook, cover each page with a plastic, protective coat. Put the pages in a three-ring binder. Illustrate a picture and glue it to the cover. A clear, plastic binder with a binder clip also makes a good cover.

❧ **Print your cookbook and sell it as a fundraiser** to support your garden projects. Give a copy to the library. Be sure to give your Thanksgiving hosts a copy of your cookbook - even if the hosts are your Mom and Dad! They will be especially pleased if it includes one of your baked or cooked recipes.

A Three Sisters Thankfulness Celebration

Celebrations create an environment where we can share our feelings of gratitude, joy, sorrow, respect, and hope. They also help us make our direction clear. What are the ingredients of a celebration?

Traditionally, Native Americans offer ceremonies of thankfulness throughout the year, but they also practice rituals of gratitude every day. Thanksgiving Day - also known as Pilgrim Day - was the first thanksgiving offered by the colonists, who celebrated it with some of the Native Americans of the Plymouth area. However, the Native peoples of America had been offering thankfulness ceremonies for thousands of years before the Pilgrims arrived.

Ideas for designing a celebration. . . .

❧ A celebration should revolve around a special theme. For example, a Thanksgiving celebration might honor an abundant harvest, Squanto's generosity, the gifts of renewal, the Three Sisters' teachings, or the power of community spirit.

❧ A bonfire, candles, corn shucks, a ceremonial harvest table, or ceremonial dress can create a special mood. Choose colors that express the mood you are trying to create. Ask the participants to wear clothing consisting of these colors, or decorate the ceremonial area with tablecloths or banners of these colors.

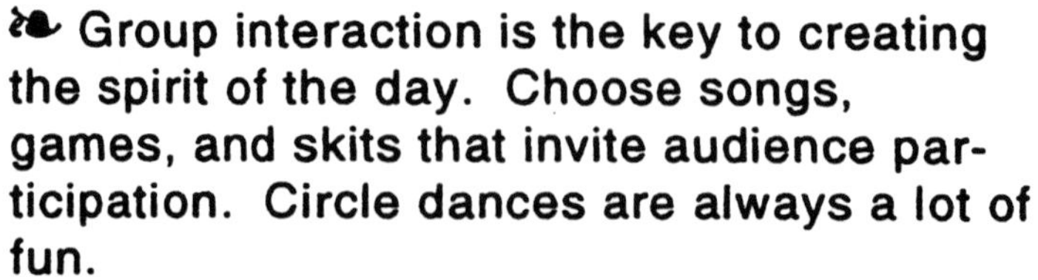

❧ Group interaction is the key to creating the spirit of the day. Choose songs, games, and skits that invite audience participation. Circle dances are always a lot of fun.

❧ A ceremony or share circle can be used to express your feelings. For example, pass a harvest seed around the circle. The person holding the seed might say: "I am grateful for the seed of friendship and I would like to sow seeds of forgiveness." Invite one participant of the ceremony to be the caretaker of this seed. The caretaker can renew the spoken words and deepen their meaning by sowing it at an appropriate time.

❧ Read about a young girl's celebrations in *I'm In Charge of Celebrations* by Byrd Baylor.

Suggestions for a Three Sisters Thankfulness ceremony for your family, school, or community center. . . .

❧ String corn necklaces. During the ceremony, put a necklace on your neighbor as a reminder of the power of every individual to make a difference in times of need. The corn kernels themselves can serve as a reminder of Squanto's gift to the world.

❧ Join in a friendship circle dance that celebrates how wonderful it feels to be alive and to have neighbors who care.

❧ In the spirit of Squanto, donate seeds or a dry bundle of corn seeds from your harvest to your neighborhood food shelf.

❧ Sing songs of thanks. If you don't know any, make up your own. Or, look in the music books *Rise Up Singing* or *Children's Songs for a Friendly Planet,* listed in the bibliography.

❧ In the spirit of the first Pilgrim Thanksgiving, organize a Three Sisters and Brothers Cooperative Games event. Some traditional Native American games are cross-country relays, corncob darts, and the hoop game.

Want To Do More?

❧ Today, many Native Americans do not think of Pilgrim Day, or Thanksgiving Day, as a day of gratitude. It is remembered by them as a harsh turning point in history. The disregard of European colonists for the rights of Native peoples as self-governing, sovereign nations created a series of events that led to their oppression. This unfortunate practice continues today. It is a shameful part of United States history, for it denies to all of us the founding heritage of this country. A sensitive, truthful - not romantic - approach to this topic will benefit Native and non-Native children alike.

Interview Native Americans and learn firsthand why they view Pilgrim's Day as a harsh turning point in their history.

Can you find a way to try to replace these bitter feelings with happy, hopeful feelings for the future? Create or support a community service project that benefits your local Native community.

GARDEN HARVEST SWAP: EATING SEASONAL FOODS

Fall harvest foods have high levels of vitamins and a high quality flavor - both of which your body will love! Prepare your own harvest foods, then swap them with friends and discover new taste treats!

❧ Visit local orchards, farmers' markets, or your neighbor's garden to discover the wide variety of fresh, seasonal foods that are available. You might find apples, honey, potatoes, squash, pumpkins, popcorn, sweet corn, maize, tomatoes, broccoli, blueberries, and other fruits and vegetables.

An experienced forager can help you discover nature's foods. Look for wild nuts and berries in the neighboring lawn, meadow, or forest. Nature's own wild edible gifts might include grapes, sumac berries, butternuts, black walnuts, wild apples, raspberries, and herbs.

❧ **If you cannot eat all of your harvest, preserve foods for the Winter!**

- Apples and pumpkins can be preserved by cooking them, then processing them in a food mill. The sauce or mash can be canned or frozen.
- Make wild grape juice or jelly.
- Dip thinly sliced apple rings in lemon juice, then dry them on a dowel.
- Carrot rounds and corn can be dried by stringing them as a necklace. When you are ready to use them in a soup, simply remove them from the string!

Herbs such as red clover blossoms, coltsfoot, mullein, peppermint, and spearmint can be dried by hanging them. Save them for winter teas.

Make vegetable soups and stews from any of your harvest vegetables. Eat some now, and freeze the remainder to warm you on a cold winter's day.

Plan a Harvest Swap. Ask everyone to bring a favorite harvest food, including the recipe.

As part of a family harvest celebration or school lunch program, organize a Garden Harvest Swap and Taste Day. Mmm, Mmm. Delicious! Publish the recipes in a Harvest Swap newsletter, complete with home-grown illustrations, or add them to your cookbook.

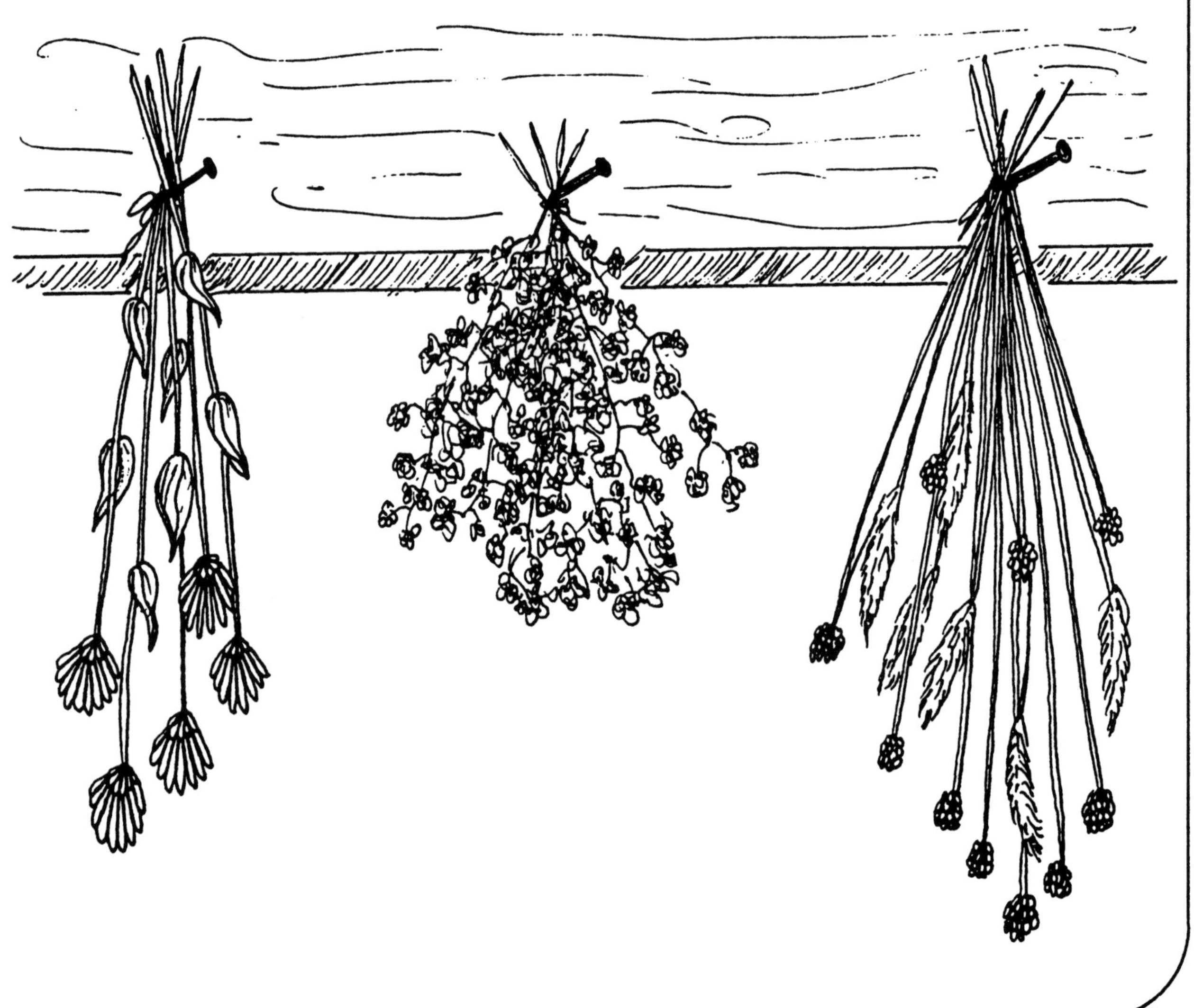

Who Made My Lunch?

Look at your lunch. Do you know where all those foods came from? Everything in it was brought to you by the earth and sun!

❧ Here is a sample lunch - and the sources of each food:

Bread - grains (wheat, corn, or rye), soil, sun.
Milk - cow, grass and grains, soil, sun.
French fries - potatoes, oil, corn, soil, sun.
Hamburger - cow, grass and grains, soil, sun.
Fruit Salad - oranges, apples, bananas, watermelon, mint leaves, soil, sun.
Salad - carrots, lettuce, celery, tomatoes, soil, sun.
Brownies - eggs (which come from chickens and grain), flour (from wheat), milk (from cows and grass), chocolate, walnuts, soil, sun.

Can you trace <u>your</u> lunch food to its source? For example, if your lunch contains milk, draw a glass of milk. Then draw where the milk comes from - a cow. Next draw what the cow eats to make milk - grass or grains. Then draw soil, which feeds the grass and grains. Draw the sun, which grows the grass and grains. Does this make you look at your lunch in an entirely new way?

Spend a week investigating the sources of your lunches. Can you discover which food is native-grown - that is, grown locally in your state or community? Does a local farm raise any of the foods found in your lunch? Which food comes from far away?

❧ **A taste test** is a fun way to compare home-grown food to food from a faraway farm or another country. Pick a carrot, cucumber, or tomato from your garden or local farm. Eat it immediately after picking it, then eat the same kind of food bought from a supermarket. Can you taste the difference? Which do you prefer? The crispy, fresh, <u>alive</u> taste of local produce indicates that nature's best is still inside. You can even taste the earth and sun! Give thanks to both!

❧ All foods come from the Earth's garden. Fresh garden harvests contain lots of vitamins and nutrients that strengthen your body. As harvested food gets older, the vitamins escape or diminish. Why might foods from faraway places have fewer vitamins by the time you eat them? These foods travel by air, truck, or ship to reach your table, and often receive special treatment during transit. This treatment usually prevents the food from becoming ripe during the trip. Can you think of a reason why ripe food does not travel well?

Home-grown food contains fewer, if any, of the chemicals and pesticides used by many large farms. It also contains a lot more vitamins. Chemicals and pesticides do not help your body grow, but vitamins do! Help your body become strong and healthy by eating locally grown foods.

❧ **Make a "Locally Grown Foods" banner** that illustrates your community's locally grown foods. Use fabric paints, iron-on fabric crayons, or applique fabric scraps to illustrate the banner.

✍ With the help of some community volunteers, make a map of your community's native food sources on a large bed sheet. Draw the orchard, beekeeper, corn farmer, dairy farmer, wild berry patch, herbs, pick-your-own strawberry fields, sheep farm, honey hives, market gardens, greenhouse, community gardens, and local fishing hole.

Want To Do More?

❧ **The next time you are in the food market, try to discover the sources of locally grown produce and foods.** Consider buying local foods to support your neighborhood farmers, as well as to eat the sweetest, freshest food of all!

❧ Visit your local food producers, such as a farm stand, dairy farm, orchard, or beekeeper. Help them by lending a hand in their daily chores.

Seasonal Birthday Treats With Sisters Corn, Squash, and Bean

Birthday celebrations can include Three Sister foods, too!

A hearty breakfast for the *Winter* Birthday child. . . .

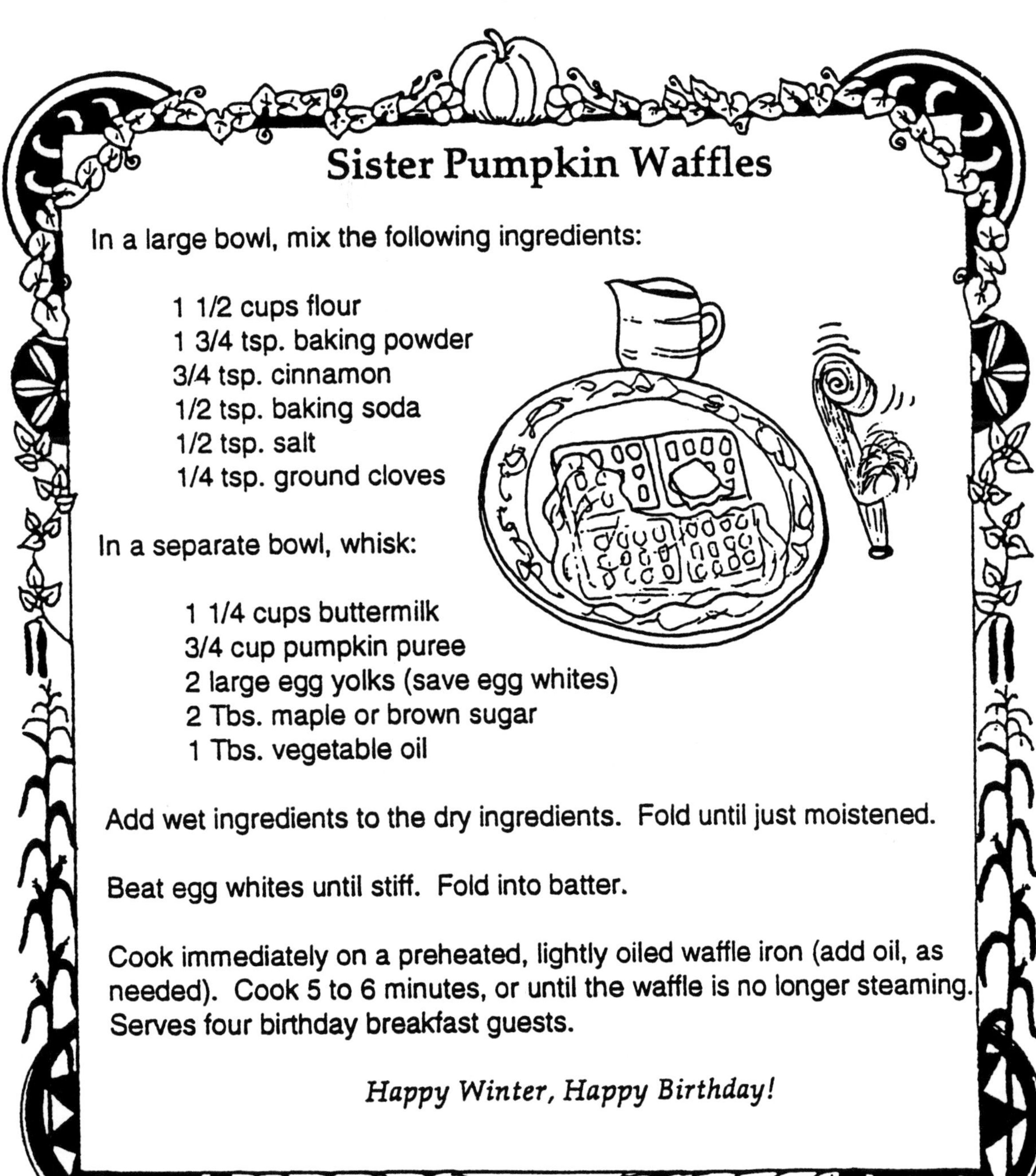

Sister Pumpkin Waffles

In a large bowl, mix the following ingredients:

1 1/2 cups flour
1 3/4 tsp. baking powder
3/4 tsp. cinnamon
1/2 tsp. baking soda
1/2 tsp. salt
1/4 tsp. ground cloves

In a separate bowl, whisk:

1 1/4 cups buttermilk
3/4 cup pumpkin puree
2 large egg yolks (save egg whites)
2 Tbs. maple or brown sugar
1 Tbs. vegetable oil

Add wet ingredients to the dry ingredients. Fold until just moistened.

Beat egg whites until stiff. Fold into batter.

Cook immediately on a preheated, lightly oiled waffle iron (add oil, as needed). Cook 5 to 6 minutes, or until the waffle is no longer steaming. Serves four birthday breakfast guests.

Happy Winter, Happy Birthday!

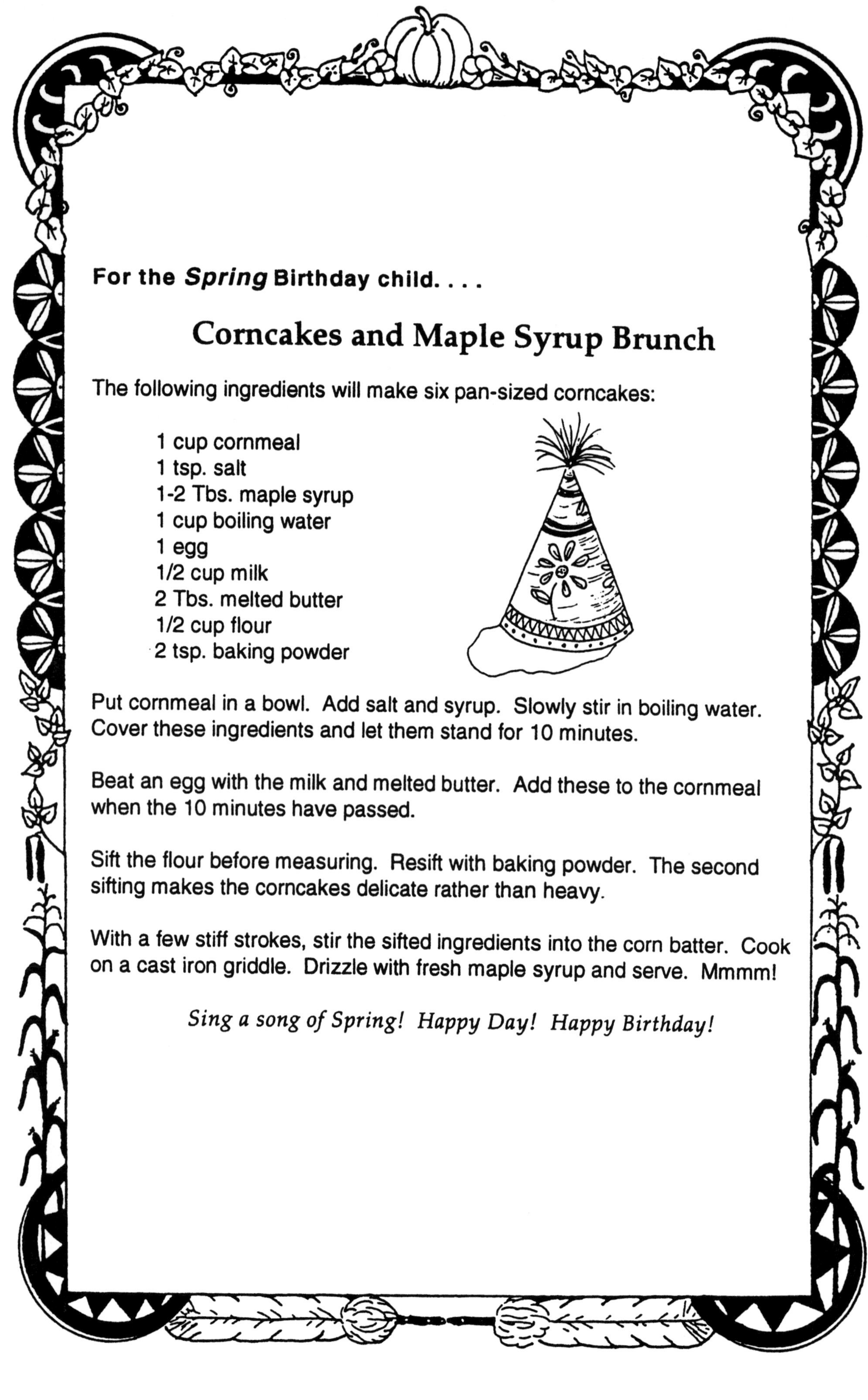

For the *Spring* Birthday child. . . .

Corncakes and Maple Syrup Brunch

The following ingredients will make six pan-sized corncakes:

- 1 cup cornmeal
- 1 tsp. salt
- 1-2 Tbs. maple syrup
- 1 cup boiling water
- 1 egg
- 1/2 cup milk
- 2 Tbs. melted butter
- 1/2 cup flour
- 2 tsp. baking powder

Put cornmeal in a bowl. Add salt and syrup. Slowly stir in boiling water. Cover these ingredients and let them stand for 10 minutes.

Beat an egg with the milk and melted butter. Add these to the cornmeal when the 10 minutes have passed.

Sift the flour before measuring. Resift with baking powder. The second sifting makes the corncakes delicate rather than heavy.

With a few stiff strokes, stir the sifted ingredients into the corn batter. Cook on a cast iron griddle. Drizzle with fresh maple syrup and serve. Mmmm!

Sing a song of Spring! Happy Day! Happy Birthday!

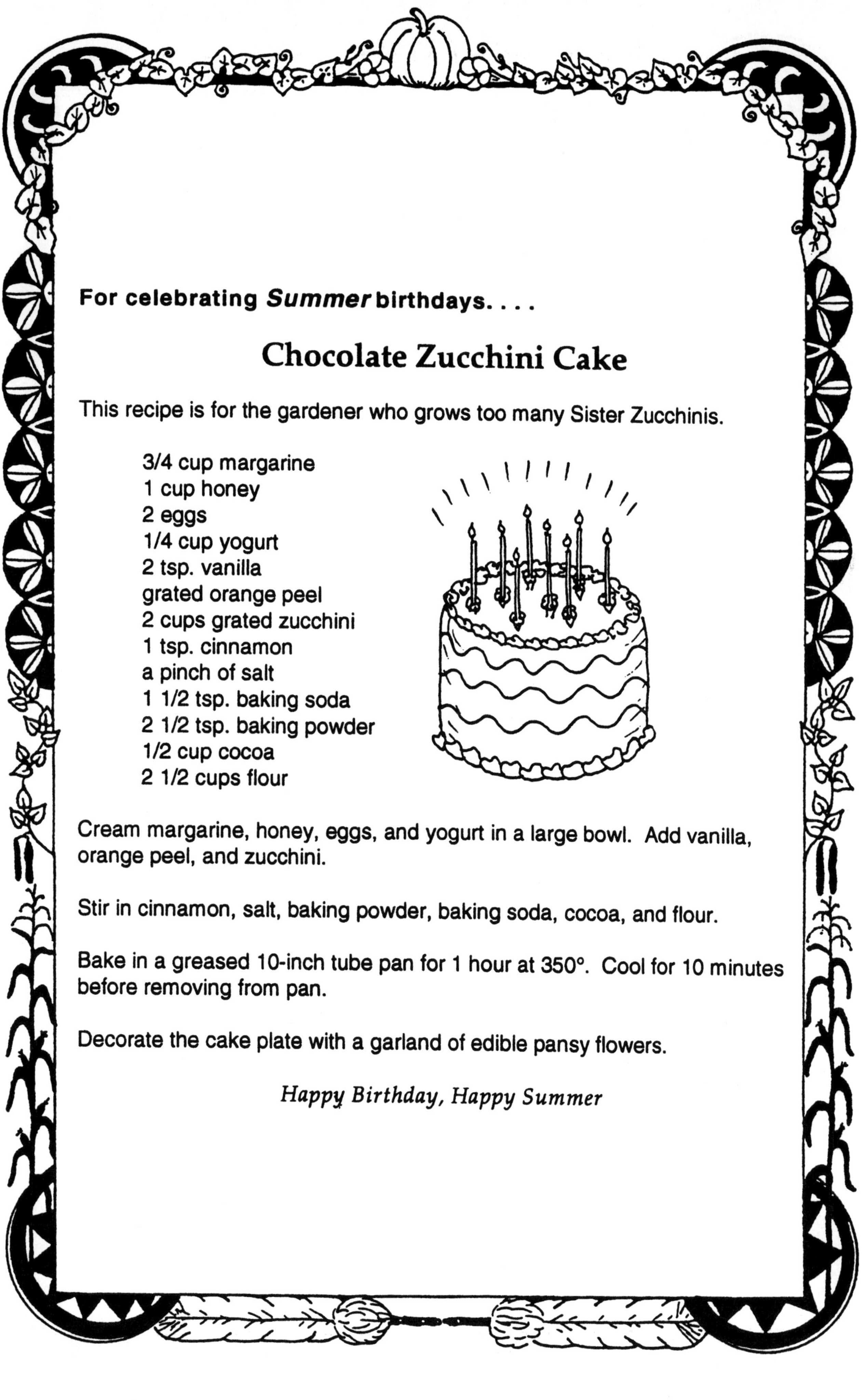

For celebrating *Summer* birthdays. . . .

Chocolate Zucchini Cake

This recipe is for the gardener who grows too many Sister Zucchinis.

3/4 cup margarine
1 cup honey
2 eggs
1/4 cup yogurt
2 tsp. vanilla
grated orange peel
2 cups grated zucchini
1 tsp. cinnamon
a pinch of salt
1 1/2 tsp. baking soda
2 1/2 tsp. baking powder
1/2 cup cocoa
2 1/2 cups flour

Cream margarine, honey, eggs, and yogurt in a large bowl. Add vanilla, orange peel, and zucchini.

Stir in cinnamon, salt, baking powder, baking soda, cocoa, and flour.

Bake in a greased 10-inch tube pan for 1 hour at 350°. Cool for 10 minutes before removing from pan.

Decorate the cake plate with a garland of edible pansy flowers.

Happy Birthday, Happy Summer

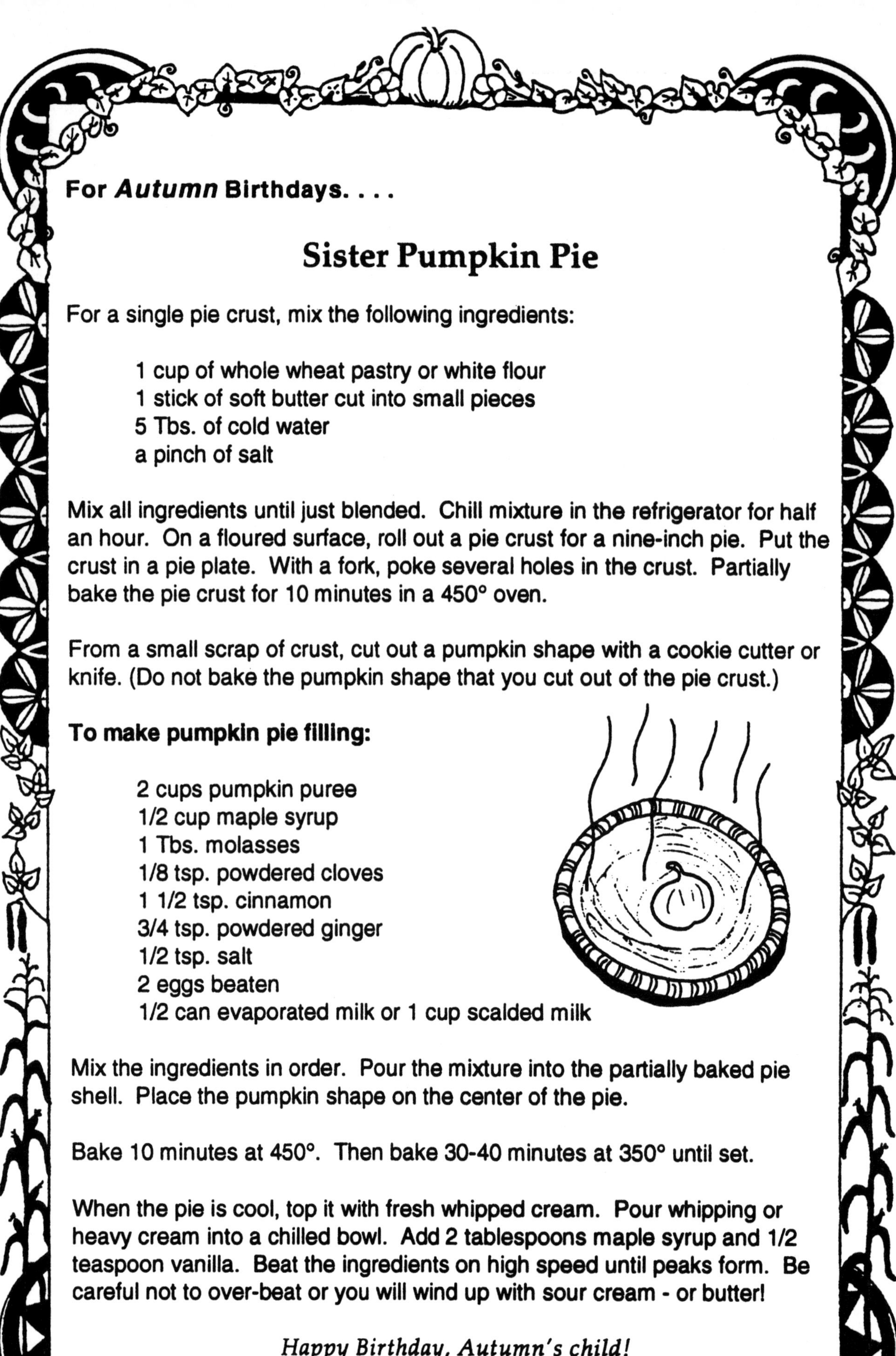

For *Autumn* Birthdays. . . .

Sister Pumpkin Pie

For a single pie crust, mix the following ingredients:

1 cup of whole wheat pastry or white flour
1 stick of soft butter cut into small pieces
5 Tbs. of cold water
a pinch of salt

Mix all ingredients until just blended. Chill mixture in the refrigerator for half an hour. On a floured surface, roll out a pie crust for a nine-inch pie. Put the crust in a pie plate. With a fork, poke several holes in the crust. Partially bake the pie crust for 10 minutes in a 450° oven.

From a small scrap of crust, cut out a pumpkin shape with a cookie cutter or knife. (Do not bake the pumpkin shape that you cut out of the pie crust.)

To make pumpkin pie filling:

2 cups pumpkin puree
1/2 cup maple syrup
1 Tbs. molasses
1/8 tsp. powdered cloves
1 1/2 tsp. cinnamon
3/4 tsp. powdered ginger
1/2 tsp. salt
2 eggs beaten
1/2 can evaporated milk or 1 cup scalded milk

Mix the ingredients in order. Pour the mixture into the partially baked pie shell. Place the pumpkin shape on the center of the pie.

Bake 10 minutes at 450°. Then bake 30-40 minutes at 350° until set.

When the pie is cool, top it with fresh whipped cream. Pour whipping or heavy cream into a chilled bowl. Add 2 tablespoons maple syrup and 1/2 teaspoon vanilla. Beat the ingredients on high speed until peaks form. Be careful not to over-beat or you will wind up with sour cream - or butter!

Happy Birthday, Autumn's child!

Want To Do More?

❧ As a special birthday treat, a parent might tell the story of the child's birth, or relate annual events that occurred in the child's life leading up to the current birthday.

❧ You might enjoy reading *Knots on a Counting Rope* by Bill Martin, Jr. In this delightful book, a young Native boy's grandfather relates the heartwarming story of the young boy's birth. The boy's year-to-year life accomplishments are promising and inspiring to all.

WINTER

Winter ❧

"AMA HEYA THE SEED CARRIER"

Winter was drawing near. The city trees were bare and the days growing shorter, the daylight fad ing rapidly though it was only five-thirty. Yet as Ama Heya stood in the kitchen watching her mother prepare a dessert with Gram's homemade applesauce, she was transported back to her great-grandmother's steamy harvest kitchen. The aroma reminded her of the sweet jams and sauces she had taste-tested under Gram's watchful eye. . . . It was as if Summer had magically returned and was blossoming here in her mother's kitchen.

During the summer harvest, Ama Heya and Gram had canned hundreds of jars of garden magic. Gram knew that the city garden in Brooklyn could not supply Ama Heya's family with food for the year, so she sealed magic from her country garden into jars, which Ama Heya brought home at the end of the Summer. The magic remained hidden in a dark cupboard until Ama Heya's mother decided the time was right for sharing it.

But Gram had other sources of magic, too. Ama Heya thought about the jars and bundles of Three Sister seeds that her great-grandmother carefully laid in a drawer beside neatly ironed and folded lace handkerchiefs. Gram cared for these seeds in an extra special way. She told Ama Heya that the seeds were like children. They must be loved. Spoken to. And never forgotten. Gram said that although the seeds lay sleeping all Winter long, they held the story - the promise - of tomorrow. Whoever cared for them carried a great responsibility for her people. Ama Heya understood what her great- grandmother meant. When Gram spoke to the seeds, she whispered to their spirits. She cared for her green children as though they were her own children - or great-grandchildren. Gram always knew which seeds were the strongest, the best to save. It was part of the great mystery that Ama Heya hoped to discover one day.

Gram often spoke about the sleeping bud inside Ama

Heya. She told Ama Heya that it was important to sing to and cradle the sleeping bud as though it were a baby. Ama Heya was not always sure what Gram meant by the sleeping bud, but she thought it had something to do with growing up and what she would one day become. Gram even called her "Little Sprout."

Sometimes Ama Heya would hide in Gram's cornfield and think about these things. In Brooklyn her brothers were always around the house, and she rarely had an opportunity to be by herself - to read, to think, to dream a girl's dream. But in the cornfield she found peace and solitude. Shaded by Sister Corn's drooping leaves, she basked in Summer's lazy quietude, listening to her sister talk to the wind. It was a wonderful place, a world made possible by Gram's magic fingers.

Now, as she stood in the fragrant kitchen in Brooklyn, breathing in the aroma of warm apples and cinnamon, Ama Heya thought of the seeds she had tucked away in her own drawer upstairs. Quietly, she started up the stairs to check on them. Did magic still exist in those corn kernels, which were as dried and shriveled as great-grandmother's hand?

Indoor Winter Garden

Even though Winter has arrived, you can still grow food! With some help from friends, you can build an Indoor Garden Center where you can grow vegetables to maturity in three months. All your need is a sturdy table and adjustable grow-lights. Or, build a windowsill garden of your very own! You can even decorate your garden center so that it resembles a Three Sisters village.

❧ **An Indoor Garden can be constructed in whatever shape or size you wish.** Plants can be grown on a windowsill or in another warm location. If sunlight is unavailable, grow-lights will produce the intense light that plants need. Grow-lights should be suspended by a chain approximately three inches above the top of the plants. Use an S-hook system so that the grow-lights can be easily raised and repositioned as the plants grow. (Look in the bibliography for the National Gardening Association's book *Grow Lab*. It contains directions on how to build your own Indoor Garden Center, or how to purchase their "Grow Lab.")

Container-variety vegetables should be grown in six-inch or larger pots. Line a tray with small stones and place the pots in the tray. Stones retain moisture, which creates a healthy growing environment for the plants. Or purchase a capillary grow-mat, which is specially designed for gardening in containers.

❧ **Ask elders or parents to help you perform your winter gardening tasks on a regular basis.** In return, invite these gardening friends to take part in a winter harvest from your Indoor Garden.

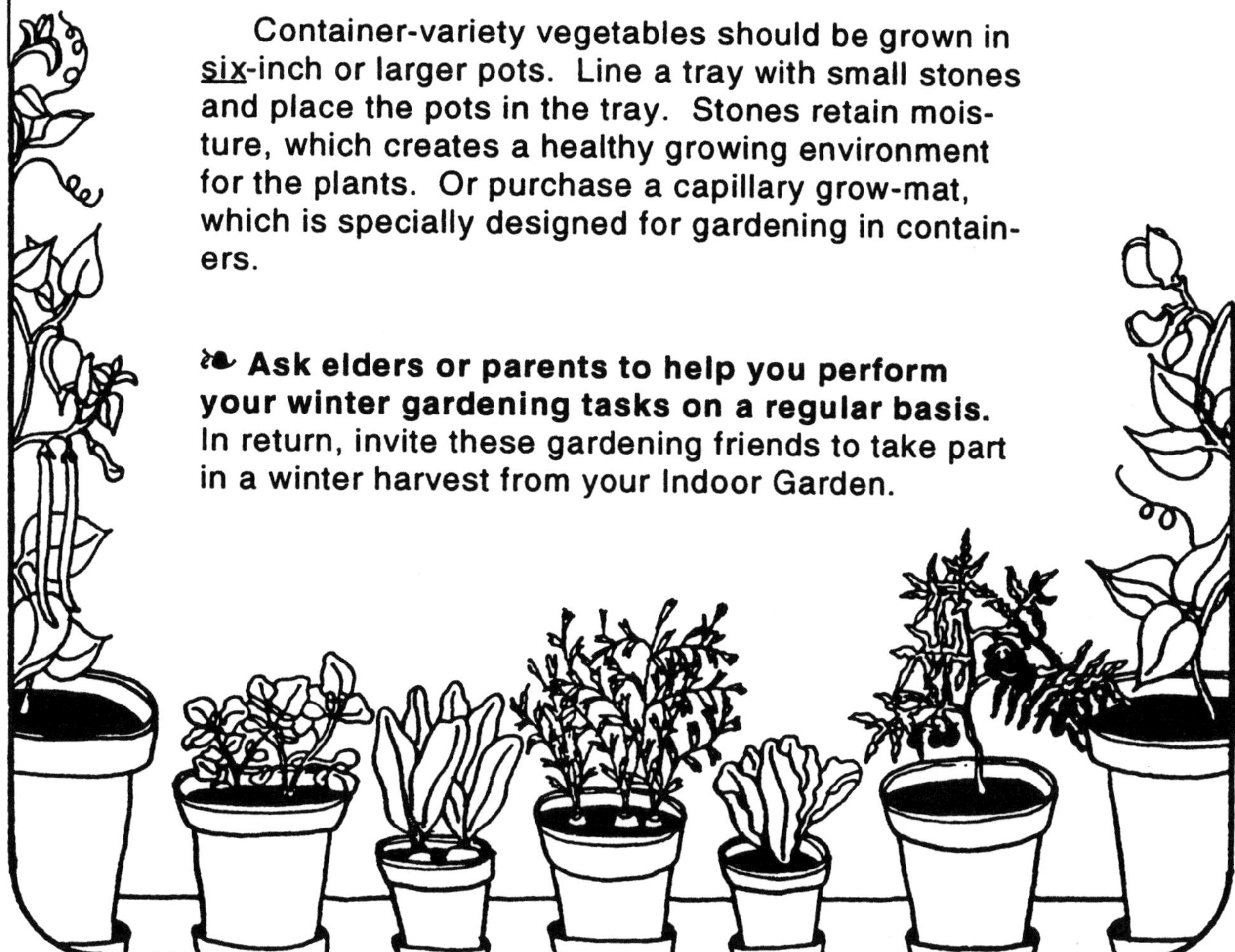

You will probably find that you can learn a lot from your elder friends, but don't be surprised if they learn a lot from you!

❧ **Would you like to grow foods indigenous to the American continent in your Indoor Garden?** Bush beans grow well. So do cucumbers, which come from the family of cucurbits and are related to squashes. Grow tiny, currant-size tomatoes, the great-grandaddies of cherry tomatoes. Miniature carrots, relatives of Queen Anne's Lace, are fun to grow. So is lettuce, which is related to wild chicory. Radishes add a spicy taste. Unfortunately, Sister Corn is not happy indoors, so it is best not to grow her seeds in the Indoor Garden.

If you are not sure what variety to grow, consult a reference book. Many reference books provide complete gardening information and cultivating tips about container vegetables for the Indoor Garden or windowsill garden. Check the bibliography at the end of this guidebook for a few suggested references.

❧ **Write for seed catalogues.** Companies like Shepherd's Seeds carry a selection of seeds that can be grown in containers. Many companies sell miniature vegetable collections, which are considered gourmet foods in the restaurant business. Look for varieties of bush beans, bush cucumbers, miniature Thumbelina zinnias, edible dwarf nasturtiums, and dwarf or gem marigolds. Other reliable container varieties include Planet Mini-Carrots, Red Currant cherry tomatoes, and Tom Thumb Lettuce. For herbs, try Basil Fino Verde Compatto and Greek Mini-Windowbox Basil. Write to Shepherd's, 30 Irene Street, Tarrington, CT 06790, and ask them for their latest Shepherd's Seeds Catalogue. (For more information, see "Dreaming of Your Three Sisters: Ordering Seeds", page 156).

❧ **Can you identify all the different tasks your Indoor Garden requires to grow healthy**

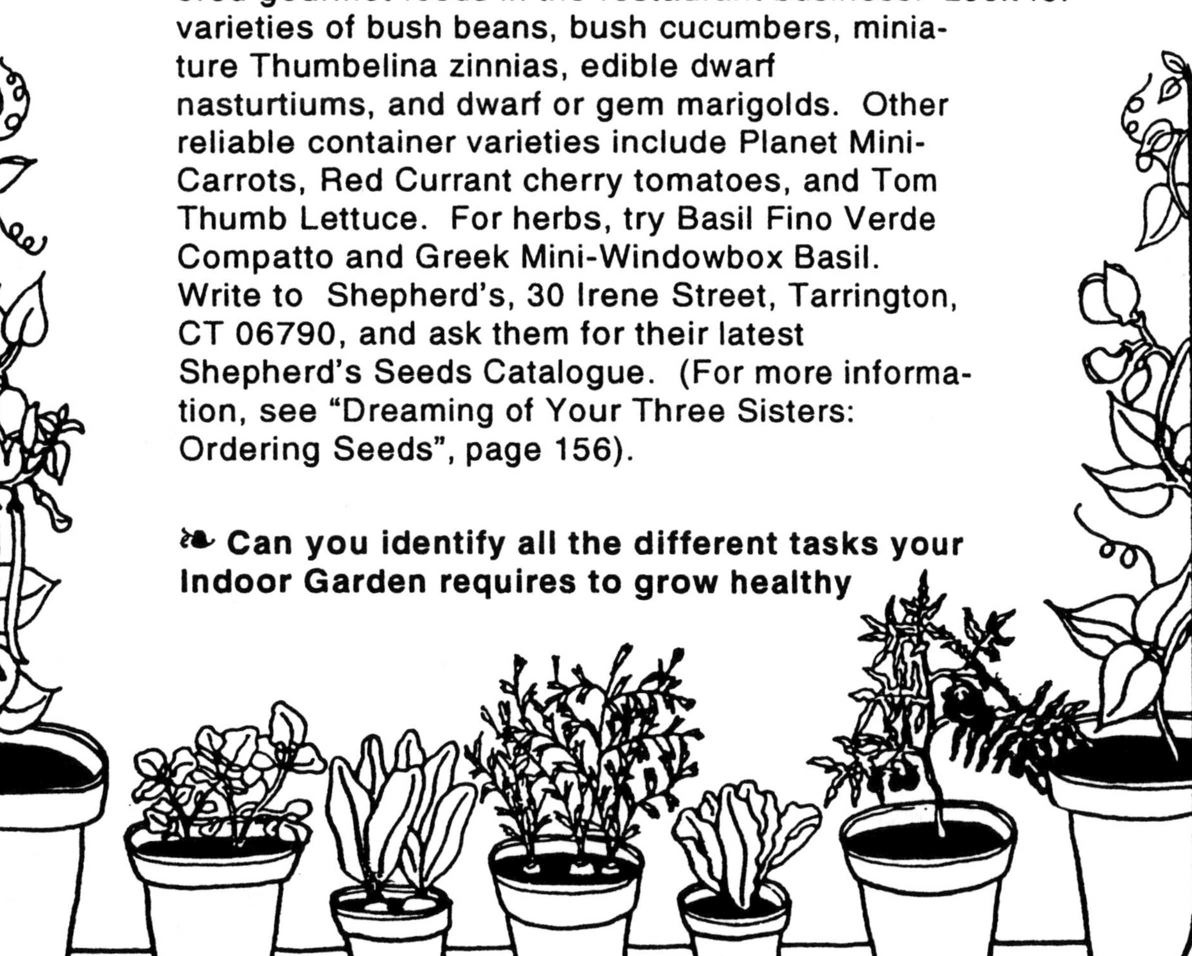

plants? Create a job board of regular chores for caretaking the plants. Include misting plants with a foliar-grow solution, watering the pots, keeping the capillary mat wet, adjusting the light levels, thinning crowded seedlings, transplanting seedlings - and so on. A weekly share circle is a good format for sharing announcements about the Indoor Garden's growth.

❧ **How can you recreate a miniature village in the Indoor Garden Center?** Create special effects for your Indoor Garden Center so that it resembles a Native garden or village. Cover it with a bark roof or woven cattail mats. The possibilities are endless for demonstrating how Native American families gardened or continue to garden today. Create a display about Native families. Demonstrate family activities by:

- sculpting people, plants, and animals
- making stick and yarn puppets
- designing people from round clothespins, cloth, and leather scraps
- making a miniature stick wickiup or other dwelling
- making cornhusk dolls

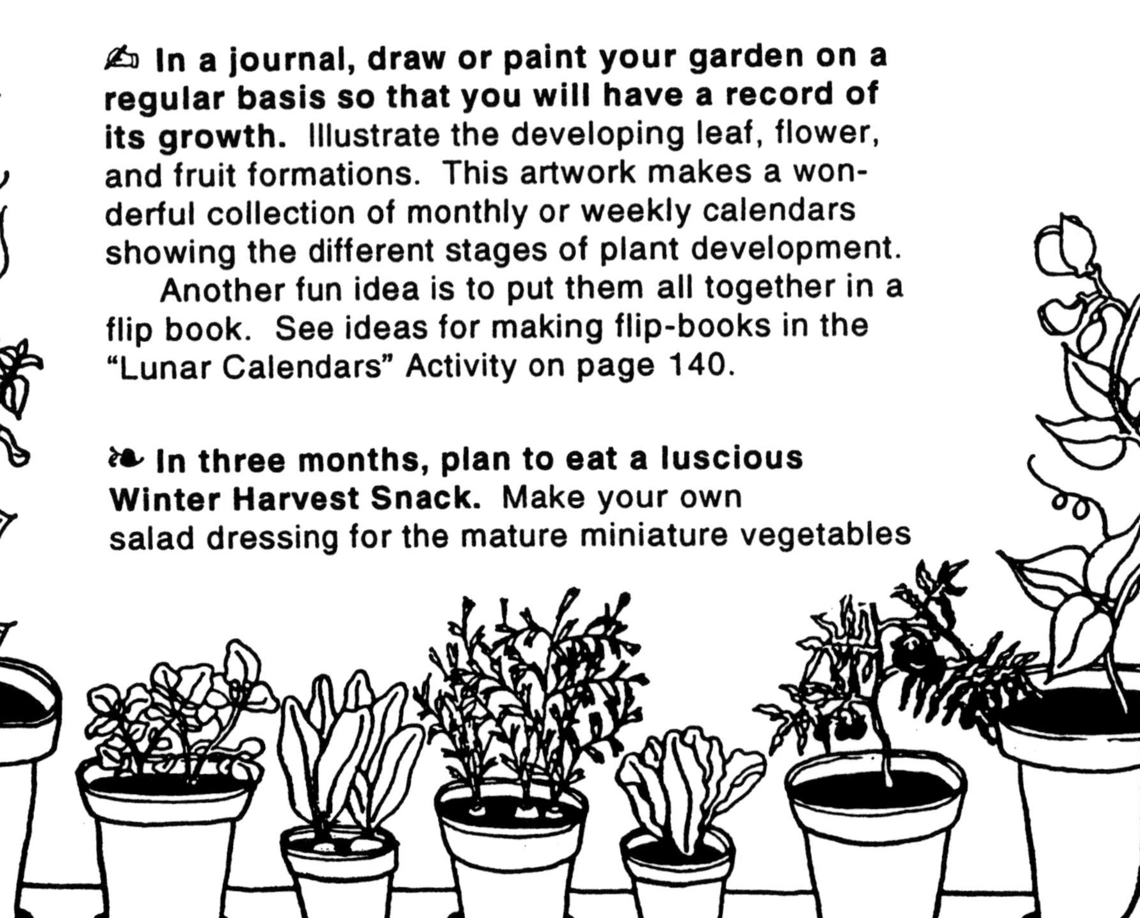

✍ **In a journal, draw or paint your garden on a regular basis so that you will have a record of its growth.** Illustrate the developing leaf, flower, and fruit formations. This artwork makes a wonderful collection of monthly or weekly calendars showing the different stages of plant development.

Another fun idea is to put them all together in a flip book. See ideas for making flip-books in the "Lunar Calendars" Activity on page 140.

❧ **In three months, plan to eat a luscious Winter Harvest Snack.** Make your own salad dressing for the mature miniature vegetables and flowers grown in your Indoor Garden Center! Invite your family, a friend, or a garden helper to join you. Celebrate the end of Winter!

Math, Nature's Way

❧ Count the leaves on a plant, noting the pattern of the leaf growth. As you count, move in the direction that the plant grows, counting in leaf patterns of twos or fours.

❧ In your garden journal, record and illustrate math concepts, such as the number of days from seed-sowing to seed-bearing or maturity. Document the number of bean seeds harvested from a plant that began as a single bean!

Three Sister Plant Adventures in the Indoor Garden

Have you ever wondered where a tiny seed gets the strength to push its way up from deep within the Earth to the light? How does it find the light? Your Three Sisters invite you to solve some extraordinary mysteries, so get ready to discover the secret life of plants!

❧ Sister Bean Adventures!

♥ **If a bean seed is planted beneath the soil in the dark, how does it get the strength to grow up towards the light?** Write down any ideas you might have about how this happens. Then look at a bean seed. Can you discover any clues for solving this mystery? Share your ideas with a friend.

Did you guess that there might be a clue hidden inside the seed? Look carefully at a bean seed, including the inside of the seed. Can you draw all its different parts?

Wrapped around the outside of the seed is the **coat**. Can you see two tiny, colorless leaves curled around a tiny stem inside the bean? This sleeping **pip** is actually the baby bean plant, or **embryo**. The bean seed itself is called the **endosperm**. It is full of baby food that will nourish and strengthen the baby bean as it tries to become a living green plant. While growing, baby beans do not receive help from a parent plant. The parent plant's job is to make a perfect seed, complete with the life forces necessary to get the young plant started in life. What a perfect package this small seed is - a little treasure box of life!

♥ **How does this little treasure box of life get started?** To find out, place a bush bean seed on a paper towel. Soak the bean seed and the paper towel. Place the wet paper towel and seed inside a plastic yogurt container. Cover the container with a lid and leave the seed inside it for a week to ten days.

- Check the bean seed on a daily basis to see what is happening inside.

- Draw the changes each day.

♥ **How does the little pip grow with nothing but moisture?** A perfect seed contains enough food, or energy, to get it started. What will it need after this exciting start in life?

After ten days, gently plant the germinating bean plant in moist potting soil in a well-drained container. Watch what happens next.

♥ **Can you make a Bean Seed Pop-Out Model** that shows how the sleeping pip develops during germination?

Bean Seed Pop-Out Model

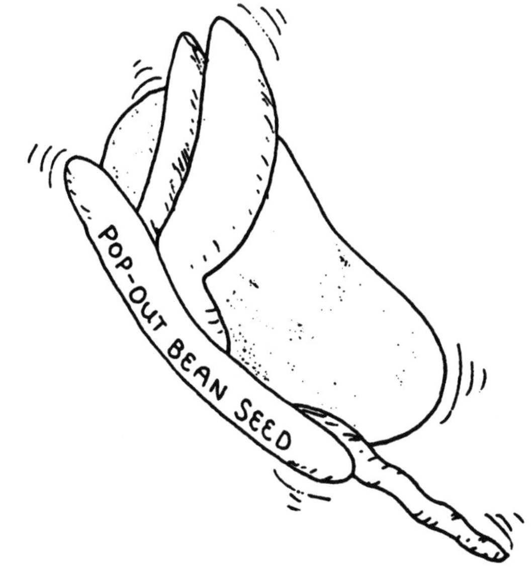

1) To demonstrate a sleeping pip on day one, cut out two identical white cardboard beans. Make them about the size of your hand. Hinge the two identical bean shapes with clear tape. Open the bean case and add a tiny, curled-up, greenish-white paper pip.

2) On day two, make a new bean case with a tape hinge. Open the bean case and add green paper that resembles the sleeping pip on day two.

3) Each following day, record the sleeping pip's stages of growth as it lies encased in a hinged bean case. As the sleeping pip emerges from its bean case, it grows long roots, stems, and leaves. Fold these root, stem, and leaf paper parts accordion-style (make the accordion parts with sturdy, durable paper so they can be folded and unfolded over and over again). Hide the

accordion parts in the bean case so that the curious bean-lover will peek inside.

❧ How would you feel if someone said you had the strength of a bean? To find out if this is an insult or compliment, try the following experiments.

♠ The Mighty Bean Experiment

How strong is a baby bean? Try this experiment to see how many pennies a bean can lift.

1) Poke holes in the bottom of a yogurt container.
2) Fill the container with moist potting soil.
3) Plant a bush bean seed as deep as your first knuckle. Or, plant a lima bean seed as deep as your second knuckle.
4) Fill the hole with soil.
5) On top of the planted bean seed, place as many pennies as you think a bean seed can lift!
6) Around the pennies, place four stick matches. The match sticks will act as a fence to hold the pennies in place when the bean seed tries to lift them.
7) How many pennies do you think a bean plant can lift? Write your estimate on a piece of paper.
8) Tape your estimate to the yogurt container. In a week you will see whether your prediction is true!

Plant bean seeds in several containers, each with a different number of stacked pennies.

♠ Bean Power Experiment

If one baby bean can lift pennies, what do you think a lot of baby beans can do together?

1) Fill a cottage cheese container with garbanzo or lentil beans

that have been soaked overnight in water.

2) Place the lid on the container.
3) Draw what you think might happen.
4) Observe the beans for several days.

If the beans are still fresh after your experiment, make a delicious hummus spread with the garbanzo beans. Make soup or a sprout dish with the lentils.

♠ Sister Bean the Acrobat

How does Sister Bean climb up a string? Try this experiment.

1) Plant a pole bean seed in a gallon milk or cider jug.
2) Put Sister Bean on a table top or desk where she will get plenty of light.
3) Attach a string from the pot to the ceiling.
4) Water and spray with a foliar solution, as needed.
5) Observe the bean for a month.

What do you notice about the way Sister Bean climbs a string? In the Northern Hemisphere, all vines spiral Earthwise, or counterclockwise. Do plants spiral sunwise, or clockwise, in the Southern Hemisphere? Write a letter to someone who lives there and ask him!

If her roots begin to crowd the pot, transplant Sister Bean into a larger container. This must be done carefully. Do not water Sister Bean for a day or two before transplanting her, as a slightly dried-out soil ball is easier to handle and will not fall apart. Carefully cut the gallon container from the soil ball. Place the bean plant in a larger container of moist potting mix. Gently tamp soil around the roots and the soil ball. Now give Sister

Bean plenty of water until she recovers from the shock of transplanting. Mist her leaves with a foliar, seaweed solution.

♠ Sister Squash Olympics Experiment

How does a baby seed know which way is up?

1) Germinate squash seeds on a moist paper towel that is attached to the inside bottom of a cardboard milk carton. Cover the seeds with clear plastic wrap.

2) Each day, carefully rotate the milk carton onto a different side.

3) Observe how the roots change direction, seeking the earth. Plants have the power to follow the magnetic force contained deep within the earth. This is known as **gravity**. A fancy word for this power is called **geotropism**.

❧ The following song will remind you how plant roots always seek the Earth's dark chambers.

"My Roots Go Down"

My roots go down, down to the Earth
My roots go down, down to the Earth
My roots go down, down to the Earth
My roots go down.

My Roots Go Down

(A wonderful song to do with children to lead into a discussion of the interrelatedness of all living things. Kids love to make up extra verses to this one - just ask for suggestions!)

♥Can you make up your own verses?

I am a squash plant growing in the garden
I am a squash plant growing in the garden
I am a squash plant growing in the garden
My roots go down.

♠ Sister Corn's Dance of Life Experiment

All plants seek the light with their shoots, much in the same way that a plant's roots seek the earth. The former is known as **phototropism**, the latter as **geotropism**. "Tropism" is movement towards something. "Photo" means light. In their dance of life, plants move up towards the light and down into the Earth. Have you ever watched sunflowers turn their heads from east to west during the day to watch the sun? Can you create a "dance of life" picture that demonstrates geotropism and phototropism?

To watch a "dance of life," sprout corn seeds in an opaque container (a yogurt container will work fine.) First, place a moist sponge in the container. Next, put some seeds on the sponge, and then cover the container with a lid. Cut a single slot on one edge of the container lid to let in light. Observe the tender young shoots. Do all the shoots grow in the same direction?

Although Sister Corn will not grow to maturity in the Indoor Garden, she can contribute to the compost pile when she has finished her "dance."

Even More Curious?

❧ "Monocot" and "Dicot" Families

Sister Corn was not always a garden plant. Her ancient relatives lived in grassy fields. Some relatives were members of her own family, Zea Mays, while others were cousins. What other plants might be Sister Corn's cousins? If you think that a certain plant is Sister Corn's relative, here is a way to find out for sure. Plant Sister Corn and the other seed in separate containers of moist potting soil. Observe them. Draw your observations of what is happening in the two seed containers. Do the seedlings look alike in any ways? Do you think they are related?

To identify plants related to the corn family, determine which sprouts have one thin, grass-like blade. Single-blade plants belong to the family of **monocotyledons**. Sprouts not related to the mono-cotyledon family have two leaves. These are called **dicotyledons**. Because these names are so long, they are often shortened to "monocots" and "dicots."

❧ The Circle Game

This game demonstrates the difference between monocots and dicots:

(All stand in a circle, facing inward)
"I am a monocot, a tall straight one,
(squat in place in the circle)
my single blade grows upward towards the sun.
(one arm up, stand up)
I am a dicot, with two leaves all,
(squat in place in the circle)
See me grow, first wide, then tall.
(two arms extending up and out, stand up)

Monocots share one family,
(everyone in the circle turns left, raising his left arm while reaching his right arm into the center of the circle to make the spokes of a wheel)
strong blades reaching to be free.
(the monocots circle around once)
Di-cots form another clan
(stand in circle, two arms up and out)
reaching out with open hand."
(all hands in the circle unite)

- JoAnne Dennee and Elisheva Kaufman

LUNAR CALENDARS: FINDING YOUR WAY THROUGH THE SEASONS

Native peoples created annual calendars that closely followed Father Sky's and Mother Earth's monthly rhythms. These calendars, sometimes documented on birch bark or animal skins, recorded the passing time. Despite the many changes in our world today, monthly rhythms continue to prevail. Nature calendars remind us that we are guided by an underlying order and harmony in the natural world.

❧ The Abenaki named their moons after seasonal tasks or events. Can you match the following moons with the month in which they might occur?

Snow Falling Moon
Hunger Moon
Sugar Making Moon
New Year's Greeting Moon
Planting Moon
Hoeing Moon
Hay Making Moon
Harvesting Moon
Corn Reaping Moon
Falling Leaf Moon
Moose Hunting Moon
Ice Forming Moon

Unlike us, the Abenaki celebrated the New Year in April because they considered Spring to be the beginning of the year.

The Abenaki calendar forecast the people's activities or rhythms, such as the need to prepare for fishing, planting, harvesting, building shelters, or other events. During Snow Falling Moon, for example, a young Abenaki might be kept busy repairing clothing to insure comfort and warmth during the remainder of the winter season. Dried corn might be ground into fine meal for sharing during winter storytelling around the hearth, where warmth, humor, and important teachings are passed along.

❧ What events mark time for you during Snow Falling month?

❧ Long ago, pictographs etched on birch bark sheets and cave walls represented passing events. Can you imagine what some of the pictures might have been?

Can you create pictographs on birch bark or paper that represent events happening in your life? In a journal, document activities occurring around your home or in your community.

❧ **Make a lunar calendar for the current year.** What names would be appropriate for the months where you live? Using the Abenaki calendar as a guide, name your months after activities undertaken by your family during a given period. Illustrate the months according to their new names. These calendars make a nice Solstice or holiday gift!

Want To Do More?

❧ **Observe the moon for at least one month and record its phases.**

What do you notice about lunar rhythms? How long is a lunar cycle? Is our current calendar based on lunar rhythms or another rhythm? What is that measurement based on?

❧ **Make a Lunar Flip Book that portrays the moon's rhythms.** There are several ways to record the phases of the moon in a Lunar Flip Book. You can observe the changing shape of the moon for a period of twenty-eight consecutive evenings and record the changes as illustrations. Or, you can copy the drawings that appear here. Directions for making a Lunar Flip Book are on the next page.

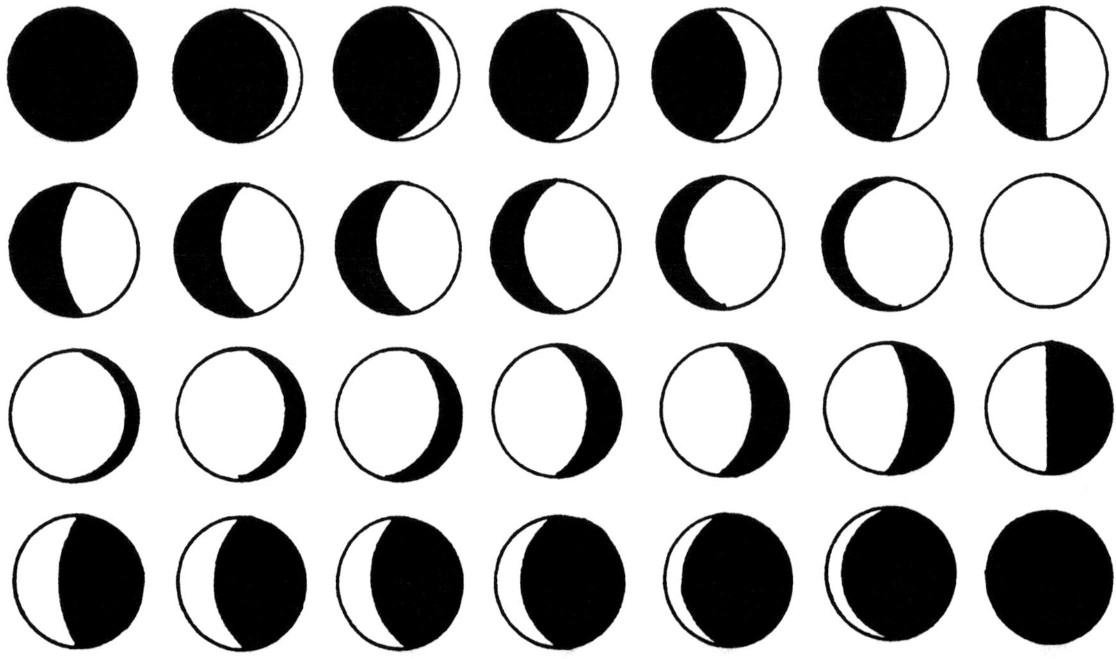

A Lunar Flip Book

you will need:

paper
blue pencil or crayon
ruler
stapler
scissors
optional: glitter for the illuminated moon

1) Measure and cut 29 pages for the flip book. The first page is for the cover, the remaining twenty-eight pages are for the lunar phases.

2) With the exception of the cover, number each page. This will help you keep the lunar shapes in their proper order.

3) Carefully record the twenty-eight lunar phases. Shadow the dark part of the moon with a blue pencil or crayon. If you wish, add glitter to the illuminated part of the moon. Or, add glitter to the area surrounding the moon so that it resembles a starry sky.

4) Decorate and title the cover page of your Lunar Flip Book.

5) Be sure the pages are in their proper order, then staple them together.

6) Flip through the book and you will see an entire month of moonlight!

WINTER CORN AND CORN-GRINDING

After you have begun your Indoor Garden Center, reflect back on the harvest. For thousands of years the Three Sisters have fed generations of Americans. Many of these meals took place well after the garden was put to bed in the Fall. Harvested corn, if properly cared for, will sustain a family through the Winter.

Now is a good time to check on the foods you preserved from your harvest. Can you prepare a winter meal from the golden riches of your garden harvest? Create an imaginative meal from your dried, frozen, stored, or canned stock of harvest foods!

❧ **How many different ways can corn products be used once the harvest season is over?** With a parent or friend, look for corn products on the ingredient labels of cereal boxes, crackers, breads, and other foods. Don't forget corn by-products, like corn sweeteners, corn syrup, popcorn, and corn oil.

Can you draw all the foods that use corn products?

❧ **How are these foods produced from freshly harvested corn?** When corn is used as a grain, it is dried to remove the moisture that would eventually cause it to rot. When dry, it is ground into cornmeal. In this granular form it can be used in the many ways you have already discovered.

Pressing machines are used to extract corn by-products from corn stalks and kernels. The by-products produced in this way are corn syrup and corn oil.

❧ **Beside providing food for humans, can you think of other uses for corn?** Are animal feed, ornamental Indian corn, and seed for next year's garden among the possible uses?

♠ Corn-Grinding

Grind your own corn-meal and discover the hidden secrets inside a kernel of dry corn.

To grind corn. . . .

Make your own mortar and pestle! A 15-inch diameter tree stump makes a wonderful, rustic outdoor or indoor mortar. Slightly hollow the stump top to form a depression for grinding. A large wooden bowl also works well as a mortar. For a pestle, find a round, smooth stone that fits nicely into the palm of your hand. Be sure the grinding stone is smooth and solid. Otherwise, pieces of rock will chip off into the cornmeal. The river is a great place to find a corn-grinding stone!

Remove corn kernels from the cob by rubbing two ears together. If you are using a mortar made from a tree stump, wrap the kernels in muslin or a cloth napkin to prevent flyaway corn. As the kernels break up into smaller pieces, remove the cloth. Continue grinding the corn until it forms a flour-like consistency. Expect to find a few large pieces of corn in the corn flour.

Observe the ground corn carefully. Does it consist of different textures? Do you see different corn kernel parts? Separate the parts into their own piles.

Examine the hard outer kernel and the soft inner germ. Are these parts the same color? Do they have the same texture - that is, do they feel the same? Does each part taste the same? If you have never tasted "fresh-ground" corn-meal, you are in for a treat!

Want To Do More?

❧ **Make a display showing all the parts of an ear of corn:** the ear, the corn seed, the hard, outer corn kernel, and the germ. Also, display some cornmeal and any other products you made from corn.

❧ **Grind blue corn, yellow corn, and rainbow corn.** Store each color separately in recycled glass jars. Cover them with lids until you are ready to bake cornbread. Or, layer the different colors of corn in a single jar so you can see bands of colored corn- meal. Colored corn makes Rainbow Corn Bread - wonderful for a special occasion!

❧ **It is fun to share your cornmeal harvest!** Put one cup of cornmeal into a recycled glass jar. A small juice bottle or jelly jar works well. Attach a corn muffin recipe to the jar. Give this harvest gift to a community elder or to the neighborhood food shelf.

❧ **Do you have lots of ground cornmeal? Make beautiful storage containers for your freshly ground cornmeal!** Wrap a 2-pound coffee can with a large piece of moist birch bark. Secure the bark by winding raffia or colored yarns around the top and bottom of the can. In addition to cornmeal, these containers are wonderful for storing entire corn ears - or dried beans.

Even More Curious?

❧ Read *Rover and Coo Coo* by John Hay. This is an unusual adventure story about a horseback trip to the corn mill.

❧ Read Joseph Bruchac's "The Story of the Corn Spirit". This can be found in *Indian Corn of the Americas: Gift to the World*, the Northeast Indian Quarterly, summer 1989, published by the Cornell University Press, Ithaca, NY.

A THREE SISTERS HARVEST KITCHEN

Autumn is the time of year for feasting - and preserving garden foods! In Winter, preserved harvest foods are ready to be made into delicious, mouth-watering meals. Create a Harvest Kitchen in your home or in your classroom at school. For a special flavor burst, prepare foods in the traditional Native manner.

❧ A complete Harvest Kitchen consists of:

a mortar and pestle for grinding corn
an old fashioned coffee grinder or vegetable grinder
cast-iron corn bread molds
a wire whisk or hand beater
large wooden mixing bowls and wooden mixing spoons
recycled jars with lids
handmade labels for labeling jars of preserved cornmeal
measuring cups and spoons
a spatula
sharp knives
a cutting board

❧ Bake a Friendship Cornbread according to the recipe below.

Friendship Cornbread

Combine in large bowl:
1 cup flour
1 cup cornmeal
1/2 tsp. salt
2 tsp. baking powder

Combine in small bowl:
4 Tbs. honey or maple syrup
2 eggs or 1/2 cup yogurt
1 cup milk
4 Tbs. oil

Mix the dry ingredients in one bowl and the wet ingredients in another. Combine the two with a few strokes. Place paper muffin liners in a muffin pan. Pour the batter into the liners. Bake at 400° for 10-15 minutes.

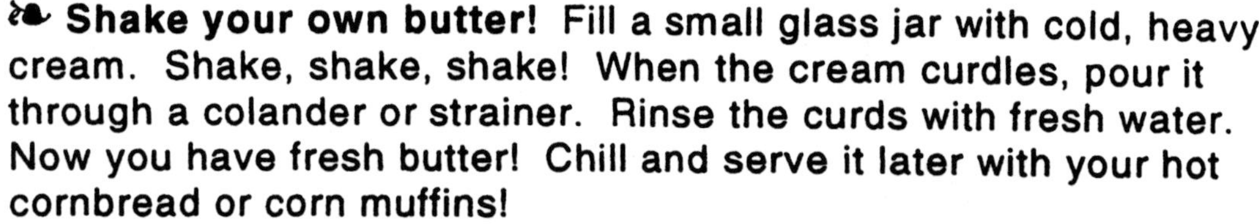

❧ **Shake your own butter!** Fill a small glass jar with cold, heavy cream. Shake, shake, shake! When the cream curdles, pour it through a colander or strainer. Rinse the curds with fresh water. Now you have fresh butter! Chill and serve it later with your hot cornbread or corn muffins!

For a different treat, prepare homemade corn muffins in your Harvest Kitchen. Add blueberries, pureed pumpkin, and whole, fresh kernels of sweet corn to your corn muffin recipe. For a complete Three Sisters meal, serve the muffins with a bean and vegetable soup.

❧ When preparing harvest foods, examine the seeds. Compare these seeds to the ones you planted.

THE HOUSE YOU LIVE IN: SELF-HEALTH

Your body is the house you live in. It is your own, and there is no other like it. It is your only permanent home during your lifetime. How do *you* care for the house in which you live?

❧ Your **body** is a wonderful, magical place. All of its parts work wonderfully, either separately or as a harmonious whole - but only if you care for it! You eat to live: food makes the blood that gives you life and strength.

❧ Your **bones** are like the strong beams of a house. You cannot see them, but you can feel them. Can you find some of your bones by feeling? Young bones are soft. As you grow, your bones become hard from the foods you eat. Which foods help to

strengthen your bones? Which ones do not? Look at the way your bones hold up your body. Do you like the way they work? Use a mirror to observe your posture.

❧ **Muscles** move your bones and give your body its soft, round shape. Can you feel or see any of your muscles? Outdoor play and good food keep your muscles strong. What is your favorite exercise? Be kind to your muscles and play outdoors regularly.

❧ Your **teeth** help you to eat and speak. They begin to grow when you are very young. Once your baby, or milk, teeth are replaced, it is possible to keep your teeth forever. How must you care for your teeth if you wish to keep them forever?

❧ What protects the inside of your body and is a soft cover for it? Your **skin**! Your skin feels the environment around you. Can you feel the air caress your skin? Your body's ability to feel things helps you to know when it is being touched, or hurt. Your skin hurts when it is cut. If your body is burned by the heat of a stove, the nerves - or feeling power beneath your skin - warn you of danger and you pull away. What can you do to keep your skin healthy? Good hygiene is one way to care for your skin. Clothing helps your body do its job by protecting your skin. How can you best clothe the house in which you live? What foods are good for your skin? Foods that make your skin glow are wonderful for building healthy skin. Yellow and orange vegetables make your skin glow. Which "glow" foods do you eat?

❧ At Halloween, everyone eats lots of candy. Candy does not feed the house you live in. Put a tooth in a glass of cola for a week. Watch what the sugar does to the tooth. Do you want sugar on your teeth?

❧ Display a skeleton holding a paper plate. Which foods help your house grow? Place calcium-rich foods on the skeleton's plate. Calcium-rich foods include broccoli, almonds, tofu, comfrey teas and dairy products. Can you name any other calcium-rich foods? Be sure to eat lots of these calcium-rich foods at Halloween so you do not end up looking like a skeleton!

❧ **Make a life-size tracing of your body,** with two arms outstretched, on brown paper. Label the drawing "Good Food for the House I Live In." Add distinguishing characteristics to the body, such as eye color, freckles, hair, missing teeth, and your favorite t-shirt. On one outstretched hand, glue a large paper plate. Glue a small paper plate on the other hand. On the large plate, draw or glue pictures of food that are good to eat in large quantities. On the small plate, draw foods that are better to eat in small portions. What wise food choices do you already practice?

❧ **"All About Me" books reflect upon your unique, wonderful self and the house you live in.** In an "All About Me" book, record pertinent data about yourself, such as your weight, height, abilities, favorite foods, meals you can prepare by yourself, favorite ways to keep your body active, great accomplishments, favorite things to do, and what you might like to do when you grow older. Memorable photos, drawings, and family stories also belong in "All About Me" books.

❧ **Try this muscle strength test.** Hold your arm straight out from your body. Ask your friend to try to push your arm down as you use your muscle strength to resist. Now hold a few tablespoons of sugar in your hand and do the same experiment. Ask your friend to try to push down the outstretched arm, and again resist with your muscle strength. What happened and why? Can you solve this mystery?

❧ Ask your doctor, school nurse, health food store, or co-op personnel for answers to questions you have about good health and hygiene.

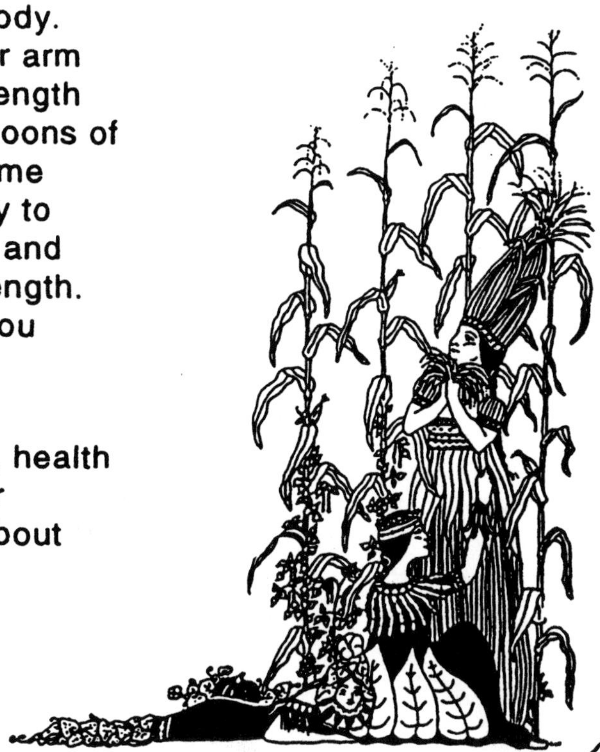

The Go, Grow, Glow, and Flow Sisters Tell About Nutrition

Cornmeal was one source of protein always available to Native peoples. But cornmeal alone cannot provide a healthy diet. Which sister do you think provided the necessary protein to complement Sister Corn? Sister Bean also belongs to a family of foods rich in protein. Together, corn and beans sustained many Native people for thousands of years! Sister Squash often accompanied the other sisters in a meal. Together, the three combine to make a healthy diet for all peoples - yesterday, today, and tomorrow.

A healthy diet consists of foods in three basic categories, plus plenty of water. Each food category helps your body do the following - **Go, Grow, Glow** - and **Flow! Go** foods give lots of energy. **Grow** foods make your body grow. **Glow** foods make your hair and skin shine! Can you guess what **Flow** foods do?

❧ **What foods help you "Go"?** Power foods give your body warmth and the energy to Go, Go, Go, whether it be for work or for play. "Go" foods contain fat and sugar. Carbohydrates or starches are contained in foods that help boost energy reserves.

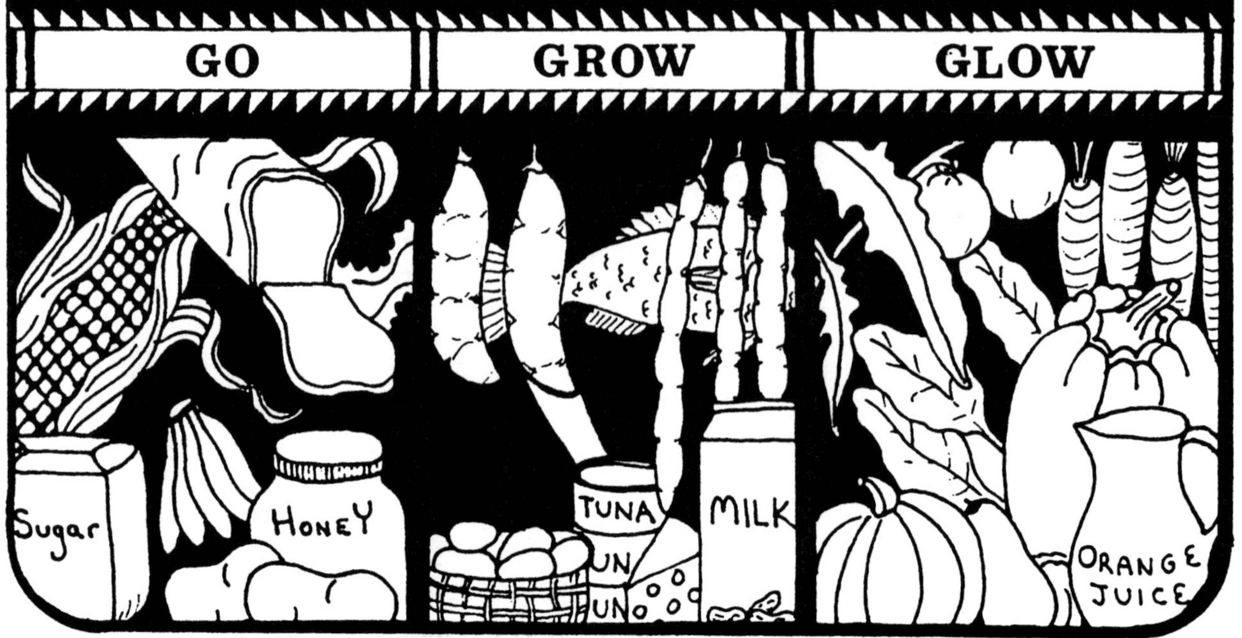

These include fruits, vegetables, wheat products, and sugar. Refined white sugar gives lots of energy - but the energy lasts only a short time. Sugar creates a craving sensation in many people that makes them eat more and more sugar. If you eat too much "Go" food, your body will have more than it needs for work and play. What happens to the extra "Go" food you eat? The excess gets stored on your body, making you fat. So don't eat more "Go" food than you can use up! Plenty of activity also helps you to "Go"!

What are your favorite "Go" foods? Beware of "junk" foods! When eaten in large amounts, junk foods are unhealthy "Go" foods. You can taste the greasy fat and sugar sweetness in some junk foods. Try the taste test yourself, and learn to identify "Go" foods that consist mostly of sugar and fat. Keep track of how often you eat these greasy or sweet foods. What healthy "Go" foods do you like? Could they replace some of the sweet and greasy "Go" foods you have been eating? Which of the Three Sisters help you "Go"?

❧ **Can you name some of the "Grow" foods in your current diet?** "Grow" foods are healing foods that build or repair parts of your body, like your bones, blood, muscles and organs. If you want your body to continue to grow, or to be able to heal and replace worn parts, you will need to eat "Grow" foods. "Grow" foods are protein foods, which come from vegetables or animals. Can you name some animal proteins? Animal proteins include animal meats and all sources of animal products - dairy, lard, beef, poultry, lamb, pork, and fish. Non-animal proteins include whole grains, seeds, and legumes. Can you name some non-animal proteins? What "Grow" foods do you eat? Which of the Three Sisters help you "Grow"?

❧ **Do you ever eat foods that help you to "Glow"?** "Glow" foods give your skin and hair a healthy shine. These foods also help you to see in the dark. "Glow" foods come from plants that are full of vitamins and minerals. Yellow, orange and dark green vegetables are "Glow" foods that contain Vitamin A. Vitamin A fights infection when your body gets cut, and helps you to see in the dark. Vitamin C is found in many fruits and green vegetables and can help prevent colds. Can you name any foods you eat that contain Vitamin A and Vitamin C? Which of the Three Sisters might help you Glow?

Nutritionists recommend eating five fruits or vegetables a day to keep your body glowing. The fresher the food, the more your body will glow. Vitamins are contained in the skin of fresh foods. When you cut open the skin, some vitamins are released into the air. When you cook foods in water, some of the vitamins escape into the air, and some are left in the water in the bottom of the cooking pot.

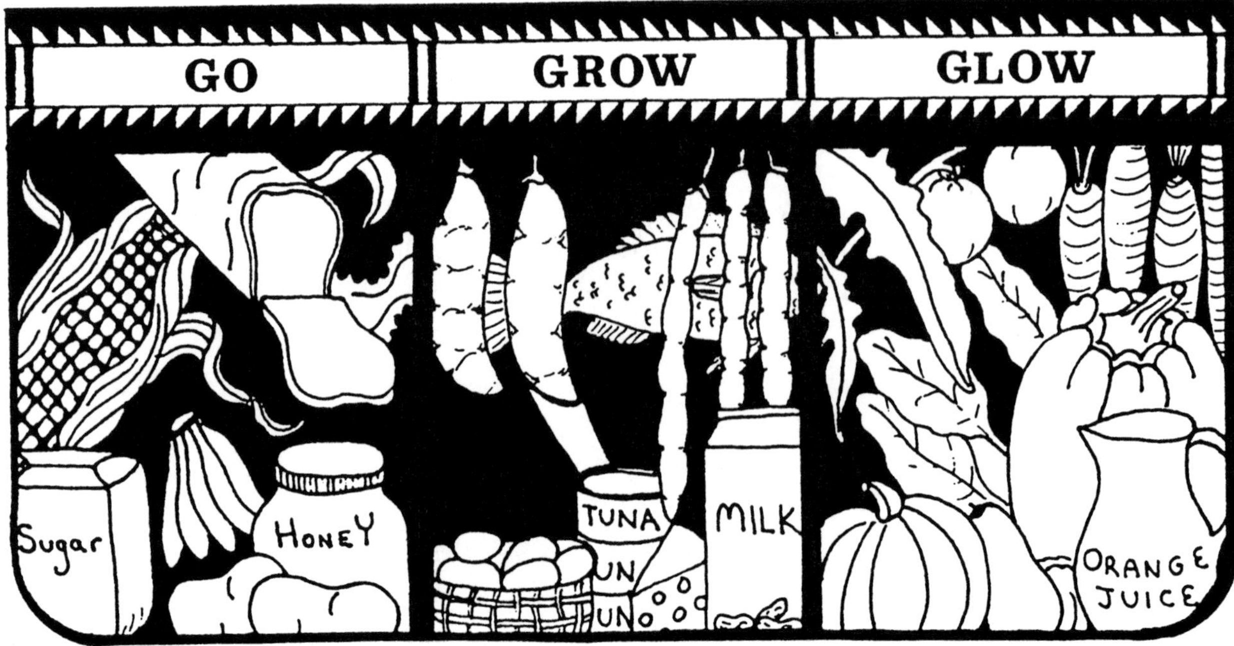

❧ **What foods help you "Flow"?** "Flow" foods keep your body flowing and purified by removing waste from it. "Flow" foods include fiber and water. Fiber is plentiful in many of Mother Nature's foods, like whole wheat, oats, roots and greens. Great quantities of water keep your body flowing, too, so remember to drink lots of good quality water to make things "flow" and purify your body each day. And don't forget about fiber which helps you pass food waste from your body.

✍ **Keep a Go, Grow, Glow, and Flow Health Journal.** Make a page for "Go" foods, a page for "Grow" foods, a page for "Glow" foods, and a page for "Flow" foods. List and illustrate foods in each of these categories. For the next month record everything you eat and enter the food in the appropriate Go, Grow, Glow, or Flow categories. What foods do you need to eat more of? Less of? Are there any foods that you feel do not fit into the Go, Grow, Glow, or Flow categories?

❧ **Prepare a Go, Grow, Glow and Flow lunch.** Make a placemat with four sections. Illustrate Go, Grow, Glow or Flow foods in each section. Before eating your lunch, sort your foods according to their Go, Grow, Glow and Flow qualities.

Dreaming of your Three Sisters: Ordering Seeds

It is never too soon to start daydreaming about your garden, even if Spring seems like a dream itself.

❧ **While dreaming about your garden, make a list of the plants you like to eat.** Like many gardeners, you might become overly enthusiastic and want to experiment with many different varieties of corn. However, it is important to limit your choice of corns to those that mature at different dates. To avoid cross-pollination, plant one variety of corn and one variety of popcorn. This will protect your crops, insuring that you harvest the variety of corn you originally planted. It will also insure that you get a pure seed for next year's seed bank.

Sometimes gourds cross-pollinate with other squashes. To keep fruits and seed true to variety, alternate sowing squash and gourds every other year. Or, avoid cross-pollination by choosing squash and gourd varieties that mature at different times.

❧ **Here are some tried-and-true varieties of Three Sisters. Remember not to plant corn of the same growing time together.**

- Mandan Rainbow Corn or Hopi Blue Corn are ornamental corns used for grinding corn flour.
- Black Aztec Corn is a sweet corn when white, but can also be dried to make a blue grinding corn.
- Tom Thumb Popcorn is a short-season, New Hampshire-heirloom variety.
- Vermont Cranberry Bush Bean and Genuine Cornfield Pole Bean are both snap beans.
- Scarlet Runner Bean, Anasazi Bean, and Jacob's Cattle Pole Bean are all drying beans for baking and stews.
- Connecticut Field Pumpkins make great Jack-O-Lanterns. Small Sugar pumpkins or New England pumpkins are great for baking pies.
- Jack-Be-Little Pumpkins are three- to four-inch, miniature ribbed pumpkins.
- Hopi Container Gourds are exciting to grow because when they are dry and hollow, they make wonderful containers for everything from water to birdseed!
- Hopi Sunflowers are good for eating. The seed hulls can be used as a dye (ranging in color from red to purplish-blue) for craft projects.

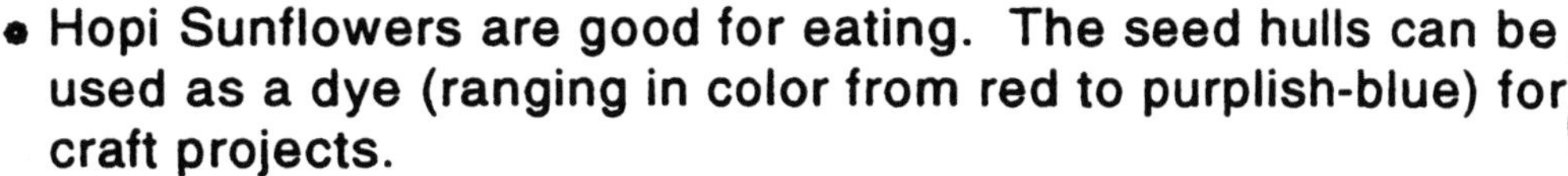

❧ **The advanced Three Sisters gardener might want to try these crops:**

- Abenaki Potatoes are organic seed potatoes. These are available only from Ronniger's.
- Seneca Horn Potatoes are also available from Ronniger's.
- Hopi Turquoise Corn is a treasure from Seeds of Change, which specializes in organic heirloom seeds.
- Sweet Scented Nicotiana has white, jasmine-scented flowers that close during the daytime, but open in the late afternoon or early evening to perfume the air. This 3- to 4-foot tall variety is available from Shepherd's Seeds.

❧ **If you need seeds, write a letter in January to one of the following seed companies asking for seed catalogues:**

For Northern growing varieties, write:
Johnny's Selected Seeds
Albion, ME 04910

For organic heirloom seeds, such as Hopi Turquoise Corn, write:
Seeds of Change
621 Old Santa Fe Trail #10
Santa Fe, NM 87501

For Hopi Blue Corn and Black Aztec Corn, which grow well in the Northeast, write:
Native Seeds Search
2059 North Campbell Avenue #325
Tucson, AR 85719

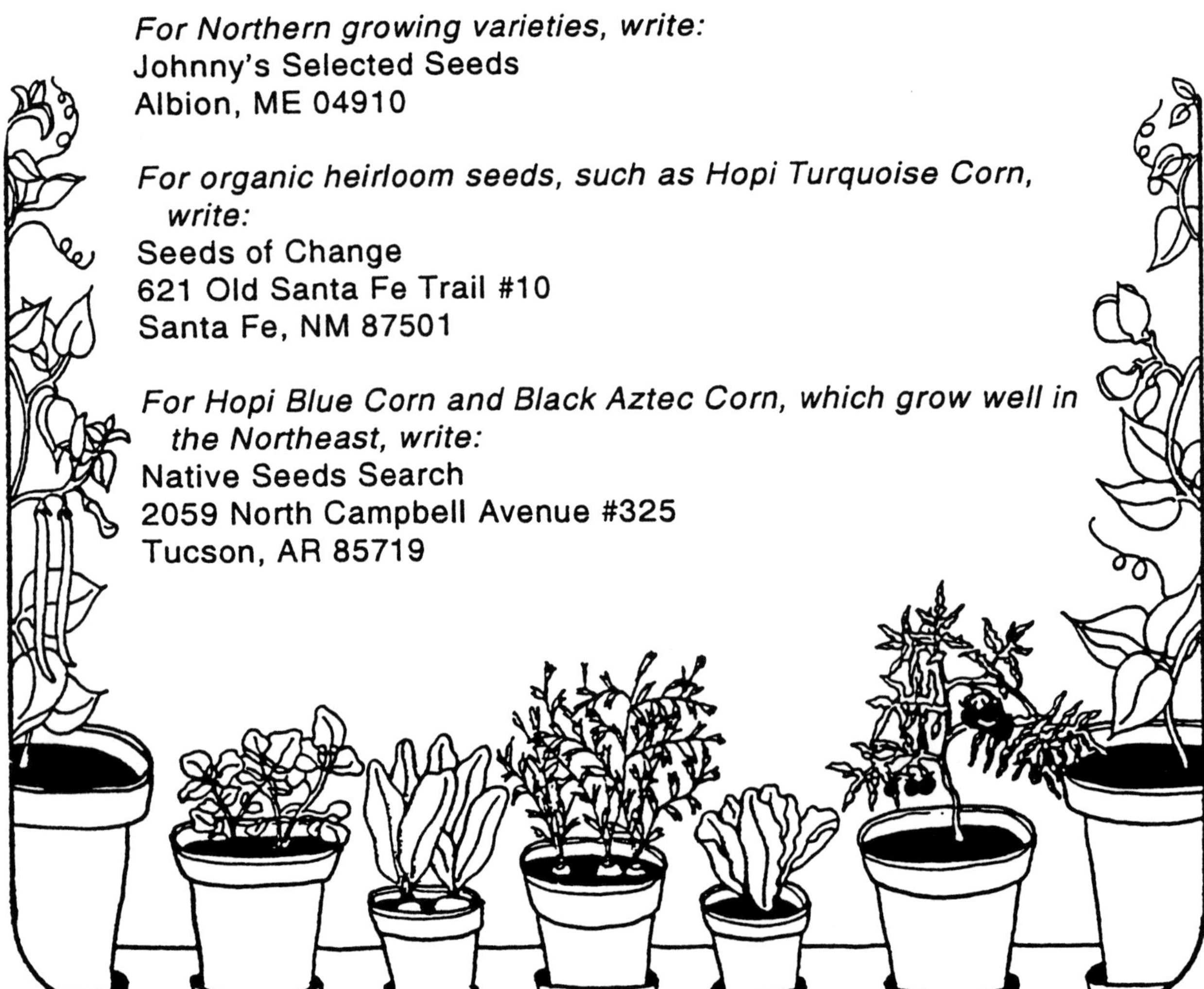

Abenaki and Seneca Horn Potatoes are available from:
Ronniger's
Star Route
Moyie Springs, ID 83845

A large variety of flowers and vegetables are available from:
Shepherd's Seeds
30 Irene Street
Tarrington, CT 06790

For gardening publications and educational gardening games as well as seeds, write:
Ecology Action
5798 Ridgewood Road
Willits, CA 95490

Many other companies also carry heirloom seeds or seeds for small containers. Do some research and see what you can find!

❧ Will Native seeds grow in my region?
When ordering seeds, look for varieties that adapt well to your region. There are a lot of good seed sources for growing Native foods. Many Native seed companies are located in the Southwest and West, but their seeds are generally adaptable to regions all over the country. Count the days between the first and last frost, then try to choose plant varieties - especially corn - that will mature during your growing season.

❧ How many plants will I need?
You can figure out how many plants you will need to grow by determining how much food each plant produces. Many good gardening books recommend a certain number of plants per person. But don't forget to plant some extra crops for hungry four- and six-legged relatives!

❧ Should I plant companion plants as well?
Determine what companion plants will help your Three Sisters flourish, such as herbs or plants that repel harmful insects. Traditionally, the men in Native American communities grew nicotiana with tobacco and planted them separately from food crops. Today, nicotiana is planted in Native gardens to keep aphids at bay as well. Nasturtium repels bean beetles and squash bugs, while sage's pungent aroma is disliked by many insects. Marigolds might not be traditional, but they are good insect-deterring companions.

On the other hand, nasturtium, nicotiana, calendula, sunflowers and cornflowers are companion plants that *attract* pollinators, like bees and butterflies. Mound-plantings might contain any combination of these companion herbs and flowers. Sunflowers and nicotiana hedges make nice border plantings.

❧ What plants, if any, must be started indoors before being transplanted into the garden? To determine which plants must be started indoors, you will need to know how many days it takes for each plant to reach maturity. Count backwards by days from the autumn frost date in your area to determine if, and when, you have to start your seeds indoors. Starting seedlings indoors, however, gives plants - especially flowers and tomatoes - a headstart on the season. You'll have a ripe tomato and a beautiful bouquet of flowers earlier than ever!

PUSSY WILLOWS SIGNAL WINTER'S END: TIME TO PLAN

On a late-Winter hike along a river, you might see young pussy willows, where once upon a time Bobcat left his tail hanging. Furry buds help pussy pillows brave the end of Winter, and prepare them for the changing of the seasons. If you see pussy willow buds during your hike, it is time to do more garden planning.

All life honors the coming of Spring. For young and old alike, it is time to play outside, and to explore the earth as she awakens from her long winter sleep. One of the first signs of Spring is the silvery, soft pussy willow. It can sometimes be found in wet places with southern exposures - even before the snow has disappeared! Here is a story written by our authors about two bobcat kittens whose curiosity got them into quite a bit of trouble....

"How Pussy Willows Came into the World"

It was a beautiful morning in early Spring. Most of the snow had melted, except for a few patches in the cooler, shadier spots. Teemo and Teeko, two charming, impish, and curious bobcat kittens, prowled outside their lair while their mother slept in the sun. Teemo stretched, yawned, and sharpened his claws on a nearby beech tree. Then he nudged his twin brother.

"Prowwhh!" he purred softly, so as not to wake his mother. In human talk it meant: "Lets explore!" Or: "I wonder what kind of mischief we can get into today?"

So the twins set off, playing their favorite games as they gamboled. They chased windblown leaves. They sniffed for mice beneath rocks and fallen logs. They scrambled up and down tree trunks. And all the while they wandered farther and farther from home.

"Let's see if we can find the rushing water that mother

warned us about," Teeko said as he practiced walking across a log. "It can't be dangerous if we only watch it."

Teemo, always ready for an adventure, heartily agreed. He perked up his ears, listening intently, and sniffed the wind. "I think it's in that direction. I smell water - and I can hear it rushing down the mountain."

The brook was swollen with snowmelt from the mountains, and as they neared it the rushing sound became a roar. Neither of the twins had seen rushing water before - all they knew was that their mother had warned them to stay away from it. More curious than fearful, they gave each other a knowing glance, sank to their bellies, and slunk towards the sound of the rushing water.

Soon they came to the brink of a little cliff. Cautiously, they peered over the edge. Below them the water frothed and boiled. Certainly it was not a cat's cup of tea, but Teemo and Teeko were no ordinary felines. They were immensely curious, and though their mother had warned them that curiosity kills the cat, they had also been told that a cat has nine lives. Teeko wanted to go down to the water's edge and practice jumping from rock to rock. But Teemo, who spied logs across the brook, decided he wanted to test his log-crossing skills. They ambled downstream to a place where the water slowed to a black crawl. Here the brook looked totally harmless as it mirrored the lighter sky between the barren trees. It was the perfect place to play! Rocks and boulders of various sizes were strewn up and down this quiet stretch. And two trees - marvelous bridges - lay across the brook. Teeko walked out onto a rock and sat down to watch whirligig beetles dance lightly across the water's surface. He observed them for a very long time.

What a curious thing, he thought. Those little creatures can walk on the water without getting wet!

"Hello, little brothers!" Teeko called to the beetles. "How is it that you can walk on the water?"

"Oh, hello there, brother Bobcat," one of them said. "My name is Whirligig. The water's surface is magical. It is soft and giving, but does not break. Watch me move

from one end of this eddy to the other." With that, Whirligig danced across the smooth surface, making only the slightest indentation in it.

"Hmmm," Teeko said aloud, musing to himself. Now he was really curious. Maybe I could do that, too, he thought. Turning, he saw Teemo carefully crossing a slippery, wet log.

"Teemo, watch this!" Teeko called to his twin.

He pranced out onto the black, glassy water. The next thing he knew, a wet, uncomfortable, and cold darkness enveloped him. He sank down, down, down. . . then popped suddenly into the spring air. He coughed and sputtered as the snow-fed brook carried him downstream.

In the meantime, Teemo had fallen from his log, and now he was as wet and frightened as his twin. As the two terrified kittens bobbed helplessly in the water, the stream gathered speed.

"MMMMEEEOOOWWW! MEWROOOWLLL!!!" they screamed.

They continued to float downstream, but soon they arrived at a place where the brook was divided by a series of tiny islands. Here the water, impeded by the shallows and a tangle of willows that grew along the stream bank, slowed. Noticing the willows that overhung the water, the kittens pleaded with them to save their lives. One of the willows thought about this for a moment before speaking.

"I'm cold, and you're very wet! But you may climb up into my branches if you promise to leave some of your soft fur for my buds to wear so they may stay warm."

The kittens hastily agreed. Whoosh! Out of the water and into the branches they climbed. The willow - and her sisters standing nearby - were suddenly graced with silvery, soft buds. As the two felines slunk away towards home, the willows called out a thank you to them, for now they were very warm indeed!

During the next month, as Spring edged towards Summer, the willows thought often about the two bobcats. And then, quite suddenly, they were surprised to see their buds burst forth into a shower of flowers. The willows were so thrilled with their new garments that they decided to honor the two bobcat kittens by giving themselves a new name.

And that is why the willows came to be called "Pussy Willows", and why their flowers are known as "catkins".

❧ **Establish a Winter Discovery Trail outdoors.** For the next several weeks, walk along the Winter Discovery Trail. Become aware of the season's rhythms as Winter prepares to change to Spring. What kinds of things do you see on your end-of-Winter hikes? What seems to be changing in Nature's cycle?

❧ **If you find pussy willow buds on the Winter Discovery Trail, bring a few branches indoors.** In the Northeast, the familiar Pussy Willow shrub grows as large as a small tree. Place some of its branches in water and watch them bloom with the promise of Spring's green world. Black bud cases will swell open to reveal fuzzy, gray bobcat kitten tails. The gray kitten tails soon become pollen-covered catkins. Finally, tiny green leaves emerge. When roots begin to sprout from the pussy willows, transplant the branches to a wet habitat - but be sure the frost has left the ground first!

❧ **Weeping willows and black willows are very large trees that are fun to observe at Winter's end.** As the end of Winter approaches, weeping willow's golden branches swell with beautiful bud cases. The branches make great material for weaving baskets, bracelets, or willow crowns. Before weaving the branches, soften them by soaking them overnight.

❧ **If you found pussy willow buds during your Winter Discovery walks, you will know it is a time to buy or swap your garden seeds.** It is also time to start collecting used milk and cider jugs, half-gallon milk containers, six-inch plastic pots, and other reusable kitchen and garden containers that can be used for starting seedlings. Collect reusable wooden popsicle sticks or tongue depressors, too. They make great plant markers for identifying young seedlings. It is almost time to being growing!

❧ **While visiting with friends or your family, retell the story of the bobcat kittens and the pussy willows.**

Winter Web of Life

Is anything happening in the winter garden, or is it simply frozen and still and without purpose? Is anything happening in your Indoor Garden Center?

❧ The winter garden may seem frozen, but many natural processes occur during the Winter. These activities enhance the growth of plants the following Summer - indeed, without Winter many plants would not be able to return at all in the Summer! What is the relationship between the Winter and Summer gardens called? A "Web of Life" process is taking place, even though it looks as though nothing is happening in the winter garden.

What is a Web of Life? A Web of Life demonstrates how the different parts of the garden work together to sustain life. It shows the "connections" between all these natural elements.

Make a Web of Life that mimics activities in the two gardens - you will be surprised at all the connections!

♥ To begin a Web of Life:

First, list all the members of the winter garden and the natural processes that take place during that season, such as:

snow	sunshine
rye grass	blue jays
ice	stones
leaves	moles
dried sunflower stalks and seed heads	

Then, list all the members of the summer garden and the natural processes that take place during that season, such as:

flowers	rain	soil
seeds	butterflies	compost
bees	robins	manure
earthworms	earthworm castings	sunshine

Can you see how the winter garden supports life in the summer garden? For example, what natural processes occur to a stone during Winter? How do these processes help the soil in the Summer? Do the wind and snow and ice help break down a stone into small bits? Think about your two lists, then create a Web of Life that demonstrates the connections between the winter and summer seasons in the garden.

♥ To recreate the Web of Life you will need:

paper
yarn
crayons or colored pencils
a hole puncher or a sharp pencil

1) Draw all the members of the garden, as well as the natural processes of both seasons, on separate pieces of paper.

2) Pick a drawing and wear it around your neck.

3) Stand in a circle.

4) Using yarn, join the natural winter processes, or the members of the winter garden, to their "sister/partners" in the summer garden.

5) Explain how the wheel of life works by telling your sister/partner how you contribute to her life.

Want To Do More?

✍ **Can you write a story or poem that explains how and why the winter and summer gardens are sisters?** Dream up a character that expresses Winter's power, and another that express Summer's power. Let your imagination do the rest! Maybe your story can be made into a play!

✍ **Can you illustrate the cycle of natural activities that take place in the winter garden and the summer garden?** Include characters from your story or poem. To create a full year's journey through the garden, add the cycles of Spring and Fall to your illustration.

❧ **Celebrate your own Web of Life** by checking your Indoor Garden to see whether any vegetables are ready to be harvested. Use some of your harvest as party food to celebrate the end of Winter and the beginning of Spring. You should have no trouble finding friends to celebrate with you!

SPRING

Spring ❧

"AMA HEYA AND THE MOON OF NEW BUDS"

The Moon of New Buds (also known as the New Years Greeting Moon) marked the beginning of the New Year for Native Americans. It was the time of year when wild, new green life began to appear in the forest, signaling the end of Winter. First, the trees produced the sap that would be made into maple syrup. Then, as buds began to form on the trees' branches, fiddleheads, wild onions, dandelions, and cowslips sprouted from the leafy, brown forest floor. It was the time of year we now call Spring.

Ama Heya loved walking in the city park during the Moon of New Buds. As her brothers dashed from tree to tree, she and her mother strolled along the winding paths, enjoying the sun's warmth on their backs. A few days ago ice had covered the stream, but now the little brook gurgled happily, its silver waters tinkling over the black, shiny pebbles in the streambed.

As they strolled, Ama Heya's mother named the shrubs and trees that only a week ago had lain hidden beneath winter's snowy quilt. She also pointed out the emerging green children, speaking of the many gifts they offered to the people: medicines, seasonings for the stew pot, fruits for jams, seed pods, and bark for making games and crafts. As Ama Heya listened to her mother, whose voice was hushed and reverent, she was reminded of the ways of her mother's grandmother, Gram.

Last year Ama Heya had visited Gram during the Moon of New Buds. Spring came early to the island of Sawanakka that year. The air was scented by the saltwater mists that bathed the thawing woodland floor.

Ama Heya remembered how her great-grandmother hummed to herself as her eyes searched the forest floor. She had been looking for the first wild foods of the New

Year. Only an experienced eye could detect them, for the green children stood silent, their green heads and necks tightly coiled beneath layers of leaves. Gram's magic fingers expertly - delicately - pushed aside winter's leafy blanket. And there, coiled in green bundles, lay what she was looking for: the young fiddlehead ferns called ostrich ferns. They resembled sleeping snails right now, but as Spring's breath warmed them they would unfurl. Their lush, green fronds would then wave in the breeze like large, bouncing feathers on an ostrich's back. Now was the proper time to harvest them, though, while they were new and young and coiled close to the Earth.

"Gali ili ga," Gram whispered in Cherokee to each of the ostrich ferns she gathered.

Gram told Ama Heya that a spring diet of leafy greens was quite a change from Winter's heavy, thick stews. She said it took some time for the stomach to adjust to the light yet powerful, cleansing greens. For this reason, Gram took only a dozen or so ferns at a time from the awakening Earth. Before cooking them, she removed the copper-colored, papery covering that curled inside the ferns' heads. As the fiddleheads boiled on the stove, mist rose up from them like an ocean fog at dawn. Gram carefully rinsed the copper-colored water that leached from the ferns. This substance, called tannin, was too rough for the stomach. Sometimes she had to rinse the ferns several times before the water ran clear. Clear water meant that they were ready to eat, Gram said.

Gram's house was filled with excitement that evening. The new food signaled Spring's steady return. Now all eyes would keep a daily watch on the dogwood tree in the front yard. When the dogwood leaves grew as large as a squirrel's ear, it was time to prepare the gardens for planting. From that day forth, the new growing season would have everyone hustling and bustling about!

Refreshed but hungry from her morning foraging adventure, Gram sat down to a snack of corn chips. As she crunched away, she shared with Ama Heya her daydreams about what the New Year - the Moon of New Buds - might bring. And she told her about the importance of caring for seeds.

"Always remember that the river continues to flow beneath the ice during Winter. Its song never ends - it simply changes tune. In the same way, a song hums inside seeds as they rest during Winter. That's why you must care for the seed like a sleeping baby. Sing to it often. Respond to its hum so it won't feel forgotten."

Ama Heya was reminded of her great-grandmother's words as she and her mother came upon the musical stream flowing through the city park. Gram would be pleased to know that Ama Heya had not forgotten to care for her seeds. On several occasions in the last few days, Ama Heya had let her seeds know how grateful she was for last summer's harvest of corn, squash, and beans. Whenever she took the seeds out of their dark hiding place, she would think of her brothers' grinning faces, glistening with butter, corn stuck in their smiles. In Ama Heya's mind, the grinning faces included all of her relatives - parents, grandparents, cousins. For when Gram gave her the seeds last Autumn, she explained that they were the descendants of ones that had been passed down to her by her elders. Ama Heya was comforted by that thought. And though she often stood all alone in her room gazing at the seeds in her hand, she was warmed by memories of her corn-loving family smiling and laughing.

Now, as she walked along the wooded path, Ama Heya tugged on her mother's arm. Spring was here - and she was impatient. She wanted the days to hurry up, to race by. She wanted the woods and gardens to be in full bloom. "Ama Heya, slow down, little one," her mother said with a knowing smile in her eyes. "Every day we must watch for the Earth's tiny changes. For now it all begins again."

Spring Equinox: Sowing Seeds of Thought for the Spring Garden

In the Northeast it is too early to begin planting at Spring Equinox, so on that day we plant seeds of thought instead. Seeds of thought remind us of the gardens and harvests of years past and of those to come. Seeds of thought are planted on the day when darkness equals light.

❧ Begin the Equinox activities by bringing the seeds you preserved from last year's garden out of the darkness and into the light! Next, collect the new seeds you plan to sow this year, the ceremonial seed vessels you made last year, and your garden plan. Place all these items on a special table, where they will inspire you between the Spring Equinox and the seed-germinating season.

To put yourself in a Spring Equinox mood, stand with your friends facing the warmth of the returning sun, and recite the following dedication.

Spring Equinox Dedication

We are the Three Sister gardeners.
Filled with the light of the returning sun,
We look into the garden of our hearts.
Though we plant no seeds in the ground this day,
We plant a seed within our hearts.

Like the Beans, we grow roots
Deep down into the Earth.
May we care for her, ourselves, and all our relations
In every way we can.

Like the Corn, we reach for the stars
With a dream for all the people.
May they be fed unto many generations.
Like the Squash, we sow seeds of joy
And celebration for this good land and our neighbors.
May we dance for life with our Three Sisters.
Ho!

- JoAnne Dennee

THREE SISTERS SEEDLING NURSERY

Make your own organic germinating mixture and start sprouting baby sisters!

To make an **organic germinating mix,** you will need:

1 part peat
1 part pearlite
1 part compost
1 part bonemeal
1 part worm castings (optional)
1 part vermiculite (optional)
a large mixing bucket
a wooden spoon
warm water
planting containers

1) Mix the first five ingredients in a large bucket (do this outdoors, if possible). Mix the ingredients gently, otherwise you will create a dust that is unpleasant to breathe.

2) Add warm water to the mixture. The germinating mix should be wet enough to form a packed ball, but not so wet that water drips from it. If the mixture is too heavy, lighten it by adding one part vermiculite.

3) Put the mixture in planting containers and prepare to sow your seeds.

❧ The Ceremony of Seed Preparation

Create your own simple ceremony as you prepare for the gardening season. Following a Native American planting tradition, soak bean seeds overnight in spring water. This will give the seeds a chance to soften their hard, outer coat, which will enable them to bring forth their true potential.

Place the soaking seeds on the Equinox table. As they soak overnight, draw a picture of what you think will happen to the seeds during the course of the growing season. Roll up the picture, or put it in a special cloth bundle, and place it near the soaking seeds. May all your wishes come true!

❧ To begin the seedling nursery:

♠ **Find some reusable planting containers that are at least three inches deep.** Peat pots, plastic planters, yogurt containers, milk cartons, cider jugs - all of them make fine nursery cradles for the Three Sisters and their friends.

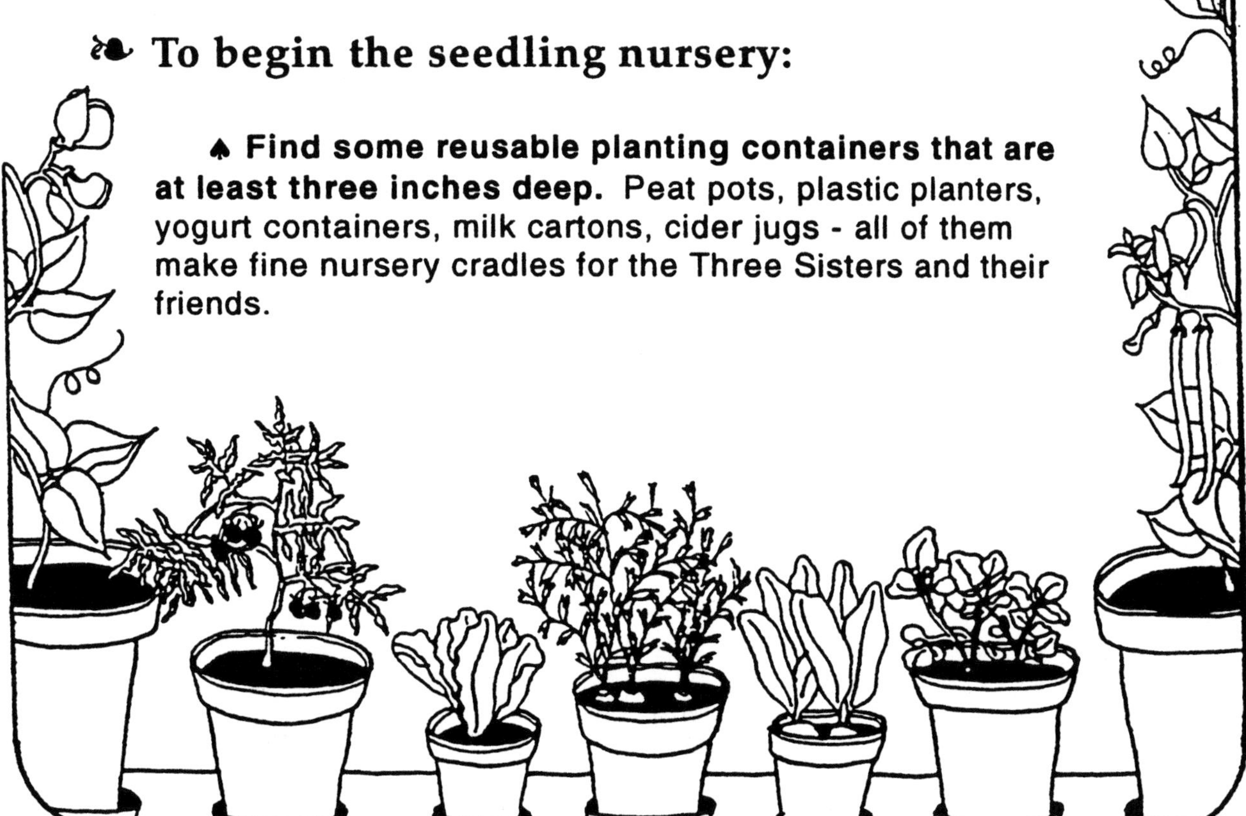

♠ **When sowing seeds, remember the rule of green thumb!** Most seeds are planted four times as deep as the seed is wide. To determine the proper depth of a certain species of seed, lay four seeds of that variety end-to-end. Place your green thumb along the row of four seeds, and note this depth on your thumb. Push the seed to that depth when you sow it. Plant a *wish* with your seed sister, too!

♠ **Six to eight weeks before planting day, start nicotiana, cornflowers, and herbs.** These can be planted one seed per square inch. Cover them with dark plastic and place them in a dark corner of the Indoor Garden Center. When they germinate, remove the plastic and place the seedlings under grow-lights. Cornflowers will enjoy living near Sister Corn, of course. Nicotiana and other herbs or flowers are happy to repel insects anywhere!

♠ **Start squash or gourd seeds four weeks before transplanting time.** Soak pumpkin or gourd seeds overnight, then plant one seed per container in large, six-inch deep, recycled containers (milk, cider, or large yogurt containers). These seeds will germinate best if the containers are covered with plastic bags to conserve moisture and insure darkness. Next, place the covered containers in a dark corner in the Indoor Garden Center. Check the seedlings daily. Remove the plastic immediately after germination. Transplant the seedlings in the garden after the last frost.

♠ **Three or four weeks prior to the last frost, soak sunflower seeds overnight.** Plant one seed per container in six- to eight-inch deep milk cartons or large yogurt containers. Poke holes in the bottom of the container for

proper drainage. Place the sunflowers in the Indoor Garden Center. If other seeds in the Indoor Garden have germinated and the grow-lights are in use, cover the sunflower seed containers with dark plastic bags. Peek under the plastic daily to check for germinating seeds. Remove the plastic at the first sign of emerging seedlings. Sunflowers will not need to be transplanted before gardening day unless they become root-bound.

♠ **Corn, though not easily transplanted, can be started indoors and successfully transplanted by following these instructions.** Start corn seed indoors only if the frost dates and your gardening schedule fail to coincide. Sow extra seedlings, as twenty-five percent of them may die after transplanting. First, soak the corn seeds. Plant one seed per container in four-inch high peat pots. (Peat pots are highly recommended because they reduce transplanting shock.) Follow the germinating instructions described for the preceding seedlings, then place the seedlings in the Indoor Garden Center. Be sure to keep peat pots moist as they dry out more quickly than plastic containers!

♠ **Sister Bean does not like to transplanted.** You must sow her directly into the garden after the last frost - be sure Sister Corn is tall enough to provide support for her sister!

☛ ***Note:*** *If you are interested in taking advantage of lunar influences, sow your herb, flower, and squash seeds so they will germinate when the moon is full. For more information about lunar planting, see the Winter activity 'Three Sisters and the Moon' in "Farmers and Gardeners of the Longhouse."*

❧ **Imagine that each container of seedlings is a mound that needs caretaking, then make up a nursery schedule of caretaking activities:**

♠ Check the moisture levels of plants and water them as necessary.

♠ Feed seedlings with fish emulsion every two weeks.

♠ Mist plants with a gentle rainfall or a foliar growth solution made of products from the sea.

♠ Check regularly to see whether the roots are growing through the bottoms of the containers. If so, transplant the seedlings into a larger container.

♠ Sing growing songs to your plants. They enjoy attention - and welcome the carbon dioxide you exhale as you sing!

A Wigwam for a Three Sisters Garden

If you would like a shady shelter in your Three Sisters garden, construct a wigwam!

❧ In ancient times, some Native Americans of the Northeast woodlands constructed wigwams as temporary shelters. These shelters were either dome-shaped or cone-shaped. The cone-shaped shelters resembled the tipis of the Plains Indians, except that they were covered with bark rather than skins. The Apache Indians called their cone-shaped shelters "wickiups." The Abenaki referred to all their houses, no matter what the shape, as "wigwams." Wigwams were used during the days of hunting and gathering, before the first farmers and gardeners came into existence.

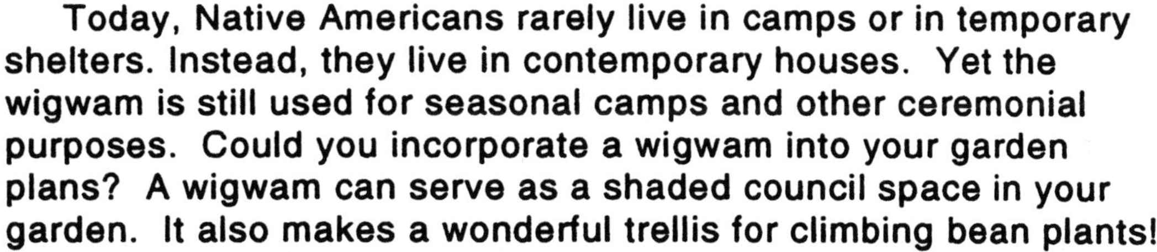

Today, Native Americans rarely live in camps or in temporary shelters. Instead, they live in contemporary houses. Yet the wigwam is still used for seasonal camps and other ceremonial purposes. Could you incorporate a wigwam into your garden plans? A wigwam can serve as a shaded council space in your garden. It also makes a wonderful trellis for climbing bean plants!

A Garden Wigwam

To make a wigwam you will need:

- a hand saw
- thirteen to fifteen poles (The wigwam poles should be made from strong trees that have fairly straight trunks. Look for sturdy trees that need to be harvested from the woodlands. The poles should be approximately two and a half to three inches in diameter and should be made from strong trees that have fairly straight trunks.)
- a strong weather-proof cord for lashing three wigwam poles together
- a post-hole digger

Before harvesting anything from the Earth, Native peoples traditionally asked permission and offered thanks. With a ribbon, mark the trees you wish to harvest. Then show your gratitude in your own way.

1) First, cut two experimental poles (these poles should be very long). Experiment with these two to find the proper length poles you will need for your wigwam. Hold the two poles up in the place where you will construct the wigwam, and determine what works best.

2) Once you have determined the proper height, plan on finding poles that are at least a foot longer than that length. This will compensate for several adjustments that will be made during the construction process.

3) Before cutting thirteen to fifteen poles to this length, choose the three strongest and straightest trees for the tripod poles. Tripod poles must measure one foot longer than the other wigwam poles.

4) Once the tripod poles are finished, cut all the remaining poles to their proper length.

For a sturdy wigwam frame, construct a tripod. The tripod will hold all the other poles in place.

1) Gather the three strong, straight tripod poles at a place just outside the garden.

2) Lay two of the tripod poles on the ground next to each other, leaving a few inches of space between them for the third tripod pole.

3) Approaching from the other direction, lay the third pole on the ground so that eighteen inches of it extends between the top eighteen inches of the two parallel poles, as shown in the illustration.

4) Lash the three poles together with a strong weatherproof cord, weaving a figure eight pattern in the middle of the 18-inch overlap. Weave this pattern five to six times around all three poles.

The lashing should be loose enough so that it does not restrict the movement of the three poles when they are placed in an upright tripod position.

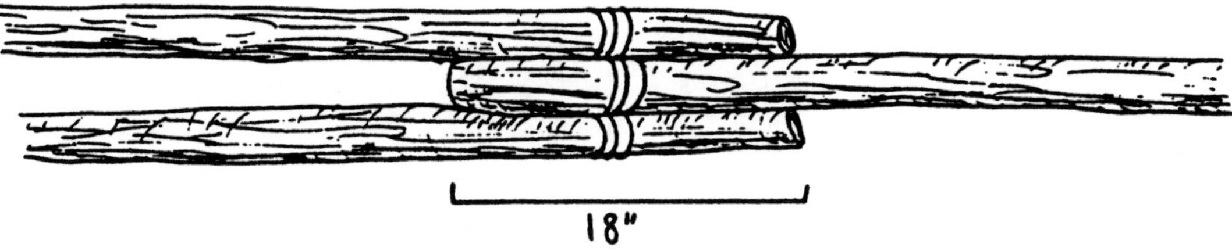

Now it is time to raise the tripod. With a trio of Three Sisters and Brothers gardeners, you can easily raise the tripod. It is fun to watch the tripod poles take the shape of a standing pyramid!

1) To move the tripod into the garden, the gardeners should grasp the lower ends of the tripod poles and lift them toward the center, pushing the lashed ends upward. Now walk the lower ends toward the place you intend to put the wigwam in your garden.

2) Place the tripod poles so that they create a triangular shape at their base, each an equal distance from the other.

3) Dig a hole six to eight inches deep beneath each tripod leg. A post-hole digger makes this an easy job!

4) Place the tripod legs in their holes and pack the holes with stones or soil. Tamp the packing materials firmly so that the poles will not move.

5) Finally, test the wigwam to insure that it is sturdy enough to withstand strong winds and gardening activities.

❧ **In the traditional wigwam, the Eastern gate remains open as the entrance.** This is where the morning sun rises each day. It is the place where thoughts of thankfulness are sent forth by many Native peoples each day at dawn. If you plan to put the doorway in the east, be sure not to enclose this space as you place the remaining poles around the wigwam. In a sunwise direction, moving from south to west to north to east, add one pole at a time to the tripod. Secure the poles in place by placing their upper ends in the crotch formed at the top of the tripod. This, together with the layering of one pole upon another, will hold all of them in place, strengthening the wigwam.

❧ **Your wigwam can be used as a living shelter, a council area, or a pleasant place to sit in the shade.** Weave a string trellis around the wigwam, beginning at the bottom and weaving up to the top - remember to leave the entrance area open! Loosen the soil around the wigwam poles. Plant climbing flowers or climbing vegetables at the base of the poles and encourage them to climb the string trellis. Pole beans or vining flowers will act as a living shade cover. Watch the plants grow whenever you seek shelter and shade for council meetings in your Three Sisters garden!

"A Story of a Three Sisters Garden in Vermont"

Not so long ago, a Three Sisters garden was created by a group of school children in Vermont. The Three Sisters garden had a wickiup in the center. The children gathered in the wickiup during the gardening season to picnic, to listen to gardening stories, and to receive guidance for the day's gardening tasks.

This is how it all began. . . .

The children foraged for thirteen tree limbs to build the frame of the wickiup. Ten of these limbs had to be fifteen feet in length, and three had to be sixteen feet. Once they found what they needed, the children trimmed all the branches from the poles. The three longest poles were fastened together as a supporting tripod. These poles were raised and set in the inner circle of the garden. The remaining ten poles were added in a sunwise or clockwise fashion by placing each pole in the crotch created by the tripod. All the poles were dug a few inches into the ground to secure them. The children knew that the traditional opening for Native shelters lies in the direction of the rising sun, so the eastern door became the wickiup's entrance. The children strung cord up the sides of the wickiup so that their soon-to-be sown climbing beans would be able to create living walls for the wickiup.

Around the outside perimeter of their circular garden, the children prepared several two-foot diameter mounds with three-foot spacings between them. The mounds eventually encircled the entire garden. Once their preparations were completed, the children compared their garden to the design they had created earlier that Spring.

Next, imitating the customs of the Native peoples, the children gathered fish bones to enrich the soil of the mounds. Local fish stores were happy to share old fish bones and shell scraps. The children aired the bones and shells so that animals would not be attracted to them once the garden was planted. They did not use raw fish meat - and they don't recommend that anyone else do it! If fish scraps are not available, crab meal, organic fertilizer, composted manure, or compost can be used. The children placed a handful of fish scraps in every mound.

After the final frost and as the full moon drew near, the children planned and held a Garden Planting Day Celebration. They selected poems, songs, and chants for the ceremony. They designed and delivered planting ceremony invitations to special guests, such as the school's principal, community elders, farmers, parents, and siblings. A Native American guest and parent, Gary Two Feathers, was also invited. The children made a sign, dedicating a section of the garden to their elders. The dedication gave thanks to their elders for feeding them and for having preserved nature for future generations. And, as a way of saying thank you for the gardening heritage that was passed down to them, the children expressed a desire to donate some of their fall harvest to local seniors and to Abenaki tribal members.

In accordance with some Native traditions, Seed Carriers were chosen among the Three Sisters gardeners. Several children were selected who had demonstrated a genuine desire to fulfill caretaking responsibilities. These children possessed a vision of abundance that benefited their friends and community. Oftentimes they were known for having planted seeds of good cause and right relations among their friends, assisting all to grow toward fullness. During the ceremony, the Seed Carriers held and cared for the seed in special seed bundles and containers that were fashioned especially for this day. Their Native American guest beckoned them forward and blessed the seeds in the traditional way. Then the Seed Carriers invited those gathered around to plant seeds of promise within their own hearts.

Getting Your Three Sisters Garden Ready for Planting Day

The last frost has passed - Planting Day will soon be here! In the Northeast, the planting season traditionally begins when white oak leaves are the size of a mouse's ear. When does it begin where you live? Are you ready to begin your preparations?

❧ **Here is a checklist of garden preparations.** These should be done two weeks or so before Planting Day.

♠ Check your garden to see whether the soil is wet or dry. If you see puddles, the soil is too wet and the garden should not be entered! If the garden appears to be dry, dig up a handful of soil and squeeze it in your hand. Does it form a tight, hard ball that does not crumble as you gently bounce it in your hand? If so, the soil is still too wet to be worked. Test it again after a few dry days have gone by. If the soil ball crumbles after gently bouncing it, get out your hand tools. The spring gardening season has arrived!

♠ Turn under any cover crops sown last Autumn. They will form part of the soil.

♠ Enrich the mounds with traditional fish fertilizer, such as seashells or fish bones, which can be found at local fish shops. Be certain to leave fish bones in the sun for several days to dry any meat still adhering to the bones. Otherwise the flesh will attract unwanted critters to your garden. Bury the bones or shells deeper than the depth you expect to sow the seeds. Fish emulsion can be used instead of shells or bones. To each mound, add one handful of compost or aged manure per Sister.

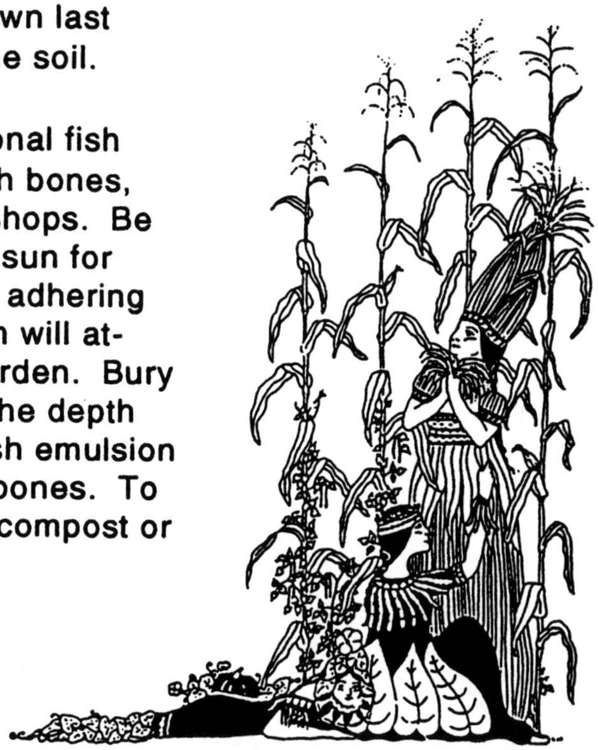

♠ Four or five days before Planting Day, harden off any seedlings you expect to transplant by taking them outdoors for a few hours a day. This will gradually expose them to increasing amounts of sun, wind, and temperature fluctuations. Tender seedlings should not remain out all night until they are almost ready to be transplanted. Cover them until the final frost has passed.

❧ Planning A Planting Day Celebration

In preparation for a Planting Day celebration, can you make a list of the different parts of the celebration that each Three Sisters gardener can volunteer to do? A list might include:

1) Who will create a ceremony for the Planting Day celebration?

2) Who will write poetry or create a skit about the Three Sisters garden to present to your guests?

3) Who will practice playing a drum and singing the songs you shared around the garden?

4) Who will tell a story about the ancient wisdoms of the garden?

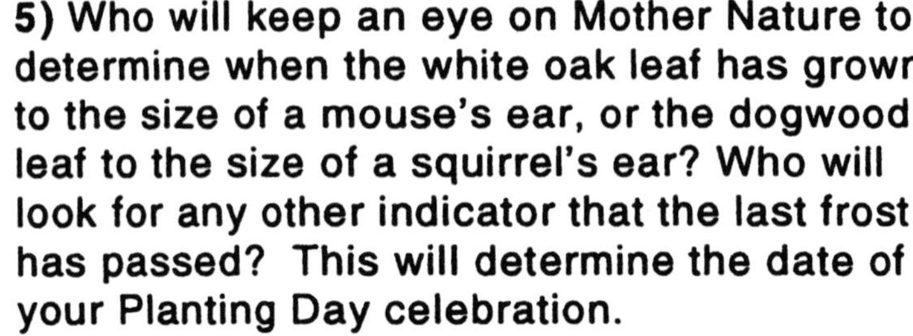

5) Who will keep an eye on Mother Nature to determine when the white oak leaf has grown to the size of a mouse's ear, or the dogwood leaf to the size of a squirrel's ear? Who will look for any other indicator that the last frost has passed? This will determine the date of your Planting Day celebration.

6) Who will write invitations to parents, elders, teachers, the school principal, kitchen staff, friends, and local farmers, asking them to join in the planting and dedication ceremony?

7) Will all the gardeners prepare food for the feast, or just some of them?

8) How will you choose Seed Carriers from among those who wish to perform this special task?

9) Who will carry tools to the garden and return them to the tool shed after the ceremony?

10) Who will acknowledge the guests? This is important, as the guests should be made to feel that they are very much a part of the ceremony.

Want To Do More?

❧ **Make special containers for holding your seeds during the planting ceremony on Planting Day.** Make clay pots or twig and bark baskets - or anything your imagination dreams up!

A Simple, Rustic Birch Basket for Seeds

You will need:

a sturdy piece of 8 1/2" x 6 1/2" birch bark
raffia or cornhusks for lacing
sharp scissors
a large darning needle or awl for making holes in the birch bark
a stream or basin of water in which to soak the bark
corrugated cardboard or a cutting board

1) Cut the basket and handle according to the birch bark pattern below.

2) Soak the bark for one half hour.

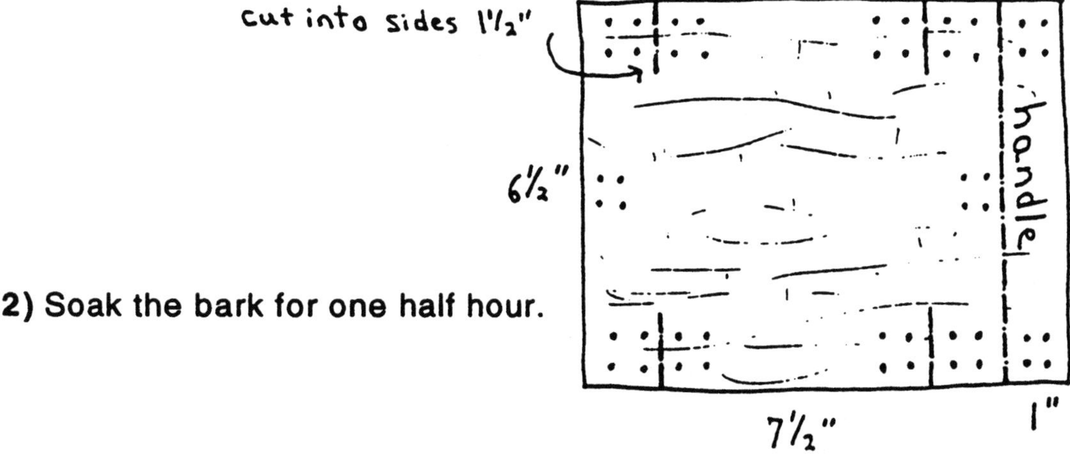

3) Lay the bark down on corrugated cardboard or a cutting board. Pierce holes with an awl or a darning needle, following the pattern shown above. Work with care to avoid tearing the bark as you pull the darning needle eye through the pierced holes.

4) Fold up the ends of the basket. Lace the strips of cornhusk or raffia through the holes in an "X" shaped pattern.

5) Attach the handle to each side. Stitch an "X" to secure each handle end to the holes made in the sides of the basket.

❧ **You can also make seed bundles to hold your seeds on Planting Day.**

Simple Seed Bundles

1) Cut leather, cloth, or felt into circles that are eight inches in diameter.
2) Close to the edge of the circles, snip quarter-inch X's, spaced no more than an inch apart, for holes to lace a drawstring cord through.

When the drawstring is pulled tight, a simple but efficient bag for seeds is created.

Even More Curious?

❧ **Research the traditional planting ceremonies that are practiced by a Native American community in your area.** Perhaps you can incorporate some of these ceremonies into you own upcoming Planting Day - and make it a special celebration!

Three Sisters Garden Ceremony and Planting Day!

Finally, the day arrives to celebrate your preparations and work in the Three Sisters garden!

❧ During the Planting Day ceremony, in addition to all the different parts of the ceremony you have created, you might invite the elders to relate their first experiences growing corn, squash, and beans. Ask them to share their special gardening insights with the Three Sister gardeners. Thank them for their gifts and for contributing to a "caretaker mind" attitude.

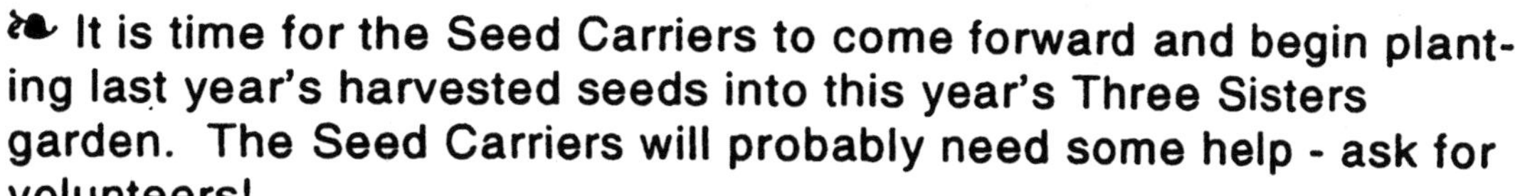

❧ It is time for the Seed Carriers to come forward and begin planting last year's harvested seeds into this year's Three Sisters garden. The Seed Carriers will probably need some help - ask for volunteers!

❧ It is also time to transplant the seedlings that have been carefully tended in the Indoor Growing Center. Below are some special recommendations for those who wish to transplant seedlings with a "caretaker mind" on Planting Day. This is especially important for Sister Corn.

Transplanting Seedlings

1) Immerse the corn peat pot in lukewarm water.

2) Carefully break off the rim of any peat pot that protrudes above the level of the soil. This will prevent the rim from acting as a wick (if the sun is allowed to shine on a protruding part of the peat pot, it will suck necessary moisture away from the tender seedling).

3) Dig a hole larger than the width of the peat pot.

4) Water the hole lightly.

5) Place the soaked peat pot in the hole.

6) Fill the sides of the hole with soil.

7) Tamp the soil gently with your hands.

8) Wish this tender corn seedling a strong and healthy life.

9) For other seedlings, remove them carefully from their containers and transplant them into moistened holes in the garden.

For the next ten days, pay "caretaker-mind attention" to your transplants. Water them daily, if needed, or at the first sign of wilting.

❧ As part of your ceremony, you might enjoy acting out or telling a story about corn. Generation after generation, families, villages, and tribal groups in North America have handed down their corn seeds. There was a time, however, when one village almost lost the precious gift of corn. There are many stories about the Corn Spirit, but central to each one is a warning to beware neglect and laziness. The following story was written by our authors today, but it keeps alive the warnings of yesteryear.

"Singing Bird and the Corn Spirit"

Fork-of-the-River village was known for its great abundance of crops. Years of hard work yielded a rich soil, and rainfall was always plentiful. Proper care, a spirit of thankfulness, and traditional ceremonies were essential ingredients in the planting, tending, and harvesting of the village's crops. Corn, beans, and squash thrived in this environment, and the people never went without food. Even in midwinter they had enough to share with visitors or passers-by.

As time went on, however, the people became lazy. Many of them wondered aloud whether it was necessary to work so hard when food overflowed their gardens. They neglected the soil and failed to replenish it with nourishing fertilizers. They stopped rotating their garden sites. Some people even forgot the value of proper care and thankfulness. Instead, they boasted of the great quantities of food they received as free gifts from the spirits.

Almost instantly, their neglect affected their harvests. And with each passing year, the people reaped less and less from their gardens. In one particularly disastrous year, the seed from the only remaining species of corn was destroyed by raccoons and crows. As if waking from a dream, the people realized they were in danger of starving.

One night, soon after the disappointing harvest, a young maiden named Singing Bird had a dream. In it, a crow led her through the forest to a clearing. With her inner vision she glimpsed sadness - and awoke with a start. Outside her wigwam, the first rays of dawn began to slant across the village. Singing Bird heard the cawing

of crows in the distance. Their cawing was so compelling she decided to search for the source of their excitement.

Singing Bird filled her waterskin as she crossed the bubbling stream near the edge of the village. Spotting the crows circling over a cluster of grandfather spruces, she headed in that direction.

Then, mirroring her dream, a crow swooped down and landed on a tree in front of her. Singing Bird waited to see what it would do. After preening its feathers for a few moments, the black bird cocked its head, made a guttural crow sound and looked Singing Bird directly in the eyes. A second later, it flew leisurely off through the forest. Well-versed in the portents of dreams, Singing Bird followed the shiny black bird, her curiosity mounting.

A bright yellow, late autumn light sifted through the lofty evergreens and leafless trees. There were no patches of snow to slow her down, and Singing Bird quickly made her way across the frozen, leaf-strewn ground.

The crow flew over a dense cluster of spruces, then disappeared. As Singing Bird squeezed through the prickly spruce branches, she realized she was entering a clearing. Senses alert, she paused to listen for potential danger. She heard the crow garbling softly. And then she heard the mournful sound of someone crying! Quietly, Singing Bird peered through the branches.

In the middle of the clearing stood a house, collapsing from years of neglect. Beside it sat a tearful old man, his clothes in tatters. Dead and dying cornstalks stood in scattered clumps around the clearing, their yellow leaves rustling in the wind.

After a few moments, Singing Bird found the courage to approach the tattered man, whose face was sad and craggy. The old man bore a remarkable resemblance to the withered cornstalks.

Apparently the old man did not hear the young maiden's approach, for he glanced up only when Singing Bird offered him a drink from her waterskin. The old man

took an appreciative swallow, and Singing Bird handed him a soft deerskin cloth to dry his eyes.

"Would you like some food?" Singing Bird asked. Ragged clothing hung from the man's bony body - he looked as if he had not eaten for days.

"Oh! Oh, yes!" the old man said, his eyes brightening. "You are so kind. It has been a long time since anyone has shown such caring."

Singing Bird brought out some dried meat and nuts and shared them with the old man. As the two of them ate in silence, Singing Bird thought about how her dream had drawn her here.

This man certainly needs some lessons in how to take care of himself and his land, Singing Bird thought. But he is so sad and so old. . . . I wonder where his people are?

At that very moment the old man was thinking: This child is wise and caring and full of life. Perhaps she can help me to live again. The Dream Spirits must have brought her here, and that is a good sign.

When they finished their meal, Singing Bird waited for the elder to speak. At last the old man turned to her.

"Once I was a powerful, honored, and respected Corn Spirit," he said. "For many years I brought your village an abundance of crops. But then your people became lazy and started to disrespect me. They banished me from their gardens, and I was exiled here among the trees, where the sun's warming rays reach but a few hours a day. Now, as you can see, I dress in rags. My home is ruined and my cornstalks withered."

After the old man had spoken, Singing Bird realized she had been sent to this clearing to reunite the Corn Spirit with his people. But the young maiden knew that such a reunion would be difficult. First, her people needed to rekindle a spark of life in the old man - it would require much caring from them. Yet, light already sparkled in the old man's eyes from the small acts of kindness Singing Bird had shown him. Even the leaves of the cornstalks looked less withered, and began to slowly lift and wave in the fading autumn sunlight.

Singing Bird assured the Corn Spirit that she would do everything possible to help him return to the gardens in his village. The young maiden stood, intending to go back to her people. In that moment Corn Spirit handed her three of the most beautiful ears of corn Singing Bird had ever seen.

"You are now the Keeper of your people's corn. Take these sacred ears back to your village and store them safely. When Spring comes, plant them in my honor. Remember to nurture the plants, as you have nurtured me today."

The sun was setting as Singing Bird returned to her village. It had begun to snow, and a cold, damp wind blew in from the east. Spring seemed far away, yet the young maiden was comforted by the three ears of corn snug inside her robe.

That night she spoke at the storytelling fire. Everyone listened with rapt attention to her dream and the story of her meeting with Corn Spirit. When Singing Bird drew the three ears of corn from her robes, everyone gasped at the beauty of the seeds. They agreed that she should be the Keeper of the corn, and entrusted her with the three ears until spring planting time.

At the close of the storytelling fire that evening, everyone in the village prayed for the health and happiness of Corn Spirit, who lived alone in the cold, snowy woods.

During the long, dark nights that followed, the people of the village wove Corn Spirit stories as they sat before their fires. At last the longest night of the Winter passed, and the hours of daylight grew steadily longer. Slowly, the daylight's strength increased. It melted the snow. It exposed the gardens, the fields, and the forest floor.

When it was time for planting, Singing Bird led her people to the fields. There they prepared the soil and planted the first seeds. Everyone participated in the plant-

ing ceremony and in the celebration that followed. The women prepared a feast of wild foods, fresh meat, and corn bread from the last of their stores. Everyone gave thanks to the food-growing spirits - especially to Corn Spirit. It was a wonderful day in the village, and when it was finished everyone fell into a contented sleep beside the fire.

A few days later, the first green sprigs of corn appeared. The people rejoiced when they saw them. Singing Bird was especially happy. She decided to visit Corn Spirit to see how the old man had fared during the Winter. Taking her waterskin and dried meat as before, she headed toward the clump of spruces that enclosed Corn Spirit's meadow.

When she arrived, the young maiden stepped carefully into the meadow. It was empty, save for seven beautiful cornstalks, which happily waved their sturdy green leaves in the sunshine. Singing Bird smiled to herself. An abundant harvest was ensured for her village. For she knew that Corn Spirit had returned to her people's gardens.

After the seeds are planted, it is up to you to let neither weed nor raven disturb your garden. Organize a Summer Garden Schedule to care for your Three Sisters!

SUMMER

Summer ❧

"AMA HEYA AND THE SUMMER'S SONGS"

When Gram's humming drifted up from the garden to the second-story guest room, Ama Heya popped out of bed and looked out the window. There was Gram, her wide-brimmed straw hat bobbing to the rhythm of her weeding. She looked like a contented child building sand castles at the beach, her cocoa-colored hands moving playfully among the earth and plants. Gram always rose early to be with her green children. She said you had to get in the garden early or "the noon would wear you out."

Ama Heya had been waiting all year to spend her summer days on Sawanakka with Gram again, so she wasted no time getting dressed. After washing her face, she headed for the kitchen. Ama Heya knew she needed a good breakfast and lots of energy to keep up with Gram in the garden. She helped herself to a large bowl of oatmeal, and smothered a slice of toast with Gram's "magic in a jar" - plum jam.

Ama Heya ran out to the garden. She saw the happiness shining in Gram's eyes as she greeted each of the sprouting plants. "I'm so happy to see you, Sister Corn," Ama Heya said. "How is Sister Bean today?"

Gram had already planted her onion sets that morning - she always planted them just when their relatives, the wild onions, sprang up. As Ama Heya walked along the border of the garden, she noticed that Gram was planting other seeds in hills she had prepared. The soil in the hills was rich because her great-grandmother had added manure to it from the farm down the road. It was Gram's way to give to the Earth before expecting anything in return.

Gram smiled at Ama Heya, inviting her into the freshly opened earth. She did not have to give her great-granddaughter instructions, for Ama Heya had tended Gram's garden for many Summers now. Gram worked quickly but respectfully as she poked shriveled seeds into each of the hills. When her gnarled yet magical, green fingers disappeared into the earth, she sang, "*Gali ili ga.*" It meant: I am grateful. Ama Heya sang with her, and together they moved to the rhythm of their song, entrusting seeds to the tender care of the Earth.

From among Ama Heya's many thoughts, a single question rose up to float upon the wind created by their song. "How does the seed know how to grow?"

And the silent song hidden deep in the seed replied through Gram's words. "All things are given the power to remember and the power to dream - people, animals, even plants. Just as the salmon remembers to return to the stream of its birth to bear its young, the corn remembers its growing song. Tapping deep into its memory, the corn seed recognizes the cradle of darkness as its mother, the earth. It sends out roots to touch her, just as a baby's fingers grasp its mother's hand. The green corn child grows quickly, as does any child in its mother's loving care. And as it grows, it dreams of tomorrow. From the single seed of its birth, it produces a multitude of new seeds. A few of these new seeds eventually become green children themselves. And as these green children sleep through the long Winter, waiting to be planted deep in the earth, they dream of the plenitude of Summer, when each ear of corn will burst with hundreds of seeds. This dream of plenty makes the children strong. It makes the children strong in their own remembering."

When they finished their planting, Gram and Ama Heya gently patted the earth that protected the seeds.

Next came the weeding. Without looking, Gram's magic fingers could tell the difference between the green grandchildren she planted and their wild green relatives who visited the garden. Nothing was wasted in Gram's garden. "We can eat these for lunch," Gram said, picking out lambsquarter weeds and setting them aside. Their tender young leaves would be tart and tasty in a salad.

Removing them from the hills gave Gram's little green sprouts more room to grow.

When the weeding was finished, Gram ran her hands over the soil as though she were tickling the Earth. The loosened soil was ready for its final scratching. With a hoe, Gram gently opened the soil a little deeper. Now fresh air and rain could reach down to and nourish the growing roots.

Before Ama Heya knew it, Gram looked up at the sky and said, "Noon is nearly upon us. Better stop for lunch before it gets the better of us!"

In the kitchen, the two chatted about the upcoming Green Corn Festival. The Festival occurred in midsummer and was the occasion for a Thanksgiving feast. The family would gather around the garden and pick the tender, green, not-yet-ripe corn. Each would offer thankfulness, and then the family would feast on the raw corn. It was a time of sharing, of stories, of celebration. It marked the beginning of a harvest of ripe, golden corn that would continue into Autumn. At the end of the final harvest, Gram would dry the remaining corn seed and plant it in next year's garden. Some of that seed she would place in Ama Heya's care. Gram's gnarled yet delicate, magical fingers would cradle the seed bundle as she spoke to her great-granddaughter, Ama Heya, in a proud, hushed voice.

"Walk tall, as your ancestors did. And remember: laying in the seed keeps alive the memory of our ancestors. Their spirit stiffens our backbone. Walk tall. In your hands lie the dreams of tomorrow. What will you dream?"

To this day, Ama Heya recounts these stories to her daughter, her son and her friends. She will never forget the many Summers she spent with her great-grandmother near the waters of Sawanakka - indeed, the people of Wyandanch still remember Gram. Wherever Ama Heya went later in her life, she made friends with children of diverse backgrounds. She also made friends with their grandmothers. For Ama Heya knew that all grandmothers possess a magic of their own.

Ama Heya continues to grow with her Three Sisters in the gardens she now tends in Vermont. She encourages you to do the same. And she encourages you to discover the wonders of yesterday, which can fill your hearts and guide you today.

SUMMER CARE FOR SISTER CORN, SISTER BEAN, AND SISTER SQUASH

Summertime is the time of year when the Three Sisters really perform their garden dance! But, like all dancers, they need care and sustenance to grow healthy and strong.

❧ Sister Corn grows straighter and taller than her two sisters, reaching for the sky. Sister Bean, her pods dangling in the wind, winds her way up and around Sister Corn. Sister Squash - or Pumpkin - creeps across the earth and lies like a carpet upon it, her prickly leaves protecting her sisters from the raccoon and deer. Take a moment to reflect upon Sister Corn's, Sister Bean's, and Sister Squash's growth and needs over the Summer. Doesn't it seem that although we give so little, the Three Sisters give us back so much?

Here are some tips for caring for your Three Sisters this Summer:

❧ Sister Corn

See how she stands tall as a child upon Mother Earth? Her long leaves are like arms that bend down towards the ground, as though she were a child reaching to hold her mother's hand. If her leaves start to fold or curl up along the edges, then Sister Corn is not receiving enough water. Soak the mounds thoroughly, please!

♠ When Sister Corn is one hand high, mound up soil around the base of the stalk so the wind will not blow her down. It is best to draw up soil from the walkways between the hills, rather than digging in the mound covering Sister Corn's shallow roots. Before hilling the soil, remove weeds by shallowly cultivating the mounds with a finger hoe or by pulling up the weeds by their roots. Be careful not to damage the tender roots and stems of corn, bean, and squash! Compost the removed weeds. Cultivate Sister Corn again when she stands knee-high. Do not cultivate her when she is higher than your knee or you might damage her roots.

♠ Side-dress corn with a fertilizer high in nitrogen, such as aged manure or fish emulsion. Side-dressing is the process of applying fertilizer to the surface of the soil near the roots of the growing crop. Do this when Sister Corn stands knee-high, and again when silk appears on her husks.

♠ You can observe a special event when Sister Corn starts to tassel! At this time the father and mother parts of the corn begin the fertilization process, which creates seed in the plant's husk. The tassel crowning the top of the corn is the father part. Golden pollen on the tassels is carried by the wind down to the mother silk, which dangles from the end of the husk. When fertilization is complete, many seeds will form on the cob. This is how generation upon generation of corn has been formed over thousands of years!

♠ If you notice yellowing leaves, give Sister Corn an energy boost by feeding her an organic fertilizer that is high in nitrogen.

> ☛ ***Note:*** *The corn in your Three Sisters garden is either meal corn or popping corn - unless you are growing sweet corn, too. Short stalks are popcorn. Taller plants are a grinding corn used for making cornmeal. Neither corn should be harvested until it is fully formed and dry in the husks - usually this will occur in late September. But if you would like to feel the invisible seeds as they form on the cob, you can lightly squeeze the husks during the Summer.*

❧ Sister Bean

It's fun to watch Sister Bean wind her way up Sister Corn! Which direction are the beans going as they wrap their way up? Are they all going in the same direction? Why is that? Sister Bean might need a little encouragement to find her way to Sister Corn. If you want Sister Bean to wrap herself around the wickiup, thread string across the wickiup's supports. Then gently weave her tendrils between and around the strings to help her get started.

♠ If Sister Bean's leaves begin to wilt, water her well. Then spread compost mulch around the mounds to help her preserve moisture.

♠ Keep an eye out for bean beetles munching on the plants. Pick them off by hand, or find an insect remedy in the 'Three Sisters' Guide to Organic Insect Remedies' on **page 349** in the "Farmers and Gardeners of the Longhouse" journey.

> ☛ ***Note:*** *Beans, unless they are the summer-eating green bean type, should not be removed from their pods until harvest time, in September or October. At that time they can be dried and shelled. Then they will be ready to eat!*

❧ Sister Squash

Watch Sister Squash as she roams and rambles through the garden! She spreads her prickly leaves everywhere, protecting her sisters from raccoons and deer. Allow plenty of room for Sisters Corn and Bean to grow by gently directing Sister Squash's vines into the walkways between the mounds or onto the grass outside the wickiup. Be sure to leave the eastern walkway open so gardeners will have an entryway into the wickiup.

♠ After the flower is fertilized and the baby squash begins to mature, side-dress the plant with aged manure. When you side-dress, cultivate lightly, scratching the fertilizer or aged manure into the top inch of the soil only.

♠ When several baby squash have formed on each plant, pinch off the tips of the runners on the ends of the plants. This will allow the plant to devote its full energy to the growth of the new baby squash. Compost these tips.

♠ Check Sister Squash regularly for the striped cucumber beetles that like to nibble at tender leaves and vines. Pick them off and crush them (oops, don't forget to say "Sorry!"). Or check the Three Sisters' Guide to Organic Insect Remedies. Be sure to pick off or spray only those insects that are doing damage.

♠ Allow beneficial, six-legged friends to remain on the plant so they can do their job of preying on undesirable insects.

Sister Squash (Pumpkin) should remain on the vine into the Autumn. Harvest time takes place when her green color turns golden.

❧ Now that you have had a chance to see how the Three Sisters cooperate and care for each other, maybe you can understand why the Iroquois name for the Three Sisters means "life support." To the Iroquois, the Three Sisters are more than food - the spirit of cooperation among these plants mirrors the Iroquois' way of life. Without this spirit of cooperation, the Iroquois would not have prospered and become powerful.

❧ How can working with the Three Sisters support you as you grow in life?

Wadogh! That means "Thanks" in Cherokee, Three Sisters and Brothers!

Three Sisters Plant Parts Art

Create models of your Three Sisters as they grow in the garden. Modeling with beeswax, plasticene, or clay is easy and fun!

❧ What do you see when you look at Sister Corn?

See how her leaves, climbing the tall central stalk, arc back towards the Earth? Do tassels shoot up from the stalk to crown the plant? If so, you should see tiny pollen-carriers dangling from the tassels. Once upon a time these carriers were covered with golden pollen and lived inside the plant. But as they pushed their way up and out along the tassels, they dropped their pollen. Now the carriers are bare, and the tassels dangle and sway in the breeze. Look more closely at an arcing leaf. Do you see an ear of corn growing from the side of the stalk? Does it point towards the sky as it grows? A green blanket of husks covers every ear. Corn silk pours out of the tops of the ears. These golden silks formed long ago when the corn was young. The silks will turn brown and wave when the corn is ripe.

Create a model of all Sister Corn's parts - her tassels, stalk, leaves, ears of corn, and corn silk.

❧ What do you see when you look at Sister Bean?

Heart-shaped leaves climb up her vine. Do her heavy pods dangle beneath the leaves, or is she still hiding her delicate bean flowers? Are some of the pods pencil-thin? Do others appear to be bumpy as they ripen? Sister Bean's vine spirals in a single direction as it grows toward the sky and clings to whatever is in her path.

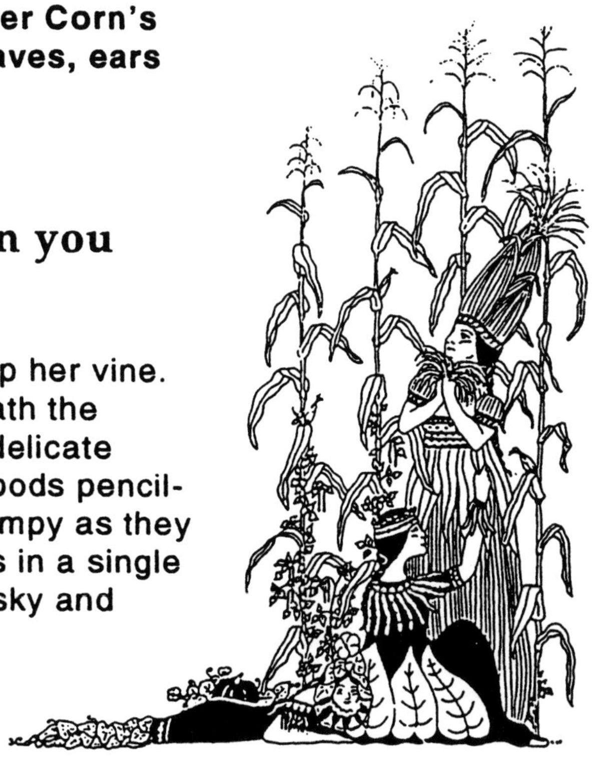

Create a model of Sister Bean. Make her vine, leaves, and pods. Show how she has a tendency to touch - and cling to - anything in her path.

❧ What do you see when you look at Sister Squash?

Her favorite pastime is to roam and ramble - there are few trails she will not explore! Her large, lobed leaves blanket the garden like a series of umbrellas, shading and cooling everything that lies beneath her. Her prickly spines keep pumpkin thieves away. Watch her crowd around the ground-loving plants she meets. Look for the hidden treasures beneath her green umbrella canopy - these orange, ribbed flowers will soon bear fruit!

Fashion a model of Sister Squash. Recreate her strong prickly vine, fruits, leaves, and tendrils. Show the way she loves to roam and ramble.

❧ **Display your Three Sisters sculptures in a miniature garden!**

Want To Do More?

❧ Create a beeswax sculpture exhibit entitled "Native Foods, Yesterday and Today." Demonstrate the history of corn in your community's gardens.

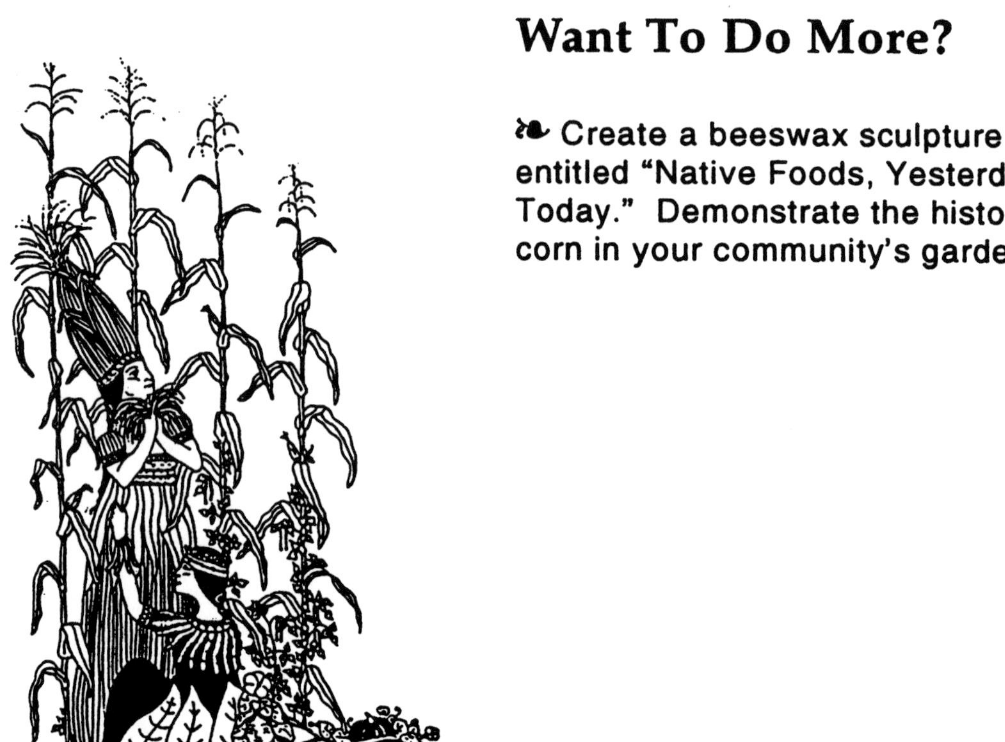

Summer Garden Pharmacopoeia: Making Hand Cream

If your hands become chapped and blistered from garden chores, or sunburn gets the best of you, prepare a homemade garden remedy. Calendula and marigold blossoms contain a soothing substance that moisturizes and heals the skin.

Turn the page for directions to make this luxuriant hand cream. . . .

Josie's Rosy Hand Cream

You will need:

a large 3-quart pot (not aluminum)
a wooden spoon
a 12- to 15-inch piece of cheesecloth or sheer material
a large strainer
a rubber band or string
recycled baby food or jam jars with lids for storing cream

1 cup olive oil
2-3 cups calendula or marigold blossom petals
2 ounces strained and cleaned beeswax (beeswax can be obtained from your local honey suppliers, or substitute several natural-colored beeswax candles)
1 ounce lanolin (available at drug stores) to create a creamier consistency
a couple of drops of rose or lavender oil to scent the hand cream (optional)

To make the hand cream:

1) After the morning dew has dried, pick vibrant calendula or marigold blossoms. Remove the petals from the hulls.

2) Measure the petals after hulling. You need enough to fill two to three cups.

3) Place oil and flower petals in a pot on the lowest heat. Do not allow the oil to boil. When the heat is at the right level, you will see small bubbles in the oil .

4) With the wooden spoon, slowly stir the oil and petals every 10 to 20 minutes. Within two hours, the rich, amber-colored resin of the blossoms should be well-combined with the oil. (Stirring can be a soothing activity in itself, and add to the enjoyment of making the cream. Stir in a clockwise direction and hum a stirring song or recite a poem.)

5) Drape the cheesecloth over the strainer and strain the oily mixture through it. When all the oil has been poured into the cloth, tie or secure the cloth with a rubber band and let it remain in the strainer until all the oil drips out. To obtain every last bit of oil from the cloth, wait until the oil has cooled enough to handle but is not cold. Gently press the wooden spoon against the cloth to remove the remaining oil.

6) Place a jar of beeswax in a pot of hot, but not boiling, water. Melt the beeswax over low heat. Keep a close watch on the beeswax as it is flammable!

7) Stir the beeswax into the oil-and-blossom mixture while both liquids are still hot.

8) Add the lanolin and the rose or lavender oil.

9) Pour the mixture into clean glass jars. Watch how the mixture cools and solidifies.

10) Can you make your own labels for your homegrown, rosy, healing hand cream? Laminate them to the jars with clear contact paper.

11) Keep the hand cream with your garden tools so that it will be available when you most need it. Use it to soothe chapped hands, scrapes, sunburn, and chapped lips.

Share your kitchen pharmacopoeia with a gardening friend and enjoy smooth, soft hands!

The Wisdom of the Shadows: Sun Time and Sundials

Most likely you have noticed that Summer brings warm days and warm nights, lightning bugs and morning dew. Have you also noticed that the days are much longer than in Winter? Why do you think this happens?

❧ Long ago, people relied on natural phenomena to determine time and to plan seasonal activities. Today, clocks and calendars provide us with similar information. Yet the earth has rhythms and secrets that are not revealed by clocks and calendars. If you would like to discover these secrets, let Mother Nature and Father Sky be your teacher. Hush-sh-sh. These secrets are revealed only to those who are willing to be still. Observe nature. Listen to the earth, and to the story of. . . .

"Shadow Dancer"

Little Sparrow scrambled to the top of Lookout Hill. On the hilltop grew a huge tree, so tall it seemed to speak directly to the sky. Little Sparrow sat beneath the tree. He had a view of the entire valley and the distant hills. If travelers approached he would be able to see them and announce their presence to the village. Yet on this day a silence fell over the land. Perhaps it was too hot for horse and traveler to venture far from home, Little Sparrow thought.

The silent heat of the day wore on. Little Sparrow was grateful for the comforting shade of the tree. He sat in its coolness, his daydreams his only company. He imagined himself running with wild horses, wrestling in the stream with other braves, visiting the animals of the forest. Little Sparrow enjoyed his imaginary journeys - it was a wonderful way to pass the time.

After a while he noticed that the tree had shifted its shade to another place. Little Sparrow moved from the hot sun into the shade. There he daydreamed once more

of wrestling in the cool stream. But the shade moved again. Little Sparrow moved with it. Once again the shade moved - and Little Sparrow was forced to again change his position. On and on he and the tree played, until Little Sparrow thought he could stand it no longer! Finally, the sun set. Now the shade of the tree seemed to rest, and Little Sparrow slept soundly in the coolness beneath it.

Little Sparrow rose early the next day. Sitting beneath the shade, he noticed that the tree began to play the same strange game again! Little Sparrow grew curious. He wondered if the tree was trying to tell him something. Perhaps the tree wanted him to stand up and look for something in the distance. Little Sparrow looked, but saw nothing. Surely, he thought, a tree that could talk to the sky must be wise in its ways. It <u>must</u> have an important message for a young boy.

Determined to discover what the tree might say, Little Sparrow moved some distance from it. Sitting in the sun's heat, he listened and waited with an open heart, watching as quietly as the stones. He squinted, hoping to detect the tree's slightest movement. All day he endured the sun's heat, waiting. But by sunset no secret had been revealed. When Little Sparrow lay down to sleep, he vowed to spend one more day of silent waiting to discover the secret of the moving shade.

The morning sun woke Little Sparrow. He rose and continued his watch, sitting some distance from the tree, as quietly as the stones themselves. Before long, Raven landed in the shade and sat enjoying its coolness for some time. Little Sparrow sat motionless. Although Raven eventually left, the bird returned often throughout the day to rest in the tree's shade. Each time Raven returned, the tree's shade was in a different place. Could the tree be playing the same game with Raven? Little Sparrow wondered.

I must listen to what the shadows say, Little Sparrow thought, for they seem to whisper to Raven. But what were the shadows saying? Little Sparrow did not know.

He decided to remain at the tree for one final day to ponder the question.

For the third and final day Little Sparrow continued his watch. The shadows whispered to the tree, to Raven - and to Little Sparrow as well! At last the secret was revealed! Little Sparrow thanked the tree, the Raven, the Earth and the Sky before racing away.

When Little Sparrow reached his village, he told a wise tribal elder all that had happened. "What does it mean?" Little Sparrow asked him.

"Little Sparrow," the elder answered him with a knowing twinkle in his eye, "you have discovered a way to know time, and with it a way that unites our people. As the tree told you, listen to the shadow. The shadow is Sun's faithful companion. Each day the Sun moves across the Sky World, traveling from one end of the Heavens to the other. Yet it always returns to where it began each day - the land of the Bright Morning Star. All the tasks that our people need to do during daylight must happen between the time the Sun arrives and the time it departs. The shadow announces Sun's comings and goings. One needs only to observe the shadow to discover Sun's location during its journey.

"You have observed well, Little Sparrow," the tribal elder said. "You have discovered an old wisdom. We shall remember what you have learned by giving you a new name: 'Shadow Dancer'."

At certain times of the year from that day forth, the Sun's shadow whispered important messages to Shadow Dancer. It told him the best time of day to plant, as well as the best time to rest. Shadows that lengthened or shortened with the seasons instructed him when to harvest or call his people together for ceremonies. Sun faithfully announced these special occasions during Shadow Dancer's life by casting its light upon a special hill or on a tree perched on the horizon. Shadow Dancer spent a part of each day sitting as quietly as the stones, and whenever the shadows whispered their secrets to him, he always paused to listen.

And so it was that Shadow Dancer learned the wisdom of the shadows and was often seen playing tag with the shadows for years thereafter.

- JoAnne Dennee

❧ **Can you retell the story of Shadow Dancer to your friends or your brother and sister?** Sit in the shade of a tree while you spin the story of Little Sparrow who, by watching and waiting, learned wisdom from the shadows.

❧ **You, too, can discover the wisdom of the shadows - as Little Sparrow did - by playing the following games:**

The Sun In The Sky Game

1) Sit in a circle on the floor with the lights out.

2) Place a candle in the center of the circle. Like the sun, the candle will cast shadows.

3) With adult supervision, carefully experiment with the length of the shadows by moving the candle, your body, or other objects.

4) Place the "sun" directly overhead.

5) Put it high and to one side in the "sky."

6) Move it lower, near the "horizon."

7) Pretend your body is the tree, and determine where Little Sparrow played in the tree's shadow.

Shadow-Catcher

1) Define some boundaries for this game of tag, and create a "safety zone" in the shade of a tree.

2) One person is the Shadow-Catcher. The other players must hide their shadows from her.

3) If she steps on your shadow, you become the Shadow-Catcher.

4) Your shadow is safe in the shadow of the tree, but, like Raven, you can only rest there for a little while.

Want To Do More?

❧ **On a sunny day, construct individual sundials.** Insert a stick into a clay ball. Set the ball (with the stick standing upright in it) in the center of a round piece of cardboard. Paint the cardboard with images of the sun and sky. Then be patient and watch the shadow of the stick change its shape and position.

Or, make a large group sundial. First, place a three-foot stick vertically in the ground. Each hour, record the wisdom of the shadows by placing short sticks at the tip of the three-foot-long stick's shadow. On each stick hang a descriptive drawing of an activity that regularly occurs at the hour the shadow marked, such as the beginning of the school day, snack time, lunch, recess, or dismissal. Or, describe the activities that take place in your home, such as waking in the morning, the time your parents leave for work, going to school, little brother's nap time, coming home from school, eating a snack with little brother, and dinner time.

❧ **Adapt the same sundial as a timekeeper for performing various gardening tasks throughout the day and season.** Keep the sundial in the garden. Record on it the time each gardening activity should be performed.

For example, early morning is the best time to water plants because most plant growth takes place at that time. Never water them during the hottest part of the day because the water droplets can act like tiny magnifying glasses and might scorch tender leaves. The best time to gather herbs is after the dew dries but before the sun shines too strongly. Transplant seedlings in the late afternoon when the heat of the day has passed and the long, cool night lies ahead. Harvest vegetables just before preparing meals - this way their vitamins will be present when you eat them!

❧ **Measure and chart your own shadow at various times of the day.** Stand outdoors in the same place each time you record your shadow. To be sure you know exactly where to stand, trace your footprints with chalk. On the hour, have a friend outline your body's shadow with chalk. Have her use a different color chalk each time she traces your shadow. Stand as quietly as the stones when she finishes tracing your shadow, and think about the following questions. Where is the sun positioned in the sky? In what ways does your shadow change each time it is traced? What secrets does your shadow whisper to you?

❧ **Are you able to "tell time" simply by looking at the sun's position?**

Even More Curious?

❧ **Make "Secret of the Shadow" drawings.** On a sunny day, trace a plant's shadow on white cardboard. How easy is it to capture the secret of the shadow? What secrets have you discovered about shadows?

Round and round the Earth is turning,
Turning always round to morning,
And from morning round to evening.

- from "A Circle is Cast", author unknown

What do the words of this song mean to you? Although it seems to us that the sun is moving across the horizon, it is we who are on a journey. We turn with the earth as she moves towards the promise of a new dawn. Many peoples on earth view the dawn as a significant moment and greet the sun with a ceremony every day. You might enjoy reading the poem "The Way to Start a Day" by Byrd Baylor.

❧ **Draw the western horizon as seen from your yard.** Every two weeks or every month, draw the position of the setting sun as it moves across the horizon. Observe the movement of the sun throughout the year. Use a sun chart to mark important garden tasks, such as the last frost date, transplanting time for hardy plants, transplanting time for tender plants, seed-sowing dates for different crops, mulching time, the dates various insects emerge, and so on.

❧ **Are you able to determine the seasons of the year simply by looking at the sun?**

Web of Garden Life

What is a Web of Life? A Web of Life demonstrates how the different parts of the garden work together to sustain life. It shows the connections between all these natural elements.

The warm winds dance, carry the Spring -
I become part of it.
I plant the corn seed in the Earth,
I become part of it.
I plant the bean seed in the Earth,
I become part of it.
I plant the squash seed in the Earth,
I become part of it.
The sun and rain fill the seed of Earth,
I become part of it.
I eat the corn, the bean, the squash -
And become part of it.

- JoAnne Dennee

❧ **To start your Web of Life,** make a list of all those who visit your Three Sisters garden.

1) Begin with animals, insects, birds, and any other living visitors.

2) Include everything Mother Nature contributes to the garden - soil, sun, wild plants, rain, moonlight, and air.

3) List everything you have added to your garden, such as compost, water, seeds, mulch, and the care you give it.

4) Draw a picture of each item on the list, one drawing per page or index card.

❧ **To Re-create a Web of Life,** get a ball of yarn, follow these simple directions, and see what happens!

1) If a large group wishes to make a Web of Life, each person should wear one of the drawings as a necklace. Simply thread a string "necklace" through the top of the illustration, place the string around your neck, and stand in a circle.

2) If only one person is making a Web of Life, lay the pictures on the ground so that they form a circle.

3) To make the Web of Life, unravel a ball of yarn and connect the elements that assist one another.

4) These "connections" demonstrate the interdependence of life in the garden.

5) When everything in the garden has been connected by the yarn-web, reflect upon what you see.

What would happen if any <u>one</u> of the elements was unable to make a contribution to the Web of Life? Drop the yarn connecting one of the elements and see what happens!

Want To Do More?

❧ Read "The Wind Eagle" In *The Wind Eagle and Other Abenaki Stories* by Joseph Bruchac, and discover how Gluskabi learns about the delicate balance in the Web of Life during his adventures.

Summer Vacation in the Lands of the Three Sisters

May your summer journeys take you around the country to other lands of the Three Sisters!

❧ **Discover more about the rich, diverse heritage of the Three Sisters and Native Americans as you travel across the country.** Attend powwows or Pueblo ceremonies if they are open to the public or you have asked for permission. Or visit the many trading posts, National parks, and museums where Native American staff conduct interpretive programs and craft demonstrations. *Indian America: A Traveler's Companion* (Second Edition) by Eagle Walking Turtle is an excellent reference and guide book. (See Bibliography.)

❧ **Buy or swap corn seed or ears at the local markets and trading posts or with the gardeners you meet during your journey.** Some of the new corn seed can be sown in your next Three Sisters garden. Grind an ear of the new corn into cornmeal and use it in your next cornbread recipe. Do you think you will be able to taste the difference between the new corn and your corn?

❧ **Learn some new stories** during your travels, and share them at your next harvest fire and dinner.

❧ If you taste delicious Native foods made up of Three Sisters ingredients during your vacation, make a **note of the recipes** and savor them again after you arrive home.

❧ **Make recipe cards of your favorite Three Sisters foods and bring them with you on your vacation.** You never know when you might meet someone who would be thrilled to try a new, delicious recipe!

Want To Do More?

❧ **Bring your appreciation of different Native cultures home** and begin a cycle of reciprocity through sharing. Can you find ways to support your local Native community? If not, adopt a Native elder through the Seeds of Change Project. This project not only acquaints you with a Native elder, but provides information about how to assist the elder by supplying him with daily living needs - such as canned foods, blankets, tools, or clothing. Write:

Seeds of Change Project
The Mountain Light Center
Box 241
Taos, NM 87571
Or call (505) 776-8474

Happy Summer! Happy gardening!

Journey Two

Farmers and Gardeners of the Longhouse

AUTUMN

Farmers and Gardeners of the Longhouse

Fall ❧

Behold! Our Mother Earth is lying here.
Behold! She gives of her fruitfulness.
Truly, she gives her power to us.
Give thanks to Mother Earth who lies here.

Behold on Mother Earth the growing fields!
Behold the promise of her fruitfulness!
Truly, she gives her power to us.
Give thanks to Mother Earth who lies here.

Behold on Mother Earth the spreading trees!
Behold the promise of her fruitfulness!
Truly, she gives her power to us.
Give thanks to Mother Earth who lies here.

We see on Mother Earth the running streams,
We see the promise of her fruitfulness.
Truly, she gives her power to us.
Our thanks to Mother Earth who lies here.

- Pawnee Tribe Thanksgiving Prayer

THE PEOPLE OF THE LONGHOUSE

The People of the Longhouse consisted of a group of six nations that shared a similar language and way of life.

❧ They called themselves the People of the Longhouse because the valley they lived in was shaped like a great longhouse. It stretched a distance of 200 miles, from Lake Erie in the west to the Hudson River in the east. The Seneca, also known as the People of the Great Mountain, were the western doorkeepers. The Mohawk, or the People of the Flint, were the eastern doorkeepers. The Onondaga, or the People of the Hill, lived in the middle of this imaginary longhouse. The Onondaga were the central fire-keepers.

The People of the Longhouse were farmers. Generally they lived in one place, tilling the same land from one year to the next. But they were also hunters and gatherers, and occasionally one nation would cross into another's territory. When this happened, the nations would sometimes make war on each other.

After many years of bloodshed the People of the Longhouse tired of war, so they came together at a council of nations and sought a way to bring peace to the land. This council of nations became known as the Iroquois Confederacy.

The Seneca, the Mohawk, and the Onondaga were three of the original five founding nations that made up the Iroquois Confederacy. The other two were the Cayuga, also known as the People of the Great Pipe, and the Oneida, the People of the Standing Stone. A sixth nation joined the Confederacy after it was formed. This nation was called the Tuscarora, or the People of the Shirt.

The peace established by the Iroquois Confederacy was so successful that it was still in existence when the first European settlers arrived in the New World. The European settlers were impressed by this lasting peace. In fact, the creators of our constitution were inspired by an important principle of the Confederacy: that each person has a voice. From this principle they developed the notion of democracy, which lies at the heart of our own constitution.

❧ **Would you like to know more about the nations of the Iroquois Confederacy?** Listen to this story written by our authors about Little Wolf, a member of the Onondaga nation, also known as the People of the Hill.

"Little Wolf and Night Fire"

The minute Little Wolf woke up that morning he sensed excitement in the village. The other nations have arrived! he thought.

He leapt from his bed and ran from his clan's longhouse to the Council Longhouse, which stood in the middle of the village and was used only for ceremonies. Already a crowd was gathering there.

As Little Wolf drew close, he saw the clan mothers from the various nations exchanging warm greetings. Nearby, young braves whooped and hugged and grinned at each other. Little Wolf could tell which ones were from which nation by the feather headdress they wore. Children and elders made up the rest of the crowd, laughing and whooping like the braves.

Little Wolf eased his way through the crowd and peered into the dusky Council Longhouse. Each of the sachems, or chiefs of the six nations, sat around the Council fire. Like the braves, the chiefs were recognizable by their headdress, but instead of feathers they wore antlers. As Little Wolf stood there, he knew he was witnessing something special, something his grandmother had helped to create.

The Council Longhouse had been built and was owned by all of the Iroquois. The residential longhouses, however, were the property of the women. This meant that the women - particularly the clan mothers - were responsible for making important decisions in their nations.

Little Wolf's grandmother was a clan mother. Recently, she had met with the other clan mothers of her nation to elect the new chief of the Onondaga, whose name was Soaring Hawk. Today, for the first time, Soaring Hawk was sitting with the chiefs of the other five nations. Little Wolf could see the pride in the new chief's face as he listened attentively to what the others around the Council fire said.

Soaring Hawk's responsibilities would be great during the coming week. Usually the Council met at least once a year to ensure that all the nations of the Iroquois Confederacy were in harmony. It was the duty of the six chiefs to find peaceful solutions to quarrels or disagreements. Usually it took time to work out differences. Often the men talked peace until the sun rose. Sometimes they stayed up two nights straight.

In these matters the chiefs represented more than the wishes of the clan mothers. They spoke the hearts of their people. In the days ahead, many hearts would pulse as one heart. A lasting peace would be strengthened around the Council fires.

Little Wolf was fiercely proud of his new chief and his nation. The Council Longhouse had been built here because the Onondaga lived in the very heart of the Iroquois Confederacy.

It was their duty to keep the great fires of peace burning at the Council Longhouse, to act as hosts whenever the six nations met ceremonially. It was a responsibility the Onondaga took very seriously. They felt honored to be the central fire-keepers.

Little Wolf could not hear what the men were saying, but he knew they were simply exchanging greetings - the Council would not begin officially until tomorrow.

After awhile Little Wolf went in search of his cousin, Night Fire. The two cousins had not seen one another since the previous summer because Night Fire's clan dwelt among the Seneca, far away to the west. Little Wolf's fa-

ther had once lived among that clan. But when a man got married, he left his mother's clan and moved into the longhouse owned by his wife's clan, and now Little Wolf's father lived here among the Onondaga.

When the two cousins saw each other they whooped and shouted, both of them speaking at once in their excitement. "Let's go to my grandmother's longhouse," Little Wolf said when he caught his breath. "I've got something to show you." And the two dashed off.

Like other longhouses in the village, Little Wolf's grandmother's dwelling was a rectangular-shaped building made of elm bark. It had a gabled roof and a door at each end. Twenty families lived in the longhouse, which was divided into ten sections, two families sharing each fire pit. Simple handmade furnishings, like a bear skin or a bench, provided comfort for the family as they sat or lay near the hearth. But the hearth was decorated with objects of beauty, too.

Little Wolf saw one of these objects of beauty as he and his cousin ran towards the fire pit where his grandmother cooked. Lying on a special bundle of cloths was a beautiful clay pipe, the finest one his grandmother had ever made. Actually, it was more than an object of beauty. Tomorrow Little Wolf's grandmother would bring the pipe to the Council Longhouse, and when the men smoked it the Council would officially begin.

The boys slowed to a walk. Lying beside the clay pipe was a quiver case. The colors and patterns on the quiver case, the supple leather and natural dyes, seem to speak to Night Fire. He glanced shyly at Little Wolf. Little Wolf nodded, reading his cousin's mind. Reverently, Night Fire picked up the quiver case and tried it on.

It is filled with a grandmother's love, Night Fire thought, running his palm over the smooth leather case. He imagined the arrows it would hold. The arrows that would cut, singing, through the air.

The cousins stared at one another. Each wore a dreamy, longing smile as he thought of his first hunt. Perhaps this year the men would invite them to go hunting and fishing!

"Let's play hoops and darts!" Little Wolf said excitedly.

Night Fire grinned as he took off the quiver case and laid it carefully next to the clay pipe. Last summer they had worked hard at polishing their hunting skills by tossing a dart through a large, rolling hoop. The game required good reflexes, swift feet, and an excellent aim. Night Fire remembered how they had whooped and hollered as they scrambled along. He had wished their time together would never end.

"Let's go!" he said, and the two ran outside.

But as the cousins entered the bright sunlight they came to a sudden halt. At the rim of the orchard, near the apple, peach, and plum trees, the gathering clans had begun to build a temporary village. Already some men and women were raising bark-covered, conical wickiups and dome-like wigwams.

It seemed to Little Wolf that the village was sprouting up very quickly, unlike corn, which took an entire summer to grow.

"It's so plentiful here," Night Fire murmured.

Little Wolf was startled by his cousin's words. But as he looked around he saw his homeland through new eyes. The fertile farmland, the towering evergreens and hardwoods, the extensive orchards - his cousin was right. It was all so wonderful! In particular he admired the Three Sisters gardens, where the women grew corn, beans, and squash. During the coming days the women would supply nearly all the food for the six nations from their bountiful garden harvest.

"Instead of playing hoops and darts, I think we had better help raise the wigwams and wickiups," Night Fire said.

Again Little Wolf realized his cousin was right. Their boyhoods were coming to an end. If they wanted the men to take them fishing and hunting, they had better act like young adults.

"Let's help your clan first," he said to Night Fire, and the two ran towards the orchard.

❧ **This story sheds light on the little-known fact that the Iroquois cultivated large areas of New York State before being removed from their ancestral lands.** Today, few Native people own large tracts of arable land since most reservations consist of poor farmlands. Still, because of their rich heritage and highly developed methods of agriculture, the Iroquois bring in abundant harvests wherever farming is possible.

Much information about the People of the Longhouse comes from archeologists, but there are other ways to learn about the culture and lifeways of these people. There are extensive stories, pictograph recordings (such as cave drawings), birch-bark scrolls, and beautiful wampum belts. These verbal and pictorial treasures document the history of the original longhouse farmers and gardeners.

❧ **Can you find out what life is like today** for the People of the Great Mountain, the People of the Hill, the People of the Flint, the People of the Great Pipe, the People of the Standing Stone, and the People of the Shirt? You might invite a Native American to speak with you about his people's present culture.

One myth commonly held about Native Americans is that all the nations wear similar ceremonial headdresses - like the ones Indian Chiefs wear in movies. Actually, the different nations of the Longhouse recognized each other by their unique headdresses, which consisted of a few feathers arranged in the nation's own particular fashion. But guess what the Iroquois Chief wore as a headdress? Deer antlers! Make your own headdress. Make ones that represent the six nations of the Longhouse.

❧ **Do you know what the Longhouse nations call themselves?** The Longhouse nations refer to themselves as the Haudenosaunee - the "people of the longhouse." But after the Europeans arrived and started a very competitive fur trade, their neighbors referred to them as Iroquois - "real snakes." Even though the times of fur trading and rivalry for trapping grounds are long past, the name Iroquois is the name that has endured.

Want To Do More?

❧ **On a relief map of the United States, locate the area where the Longhouse nations lived.** This area stretched from Lake Erie in the west to the Hudson River in the east. The St. Lawrence River between Canada and the United States formed the northern border. Can you find some of the other rivers and waterways where the People of the Longhouse may have fished? What type of foods came from these waterways? Which forests provided game foods?

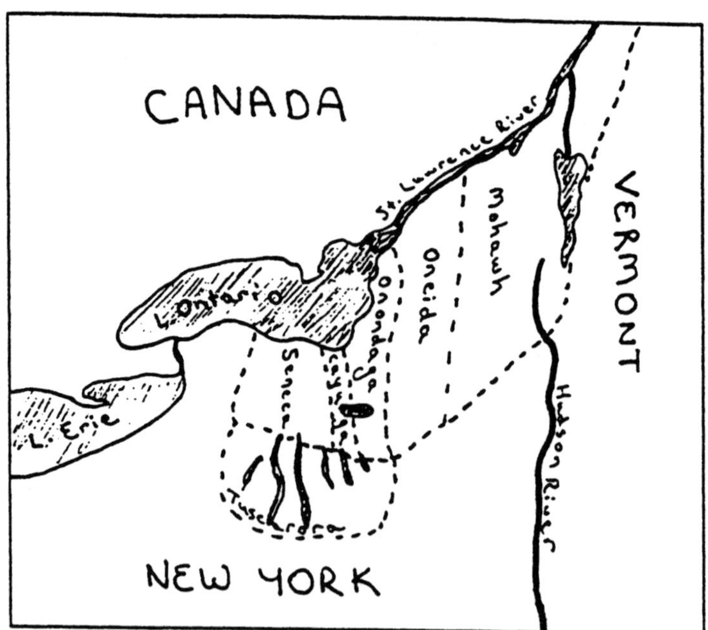

Draw a map of the Longhouse nations that includes these landmarks.

❧ **Create a Council or Peace Corner**, a place for sitting with friends or family members to talk and work out conflicts or differences of opinion. The Council or Peace Corner might have a rug, pillows, a round "council table," a candle, a talking rock, and photographs or drawings of people working in harmony.

Establish some guidelines for creating peace around the council table. Examples might include making eye contact when someone speaks, speaking only in the first person ("I" statements), taking a deep breath and observing a moment of silence before responding to the other person. Consider what the other person said, then rephrase what you think you heard her say to you. Offer suggestions for resolving the conflict. Agree on a recommendation to resolve the conflict. Invite a third party to act as a mediator if any of the guidelines are repeatedly broken.

Even More Curious?

❧ If you happen to be in the Adirondack Mountains southwest of Plattsburgh, **be sure to visit the Six Nations Museum in Onchiota, New York,** which is maintained by the Fadden family. Iroquois traditions are still practiced in this cabin museum. They are brought to life by the Faddens, father and son, who relate the wampum belt stories. The museum is open Memorial Day through Labor Day.

THREE SISTERS IN THE LONGHOUSE GARDEN

This guided journey will take you back to the days of Summer, when the Three Sisters were growing in the garden. Sit beside the garden as you experience this guided journey, and make observations as you listen.

It is a hot summer day. Many moons have passed since the garden was planted last Spring. Today the results of that hard work is apparent for all to see.

Take a moment to meet Sister Corn, Sister Bean, and Sister Squash. Notice how they work together.

Sister Corn is the one growing straight and tall, reaching her crown toward the sky. See how proudly she stands upon the Earth Mother! Look at her leaves bending down toward the earth. What could she be reaching for? Look at her tassel crown. Earlier in the Summer, the pollen from her crown was carried by the winds down to her silk, and in this way seeds were able to form on her cob. For thousands and thousands of years, Sister Corn has produced generations of seed, which have fed generations of people!

Look for Sister Bean as she winds her way up and around her Sister, the corn. Who is holding up whom? Notice the direction the beans wrap themselves. Are they all going in the same direction? One thing you cannot see is the food fixed by Sister Bean's roots. As she blossoms, she draws nourishment from the air and generously shares it through her roots with Sister Corn, who stands close by.

Sister Squash (Pumpkin) lies like a carpet upon the earth. Why does she roam and ramble like that? See how she shades and cools the earth for her sisters. What might her prickly leaves protect her sisters from?

❧ **Now you have had a chance to see how the Three Sisters cooperate and care for each other.** The Iroquois name for the Three Sisters means "life support." By this they mean that the Three Sisters are more than simply food for the living. What else did the Three Sisters teach you today as you sat in the garden with them? The Three Sisters remind us to look at each living thing in relation to other living things. How do other living things cooperate with, or support, one another?

❧ **Look for other life-support partners in the garden that cooperate with the Three Sisters, or with each other.** Consider sun, rain, clouds, air, soil, insects and birds. What do each of these partners contribute to the garden? What do you see, smell, hear and feel as you observe life in the garden?

❧ **Can you make a spider's web drawing in your journal?** Pretend that each strand of the spider's web represents one of the partners of the garden. What does each strand of the web contribute to the garden?

Can you write a poem or story about what you think this web means?

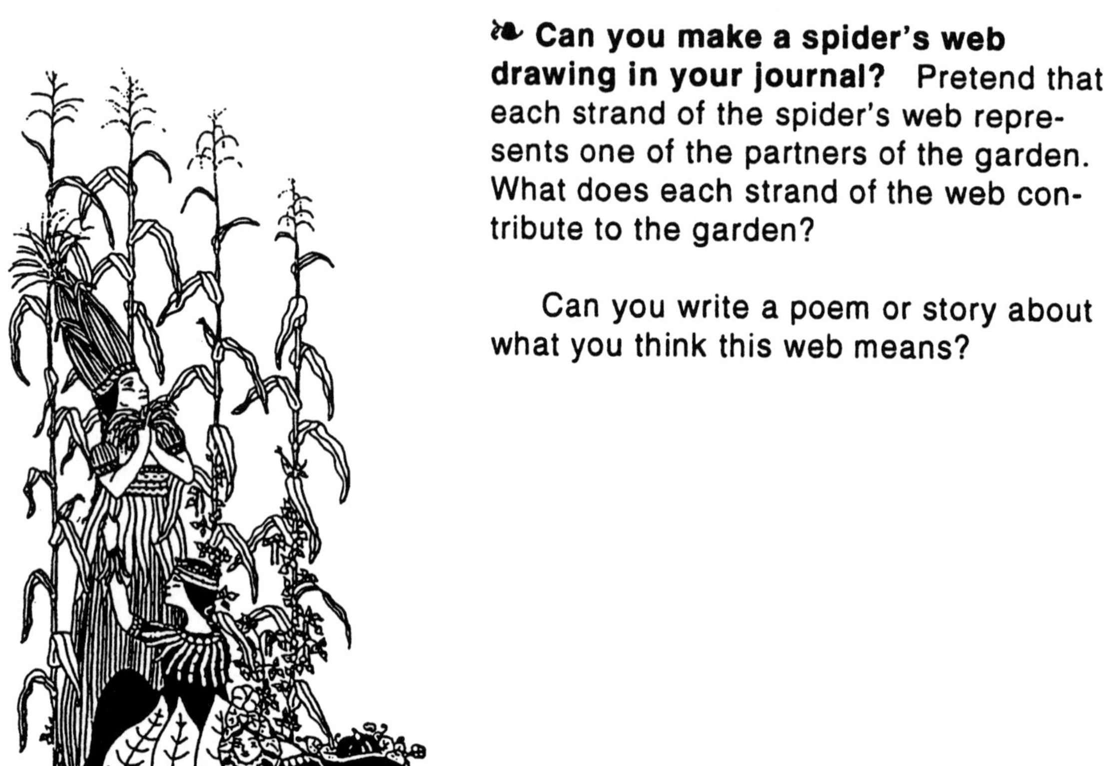

Beginning Your Longhouse Garden of the Three Sisters

So you're beginning your first Longhouse Garden of the Three Sisters - Hurrah! Now you have an opportunity to prepare and feed the earth, giving her all she needs before asking for something from her in return.

❧ If you don't have a garden, however, don't worry! Visit a gardening friend or farmer and watch their fall preparations. You might even offer a helping hand - it will certainly be appreciated! But, if you are about to begin a Longhouse Garden of the Three Sisters, consider the following suggestions:

♠ **Consider a location** where other activities will not interfere with gardening, where the soil is healthy, and where water never collects on the ground after rain or snow- melt. Find a place where your plants will receive a minimum of six hours of sunlight daily.

♠ **Ideas and plans for a Three Sisters garden** are described and illustrated in the Fall chapter of 'Three Sisters, Three Garden Designs' in "First Farmers and Gardeners ," page 52. A more elaborate plan is illustrated in the Spring chapter entitled 'A Suggested Plan for your Three Sisters Longhouse Garden' on page 310 of "Farmers and Gardeners of the Longhouse."

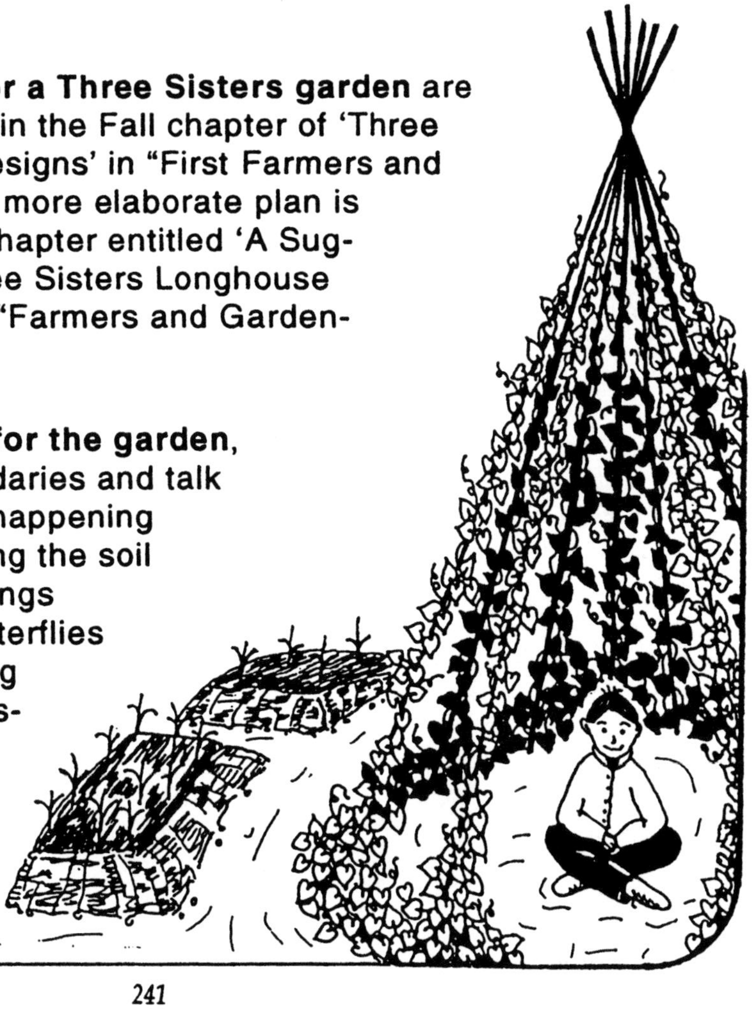

♠ **Mark off the area for the garden,** then sit around the boundaries and talk about what you imagine happening there. . . earthworms tilling the soil from below, young seedlings growing in your care, butterflies and honeybees pollinating vegetable and flower blossoms, delicious foods to be eaten and shared. Give thanks to the Earth for the rich soils that will sustain your garden. What could you give the Earth in return for gardening here?

♠ **Invite a neighboring farmer, gardener, or parent** to plow, dig, or rototill the soil.

♠ **Create a compost area**, which may be a simple mound in the corner of the garden. Put compost plants in a heap, adding a few shovelfuls of dirt between the layers. Or place plant material in a compost trench dug in a convenient location in the garden. Cover the pile with soil and bury it. Don't forget to check next Spring to see what happened!

♠ **Remove grass and other plant roots from the garden.** Shake soil from the roots and return the soil to the garden. Compost grasses and other plant matter.

♠ **Remove rocks,** but save them for outlining garden borders or planting areas.

♠ **Designate the growing areas and garden paths** with stakes and string. By knowing where to walk in your garden, you can avoid compacting the freshly turned soil. This will also help you to identify areas that need soil amendments. You can conserve resources If you add amendments only to the growing areas, and avoid putting them in the walking paths.

♠ **Fertilize the garden area** with aged manure, leaves, compost, and/or organic fertilizer. Test the pH levels of the soil to determine whether the soil is sweet or acidic. Make the recommended pH adjustments, adding lime or wood ash to the growing areas only. Till or turn under the soil amendments with a pitchfork.

♠ **Tuck a few spring bulbs into areas of your garden** where you expect to grow flowers.

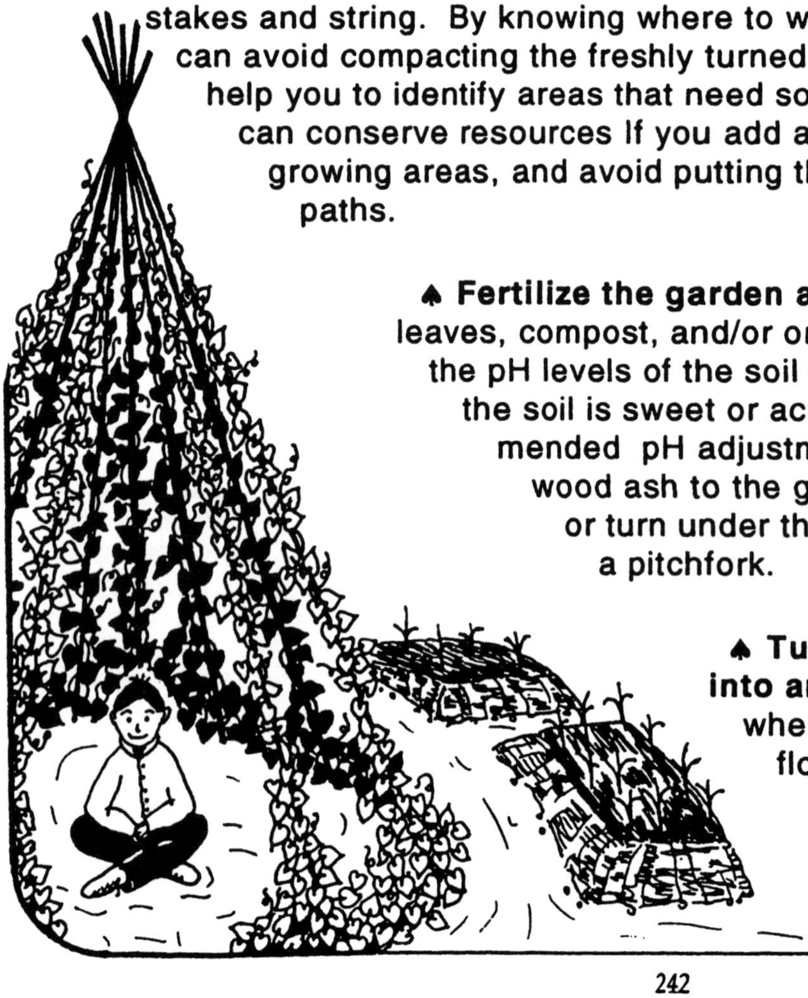

♠ Finally, **plant a cover crop** of annual rye grass, buckwheat, or clover. Which one is most suitable for your gardening plans? Which are best suited for growing before first frost? Any garden center can help you with these questions. Cover crops prevent weed seeds from taking root in your freshly plowed garden. They also prevent loose soils from blowing or washing away. And, when they are tilled into the garden in the early Spring, they nourish the earth with nutrients. Why do you think these plantings are called "cover crops"?

❧ **While the garden rests during Winter, dream about the seeds you planted.** Envision the awakening of life forces in the garden next Spring. Think about the cycle of giving (during Spring) and receiving (at harvest time).

You have been caring and generous during the preparation of your Longhouse Garden - you are in good relationship with the Earth! How does it feel to give to the Earth before receiving from her?

After the Harvest: Putting Your Longhouse Garden to Rest

If your garden was planted last Spring, an abundant harvest may await you this Fall. After the harvest has been brought in, it is time to consider how to put the garden to rest.

❧ The time for putting a garden to rest depends upon the completion of the growing cycle of its plants. Will it be September, October, or November where you live? In what ways can you give back to the Earth in return for the bounty she provides?

♠ **Turn the garden wherever corn was planted.** Although these heavy feeders draw up lots of soil nutrients, you can replace the depleted nutrients by **planting a winter cover crop.** Cover crops are plantings which will nourish the garden with nutrients when they are turned into the earth the following Spring. Before frost, sow winter rye by gently broadcasting the seed across the turned area. Lightly tamp down the seed, then be sure to keep it moist until it germinates. Rye will grow a little before the snow begins to fall, and can be turned under next Spring. It will add rich organic matter to your garden soil.

♠ **Check your soil pH** with a simple pH test kit, which can be purchased at a garden center. Lime or wood ash will sweeten acidic soils. In the Fall, add the recommended amount of lime, if needed, or apply wood ash at half the recommended rate for lime supplements.

♠ To create some spring color, **tuck a few crocus or small spring bulbs along the edges of your garden.** You can plant them in the Fall, right up until the moment the ground freezes, as late as November in New England.

EARTH RHYTHM CALENDARS

By observing and recording seasonal rhythms, you can plan garden tasks according to the natural patterns and cycles of the land. An Earth Rhythms Calendar will enable you to record your observations and document the rhythms of the Earth through each changing season. The calendar may become a useful reference for gardening and harvesting activities.

❧ Before making an Earth Rhythms Calendar, **observe the moon** for a period of at least one month, and record its phases during that time. What do you notice about lunar rhythms? How long is a lunar cycle? Is our current calendar based upon lunar rhythms or another rhythm?

❧ **What natural activities do you notice** as you observe the Earth throughout Autumn? Are leaves changing color, geese calling, cool winds blowing, pumpkins ripening, chipmunks and squirrels scurrying for nuts? Divide each month into a weekly calendar. Record and illustrate the natural events that are taking place. Include Winter and Spring months in your calendar. You might notice that certain garden tasks are performed when certain natural phenomena occur. You might also notice a seasonal and yearly rhythm in which Mother Earth and the garden are in harmony.

❧ On the following page, you will see an **Earth Rhythms Calendar**, adapted from *The Curious Naturalist* by John Mitchell. The events represented on the calendar occur in an area of New England. Perhaps these events happen at a different time - earlier or later - where you live. Or perhaps the events where you live are different altogether! How does your Earth Rhythms Calendar compare to this calendar?

New England Calendar of Earth Rhythms

September:

Week 1 Bird migrations begin (especially Swallows and Warblers)

Week 2 Apples ripen • Green darners migrate • Goldenrod blooms

Week 3 Hitchhiker seeds • Monarchs and Broadwing Hawks migrate • Autumnal Equinox

Week 4 Mushrooms appear after rain • Blackbirds flock

October:

Week 1 Fall fruits ripen • Sharp-shinned Hawks migrate

Week 2 Foliage changes • Juncos arrive

Week 3 Nuts ripen • Milkweed pods open • Robins and Sparrows migrate

Week 4 Chipmunks go underground • Grosbeaks arrive • Airborne seeds disperse

November:

Week 1 Canada Geese migrate • Raccoons and other mammals active • Tamarack turns gold

Week 2 Red-tail Hawks and Ducks migrate • Witch Hazel blooms

Week 3 Wasps leave nests for nooks • Deer herds gather

Week 4 Leaves disappear from trees • Pine Grosbeaks flock

December:

Week 1 Redpolls arrive • Starlings and Crows flock

Week 2 Mammals hibernate • Ruffed Grouse is active

Week 3 Winter Solstice • Winter constellations • Partridge berries ripen

Week 4 Orion appears • Animal tracks in snow • New birds at feeders

January:

Week 1 Mice feed on grass and bark

Week 2 Adult Stoneflies emerge

Week 3 Hunger Moon • mating season for Raccoons and Minks • January thaw

Week 4 Honeybee flights

February:

Week 1 Ground Hog Day • Foxes yelp • Redpoll flocks arrive
Week 2 Great Horned Owls nest • Skunks mate
Week 3 Barred Owls call
Week 4 Foxes mate • Redwing Blackbirds arrive • Sap rises

March:

Week 1 Geese and Ducks fly north • Pussy Willows appear
Week 2 Blackbirds and Song Sparrows return
Week 3 Spring Equinox • Hardy flowers bloom
Week 4 Skunk Cabbage and Wild Leeks appear • Robins and Sparrows arrive

April:

Week 1 Wood Frogs call • Morning Cloak butterflies emerge • April showers
Week 2 Spring Peepers call • Tree Swallows return • Forsythia blooms
Week 3 Spring Azure butterflies emerge • Toads call • Ferns unfold
Week 4 Quaker Ladies bloom • Catbirds and Barn Swallows re turn

May:

Week 1 Violets bloom • Birds nest • Shadbush blossoms
Week 2 Dandelions appear • Insects chirp • Tadpoles hatch
Week 3 Lilacs bloom
Week 4 Apple trees bloom • Buttercups unfurl

June:

Week 1 Bullfrogs chorus • Young mammals leave nest • Blue Flag Iris bloom
Week 2 Young birds leave nest • Daisies and Hawkweed bloom • Bats appear
Week 3 Summer Solstice • Swallowtail butterflies flutter • Meadow crickets chirrup
Week 4 Mosquitoes • foxglove

❧ *Round out this seasonal nature calendar by adding your own observations of Summer's events.*

Want To Do More?

❧ **What seasonal signs tell you it is harvest time?** How do you know when different garden foods are ready to be harvested? Supplement your Earth Rhythms Calendar with interviews from the older people in your neighborhood or with information obtained from the Farmer's Almanac. Even old wives tales are a good source. You can also talk to local gardeners, or consult gardening calendars for useful information.

THE GREAT BEAR AND THE GREAT GIVE AWAY

Many Native people consult the natural rhythms of the night sky to determine the proper times for planting and harvesting. What can the night sky tell you about your schedule of autumn gardening activities?

❧ The season of the Great Give Away is a time when all share the bounty of the harvest. This season occurs shortly before the "Great Bear" - also known as the Big Dipper - comes down from the sky. How can a Great Bear come down from the sky? Perhaps the following story will give you some clues.

Among the Woodland peoples, there many stories about a Great Bear that once roamed the earth. This version of Great Bear was created by our own authors, but is based on the traditional stories of old.

"The Hunt of the Great Bear"

The Great Bear caused much alarm in the villages. It had an enormous appetite. The more it ate, the bigger it got - and it would eat anything! The Great Bear grew so large as it wandered through the villages in search of food that its enormous body shook the forest like thunder. With a swipe of its great paw, the beast felled huge trees in its path.

The Woodland peoples grew increasingly alarmed. They had no idea what to do, or how to rid themselves of the enormous beast. Then, for three nights in a row, three warriors had the same dream. Whenever someone has a dream for three nights in a row the Woodland people pay attention. But when three people have the same dream for three nights in a row, the people really pay attention!

In the dream, the warriors chased the Great Bear far from the villages, which enabled the people to return to a normal life. Inspired by this dream, the warriors decided to go in search of the Great Bear.

It is said that they chased the Great Bear long and hard across the countryside, through miles and miles of meadow and forest, showering the air with their arrows, sometimes hitting their target but never seeming to fell him. And it is said that where the arrows struck, the Great Bear shed drops of blood onto the trees, making the leaves of all the trees in the Northeastern forests glow red that Autumn. Eventually, after a long, difficult hunt, the Great Bear ran to the high peaks, seemingly to the top of the world. And here, with the warriors close on his trail, he leapt into the skies, never to set paw upon the Earth again.

❧ **When you look into the skies, can you see the Great Bear?** Can you see the four stars that make up its outline, shaping its body in the form of a square? Do you see the three stars behind it?· Some say those three stars are the three warriors - to this day they're still chasing that bear!

When the Great Bear nears the horizon, you will know that a new season has arrived. It is time to prepare for the harvest, when all share the bounty of the Great Give Away!

❧ **Just before bedtime, can you see the Great Bear in the western sky during the autumn weeks leading up to Thanksgiving?** If you watch the Great Bear each week, you will discover some of the mysteries of the night sky. During Autumn, the Great Bear is said to be preparing for hibernation. It is feasting in order to fatten up sufficiently for the Winter! Can you see the Great Bear moving closer to the horizon as it gathers the last morsels? It is said that after the Great Bear has found sufficient food, it will descend below the horizon to rest in a cave where it will hibernate, not to be seen again until Spring. But if you live in the North like the Woodland peoples, you can see the Great Bear sleeping in his cave all through the Winter!

❧ **Make a Great Bear constellation and place it on a western wall.** Now locate the Great Bear in the evening sky. During the next month, as the Great Bear searches for a place to hibernate, follow its progress towards the horizon by moving your constellation along the wall. Do you know why the stars appear to move in the skies?

❧ **The Great Bear is a good direction locator.** It can help you find North. Draw an imaginary line from the Great Bear's front foot to its head. Then continue the line straight up into the sky. Eventually you will come to a star that makes up the end of the Little Dipper's handle. This star is called Polaris, or the North Star.

❧ **Can you make a Great Bear constellation to put in your nature journal?** It can be a simple design, made from rice and dark paper. Show how to find North. Mark the locations of North, East, South and West on the borders of your page.

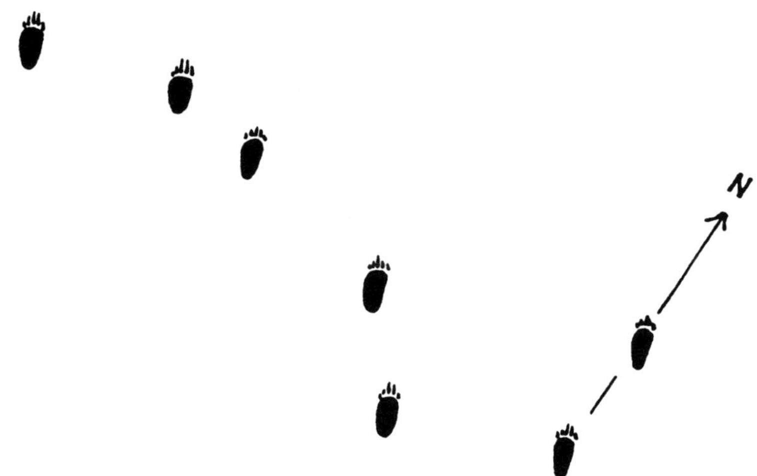

Want To Do More?

❧ The night sky has been a source of information for peoples and nations throughout history. Today, many people still count days and track the calendar year by observing the night sky. Evening travelers use it as a direction guide. It stirs the imagination of storytellers during long winter nights, and is a source of inspiration about the world beyond.

During the season of the Great Give Away, organize your friends and neighbors for an Autumn Skywatch. Ask them to bring something to give away from their harvest. As you stare up at the sky that evening, retell the story of the Great Bear.

A HARVEST BEE

Traditionally, Native Americans organized a harvest bee during the time of the Great Give Away. While the women husked the ears of corn, the men passed the time by telling stories. Harvest bees still take place around a fire and beneath the moon, often lasting through the night.

❧ Would you like to plan a Harvest Bee?

- Who will you invite from your community to attend the Harvest Bee?
- Decide how you will share the husking and storytelling tasks.
- Where will you recycle garden compost materials left over from the Harvest Bee?
- How and where will you store the harvest?

❧ At traditional harvest bees, a search is made for the perfect ear of corn, which has straight rows of uniform-sized kernels and four kernels at the tip. This perfect ear of corn is named the Corn Mother. The Corn Mother is carefully wrapped in a special seed bundle and saved for next year's garden.

❧ **Oddly shaped or unusually colored ears of corn are often an inspiration for creating a story.** What story could you tell or write about the oddest ear of corn found at harvest time?

Want To Do More?

❧ A Harvest Mural

A harvest mural is fun if you can get a few friends together. What scenes might best depict the harvest activities in your community during Autumn?

- Is the ripening corn being consumed by both raccoons and humans?
- Is the local apple orchard brimming with activity? What kinds of activity?
- Are there pumpkin fields nearby? How is the pumpkin harvest brought in?
- Does anything happen beneath the Harvest Moon?
- What kinds of food might be harvested for animal feed? What machines perform this work?
- What are chipmunks doing during the harvest?
- What kinds of food are people preserving for the Winter?
- What happens to wood piles in Autumn?
- Who or what are leaf peepers, and what are they doing?
- What kinds of activities revolve around fallen leaves?
- Do special harvest decorations appear on houses or in yards?
- How do people in your community help each other with harvest chores?
- What does the local food shelf look like this time of year?

❧ Many Native peoples believe that the Great Spirit provides for all. In the tradition of Native hospitality, excess corn is shared, traded, and even given to those whose harvests are less abundant. In this way all are cared for, and the cycle of the Great Give Away remains unbroken. **Celebrate this Native American practice by sharing your harvest with your community.**

Harvest Math, Nature's Way

❧ Harvest corn provides many wonderful opportunities for Math, Nature's Way.

- Can you estimate the number of seeds per ear of corn? One way to do this is to count the number of seeds in one of the rows, then multiply that number by the number of rows.

- Count the number of seeds in sets of 2's, 4's, 5's, 10's - or whatever number you'd like. To find the total number of seeds, add the sets. Or, multiply the sets by the number of seeds in the set.

- How many plants did you sow? How many ears did you harvest? What was the average yield of ears per plant?

- Weigh the corn before and after drying it. What difference did you find?

- How much corn seed did you sow when you planted the garden? What harvest weight resulted from that sowing?

- What was the average yield in weight per plant?

- How many cups of corn seed did you harvest? Can you convert that measurement to pints and quarts?

- Substitute bean seeds for corn seeds, then repeat the above questions.

- Estimate the weight of pumpkins, then weigh them. How close was your estimate to the actual weight?

- Can you estimate the number of pumpkin seeds per plant?

    - How much pumpkin seed did you sow? How much pumpkin seed did you harvest?

    - How many pumpkin seeds do you need to sow to have enough pumpkins for one person?

Days of the Longhouse Harvest

Long ago, a people dwelled in the longhouse villages of the Mohawk Valley. They excelled as farmers. Their beautiful orchards covered the face of the land. Their corn, bean, and squash fields ran to the horizon. These people were called the Seneca.

❧ When the Europeans arrived in this country, they marveled at the Seneca's farming abilities, for the Seneca often brought in harvests four times more abundant than non-Native farmers. Periods of starvation rarely existed among the People of the Longhouse because the harvest was shared by all the people of the community.

❧ Listen to this story about Night Fire, a young Onondaga boy who was a neighbor of the Seneca. The story takes place at a time of the year when the spirits of the Three Sisters call the people to participate in the harvest festivities. Although this is not a traditional story, a very special day is brought to life in this story created by our authors.

"Night Fire and the Day of the Great Give-Away"

Nighttime closed over the village like a blanket as Night Fire walked beneath the moonlit, starry sky. He wondered when the harvest ceremonies would begin. In less than a week, he thought, gazing up at the Great Bear. Every evening the three warriors chased the Great Bear farther down the horizon.

As he strolled past the garden, the corn rustled in the breeze. He could almost hear it sing in a whispery voice to a cloud that passed fleetingly across the face of the harvest moon: "We are ripe and ready for the Great Give Away." Night Fire took a deep breath of the fresh evening

air. The night sky sparkled, matching the spark in his heart. He could hardly wait for the harvest festivities to begin!

Finally the day arrived. At dawn the people gathered in the garden to burn a sacred herbal offering. All of them spoke words of thankfulness for the abundant harvest, their words rising up on the smoke to be carried away on the wind. When the offering was finished, the women and girls began harvesting the corn, tossing the ears into baskets strapped upon their backs. As they worked, the baskets weighed on them like playful children, swaying to the rhythms and sounds of the harvest. Before long their baskets were filled to overflowing.

Night Fire stood nearby among some men, awaiting his turn to carry a full basket to the longhouse. The men and boys had had little to do with caring for the gardens while the Three Sisters grew in earthen mounds. Their roles came at either end of the growing season. In the Spring they had made a home for the Three Sisters by clearing a field, then burning the felled trees. Ash left over from the charred trees had been tilled into the soil to sweeten it. Now, at harvest time, they helped the women by carrying baskets and providing entertainment.

That evening the harvest husking bee took place beneath the moon. There was much laughter and singing as the corn was shucked and a feast prepared. Some women braided together ears of corn for drying, while others tended to kettles of soup made from fresh corn. Still others roasted ears of corn over the fire pit. Children gathered the husks that lay upon the ground and fashioned dolls and corncob darts from them.

As the evening progressed, storytellers gathered around the fire pits to tell tales, their voices rising wistfully on the smoke. The storytellers painted pictures, images of the time before the Three Sisters became the Onondaga's "life sustainers." In the olden days the Onondaga had been hunters and gatherers. They had traveled twice a year in search of food, moving from their summer camp to their winter camp. Instead of longhouses, they had lived in

wigwams. These shelters were simple to put up and take down, which made it easy for the people to move from one location to another.

Night Fire sat quietly among the storytellers. He had heard these stories many times, but his people's history never ceased to fascinate him. One legend said that game had become scarce because the Onondaga had "fallen out of right relationship" with the rituals of hunting. Another legend said that the people had become farmers because they wanted to reside in permanent villages. Night Fire thought both legends might be true. Today the men still hunted. Yet the Onondaga were grateful for the Three Sisters gardens, which provided most of their food.

Night Fire was grateful for these easier times, too. He loved the harvest ceremonies - there was so much laughter and happiness! Still, he wished he were old enough to hunt with the men. Maybe next year, he thought dreamily. Then the story of his first successful hunt would be told around the harvest fire!

❧ **How has life changed for the People of the Longhouse?** In ancient times, Native peoples depended on wild foods and lived in rustic housing, such as wigwams or wickiups, which were moved from one seasonal camp to another. Later, when the People of the Longhouse became farmers as well as hunters and gatherers, they lived in semipermanent villages consisting of bark-covered longhouses. Later still, these accomplished farmers constructed permanent dwellings, such as log cabins.

Sadly, the Europeans who settled in the Mohawk Valley forced the People of the Longhouse off their ancestral lands. Today many Native peoples reside on reservations, or live in local neighborhoods like your own. And just as your own great-grandparents, grandparents, mothers, and fathers have changed over the generations so, too, have the People of the Longhouse changed.

Yet the People of the Longhouse still carry on the Three Sisters traditions. Though their life today may appear to be very different from what it was long ago, their traditions live on and are passed from one generation to the next.

❧ Does your family have any family heirlooms or traditions from long ago that are still meaningful today?

❧ Braid together three ears of Indian corn. Hang them up to remind yourself of the abundant harvest season and the gift of corn. Write a poem about the harvest season and this gift.

✍ Draw a picture of a harvest bee that took place long ago. Now draw a picture of one that takes place today.

SEEDS: SOURCE OF LIFE, FORCE OF LIFE

Many ancient practices revolve around saving seeds. You may come to appreciate the importance of this practice as you learn about the long history of seed-saving in this country.

❧ **Seed-saving is a practice whereby elders pass down seeds to their grandchildren and great-grandchildren for planting.** Though some say the practice began out of necessity, it was, and still is, done with great love and care. Today many parents and grandparents share or pass down these gifts of life to their children and grandchildren.

♥ Can you name some seeds that have been passed down?

❧ **Among Native Americans, Seed Carriers are chosen to perform an honorary role for their people.** They are responsible for planting seeds in the earth, as well as in the hearts of their people. In this way they provide the nourishment that sustains their nation, both physically and spiritually. Seed Carriers also prepare and care for ceremonial seed bundles. Since there are several Seed Carriers in a nation, they rotate responsibilities for monthly verifications of seed health, checking for mold, moisture or dehydration.

Traditionally, Seed Carriers were people honored for their capacity to plant seeds of "right relationship" and seeds of "good cause" among their people.

♥ Are there ways you can help sustain the people of your community from year to year through gardening?

♥ Can you become a Seed Carrier, maintaining the health of your harvest seeds from Fall to Spring, and planting seeds of right relationship in the hearts of your people?

As a Seed Carrier, try planting seeds of good cause among your fellow gardeners.

Drying Seeds Harvested from Your Garden

The Three Sisters and their friends have provided a fine harvest, and now it's time to think about saving seeds to begin next year's garden cycle. Begin a seed bank for your family, school, or neighborhood. Can you design interesting seed packets to contain your seeds?

❧ You can become self-reliant by saving your seeds this Fall. The seeds you sow next spring will be your very own second-generation seed! Any surplus seeds can be shared, exchanged, or sold as a fundraiser for future gardening programs.

♠ **To dry corn and popcorn seeds**, remove the silk from the ears. Then pull back the husks to allow the air to dry the corn seeds thoroughly. Hang the corn in braids. Drying takes approximately one month. Both popcorn and meal corn are dried in this fashion.

When you are ready to use the dried ears, remove the kernels with a flick of your thumb. Save some seeds to be used for planting next year's crop. The rest can be put aside for popping or grinding, ready to be eaten as snacks or for meals - whenever the spirit moves you! The husks are valuable, too. They can be pressed flat, then dried for use in future craft projects.

♠ **To dry bean seeds**, allow them to remain on the plant in their pods until just before frost. This way the seeds will grow to their full, mature size. Periodically, you will need to open some of the pods to see whether the beans are dry. It is hard to resist looking into these "treasure boxes," but be sure not to open too many pods or you will not have enough seeds for next year's planting. When at last the frost arrives, harvest the mature, brittle pods from the bean [illegible]. If any signs of moisture remain, allow the seeds to air-dry for a few days.

Shell the bean pods one by one. Or try the following quick, traditional method, which allows you to shell many beans at once. Place brittle, dry bean pods in an old grain sack. Gently thrash the sack on the ground. Next, put the beans in a basket, then gently toss them. The sifting action will separate the pods from the seeds. Place different varieties of seeds in separate piles, then put them in baskets or in recycled glass jars - be sure the baskets or jars have lids! Label the containers. Store them out of direct sun or heat. That way they will be ready for use when you make soups, stews, or baked beans.

♠ **To dry squash seeds**, cut open the squashes prior to cooking them. Scoop out the seeds. Rinse all the squash pulp from the seeds. When the seeds are clean, lay them out on cookie sheets, paper towels, or cloth towels. Allow them to air-dry for several days out of direct sunlight. Turn the seeds occasionally to insure that they dry completely.

❧ **Prepare well-labeled, appropriate storage containers** so that the seeds remain moisture-free and are protected from sunlight, heat, and extreme cold. Traditionally, cloth bundles or baskets - even gourd containers - were used to store seeds. Design your own storage containers from materials at hand. Be sure to write the name of the seed variety and harvest date on the containers.

❧ **You might enjoy designing, illustrating, and naming seed packets to contain your seeds.** Here is some important information you might want to include on the package:

Seed Packets

- name of seed variety
- days to maturity
- heirloom year (the year of the original parent plants)
- number of seeds per packet
- the year the seeds are packaged
- planting tips
- any Three Sisters gardening wisdom you care to pass along

Preserving and Eating the Seeds of your Harvest

Did you ever stop to think about all the varieties of seeds you eat? If you enjoy eating seeds, it is easy to preserve your own seed harvest.

❧ Here are some ways to preserve edible seeds from your harvest:

♠ **Popcorn** is a delicious treat that has been enjoyed for centuries. You probably know that each popcorn kernel contains just enough moisture to cause it to burst when it is heated. Storing the kernels in glass jars will help prevent this moisture from escaping. (If the glass jar is large enough, you can leave the kernels in place and store the entire cob!) If you have ever tasted homegrown popcorn, you will find that the process is well worth the little effort involved!

When you need to grind some corn for cooking, simply flick some kernels from the dried cobs with your thumb. In a wooden bowl, grind the kernels with a stone. Or, grind them by hand with an old-fashioned vegetable grinding mill. If you have never eaten cornbread made from freshly ground cornmeal, don't miss the chance for a great taste treat! How much corn does it take to make one cup of ground corn meal?

♠ **Dried beans** from the garden - such as scarlet runner beans, pinto beans, white soup beans, or anasazi beans - make a great side dish. They can also be added to winter soups. Plan a bean snack or meal, like tacos. Allow plenty of time for the beans to soak before cooking. Some beans have to be soaked overnight! How much do the beans expand after soaking and cooking?

♠ **Sunflowers** are composite flowers. This means that within each large sunflower head there are several hundred tiny flowers. Look closely at these formations. Below them are chambers called ovules, which cannot be seen. As the tiny flowers mature, pollen drops from them into the chambers. Slowly, seeds grow in these chambers. When the sunflower heads are nearly mature, stripes begin to form on the seed husks and the dried blossoms fall off. As harvest time draws near, the large, dry sunflower heads will begin to droop. When the heads are sufficiently dry, remove the seeds. Be sure to do this before the seeds fall out onto the ground! You can eat the hulled seeds raw, or roast them on a cookie tray in a moderate oven for ten minutes or less. Don't forget to share some sunflower seeds - or the entire head - with your wild friends!

❧ **If you enjoy eating seeds from your garden, research other edible seeds.** In a journal, keep track of all the seed foods you eat during the next week or month.

WILD EARTH GARDEN FOODS

Learning to forage entails more than merely practical skills. Not only will foraging put you in touch with the rhythms and adventures of wild food-gathering, but it will enable you to experience the rich history of the foodways practiced by local Native Americans. Start your own seasonal wild food charts. They will remind you when to harvest wild edibles each season.

❧ The first peoples were hunters and gatherers who obtained their foods from the wild "Earth Gardens" of this land. Since they were so closely connected to the Earth's rhythms, the Native peoples learned from the Earth the many ways they could care for themselves. They had no textbooks or scientific learning. How did the earliest Native Americans learn which gifts of the Earth were safe to eat? They had a highly developed sense of watching and listening to the ways of the Earth.

❧ **Have you ever eaten wild foods from the Earth's Garden?** What kinds? What do you need to know before eating from the Earth's Garden? An experienced forager is an important friend when you search for edibles! Peterson's "Guide to Wild Edibles" is a valuable resource to take on a field trip. But be sure to bring along an experienced guide who can provide helpful identification tips.

❧ **Speculate about all the possible ways you can determine which wild foods are good to eat.** Explore plant specimens in the field as you consider characteristics such as:

- How does the plant smell?
- Are its leaves waxy or smooth? Do waxy leaf textures seem edible? What shape are the leaves?
- Does the plant's shape or any of its other characteristics resemble food found in your garden or at the market?
- Does the color red seem to flash a warning sign

that means “Danger”? Do any warnings, like “Leaflets three, let it be,” seem to apply to this plant?

❧ **How might you harvest wild foods from the Earth's Garden?** Bring along a digging stick for roots and tubers. Make a small basket or pouch for gathering leaves, stems and blossoms. Before picking, look around to be sure there is an abundant supply . This way you will insure that future generations of plant life will provide harvests for human and animal communities. Take only the part of the plant that you need, such as a berry or a leaf. Be careful not to damage the stem of the plant when picking its leaves or berries. It feels good to know you are leaving plants that will replenish the species. The Native people give thanks when receiving the gifts of the Earth. You might want to give thanks in your own way.

SEASONAL EARTH GARDEN FORAGING HIKES

In the Fall, look for familiar berries, like raspberries and blackberries. Look, too, for wild apples and nuts. Raspberries grow in sunny spots, on high prickly stems. Their thorns will remind you not to be too greedy when you harvest. Be sure to leave some fruits and nuts for your two- and four-legged friends!

❧ You can harvest wild foods in the Winter - a time of year when you least expect to find food growing! **Wintergreen is abundant during Winter.** These somewhat leathery, oval, deep-green leaves trail along the earth as a groundcover. Sometimes the little, red, edible Wintergreen berry calls to the hiker from beneath the snow. For that familiar Wintergreen flavor, chew one leaf as a breath freshener. When finished, spit out the leaf which will rapidly decompose. Oh! Don't forget to say thanks! If you would like a delicious tea to warm you after your Earth Foods Hike, pick a few more Wintergreen leaves and some berries and brew them at home.

♠ Look for **blueberries in the Summer**. They have tiny leaves and grow in clusters on low and high bushes beneath the forest canopy or along its edge. Some plants produce berries that are blue but which are poisonous. Be sure an experienced guide explains the difference to you. Gather edible fruits and add them to muffins, breads, pies, or pancakes. Or, serve raw fruits and nuts in a bowl topped with freshly whipped cream - that is, if you have any berries left by the time you get home!

♠ **Spring dandelion greens** make great additions to salads. On almost any lawn, look among the low whorl of greens hugging the earth for leaves that have lion-shaped teeth. Wash the young tender greens, then toss them with dressing. Fiddlehead ferns are a delicious treat if you can find them!

Want To Do More?

❧ **Observe wild edible plants throughout the year** so that you can learn to identify them as they go through their plant cycles during Spring, Summer, Fall, and Winter. Make a Wild Earth Foods Journal. In it, record plant growth and plant cycles. One way to do this is to divide a page into four sections, each section representing a season. Illustrate a plant's growth habits during each of the four seasons.

❧ **Serve wild edibles as a snack or as an accompaniment to a salad.** Consult a reliable reference to determine which parts of a plant are healthy, and which are toxic or poisonous. Also, be sure to learn the proper, safe way to prepare wild foods. Many wild foods may be harsh on your system because domesticated stomachs are not used to them. So be sure to eat these wild foods in moderation until you develop a tolerance for them.

❧ **What other creatures survive on wild edibles of the Earth Garden?** Make a list or drawing of these creatures and the plants they eat.

❧ **The following Earth Garden Foods list can serve as a helpful guide to year-round edibles of the Northeast.** Make your own seasonal Earth Garden Foods chart of foods you can forage where you live. Be sure to make a note of any wild foods you discover.

Seasonal Earth Garden Foods

Autumn:

- Apples
- Plums
- Cherries
- Grapes
- Mushrooms (Warning: We do not recommend foraging for edible mushrooms with children.)
- Nuts: Acorn, Butternut, Black Walnut, Beechnut, Hickory

Winter:

- Rosehips
- Wintergreen

Spring:

- Maple Syrup
- Wild Onions
- Marsh Marigold (Cowslips) leaves
- Fiddleheads (Ostrich Fern)
- Dandelion Leaves
- Wood Sorrel leaves

Summer:

- Jerusalem Artichoke tubers
- Strawberries
- Raspberries
- Blackberries
- Blueberries

Even More Curious?

❧ **Would you like to know more about a particular plant?** You can learn a lot just by looking at it! Choose a plant and enter it in your nature journal, complete with illustrations and observations about its smell, texture, color, and shape. Is the plant edible or inedible?

❧ **Whenever you discover a new wild edible, draw a picture of it or make a rubbing of the plant.** Make notes about the plant, its habitat, the date you discovered it, and its location. This documentation will prove helpful as you learn more about the wonderful world of wild earth foods. Soon you will have enough drawings and notes to help you forage edible foods throughout the four seasons. Here are examples of the kinds of notes you might want to make in your journal:

Plant's Name (drawing or rubbing of plant)	**Habitat Drawing** (forest, stream, meadow)
Drawing of Person Eating Edible Plant Part (berry, leaf, root)	**Plant Use** (tea, poultice, food)

Food Gifts from the Bees

Gardens are not the only source of food at harvest time. Most people know that honey and beeswax are gifts from the bees, but what is bee's bread?

❧ **Have you ever used bee products or tasted the foods a bee eats?** It might be fun to visit a food co-op or a beekeeper to discover some of the many foods, health aids and other beautiful products (such as beeswax candles and soaps) that are made from the gifts of the bees. Before you go, make a list of all the foods or other gifts from bees you can think of, as well as any questions you might wish to ask. After your trip, write down the names of all the foods and bee products you discovered. What did you find?

❧ If you return home with bee pollen, honey, and a honeycomb from the co-op or beekeeper, **you can have a Bee Food Feast.** Bee pollen is a strong-tasting food, so take a bee-size nibble at first. Did you know that pollen is a special gift for people who have allergies? Small doses of bee pollen each day will build up your immune system and create a healthy resistance to allergies. But what about bees? What do you think they do with the pollen? Bees store pollen in the hive and eat it as bee bread.

❧ **Look at a honeycomb.** Do you see six-sided cells stored full of honey? The comb is waxy. Small tastes are recommended at first, unless your stomach is used to bee foods. What do you taste?

Now try a taste of pure honey.

- How does honey help your body?
- Is it possible to eat too much honey?
- What foods do you eat that contain honey? Can you make a list of them?
- Check food ingredient labels on the foods you buy to see if they contain honey. Add them to the list in your Earth Garden Foods chart.

❧ **Which flower does honey taste like?** Try honey made from different flower sources. You can actually taste the different flavors of different flowers! Try the taste test yourself by savoring differently flavored honeys, such as clover or wildflower. On the school lawn or in the meadow in late Spring or late Summer, look for purple clover blossoms. Pull out the individual sections that make up the blossom and you will see the white ends that were hidden in the flower head. When you suck on these tips you will probably understand why bees love purple clover. White or pink clovers are fun to try as well, though they are not nearly as sweet. What is honey useful for in human diets?

Want To Do More?

❧ Remove the honey from the cells of a honeycomb. The wax that remains can be strained and melted down into beeswax. If you have never rolled or dipped your own beeswax candles, you might want to try making some. It is fun to burn them on special occasions or during special events - such as thanking the bees for their wonderful and important gifts!

You might find beeswax suppliers listed in the yellow pages. Or ask a local orchard for information. You can also write to your local Extension Service or your State Department of Agriculture. Another source is the A. I. Root Company. P.O. Box 706, Medina, OH 44258.

❧ **After your bee adventures, can you illustrate the inner cells of the beehive in your nature journal?** Here are some things you can show:

- What does the inside of a hive looks like?
- What are the different kinds of bees that live within the hive?
- Where are bee products are stored within the hive?

❧ Can you write about the variety of bee products you are familiar with?

❧ Do you have any interesting ideas about bees?

Bee-lieve it or not. . . .

- It takes two million flowers to make one pound of honey!
- Honeybees must fly the equivalent of two and a half times around the world to make one pound of honey!
- All the work of the hive is done by female bees!
- One honey bee, working as hard as possible, cannot make a pound of honey in her lifetime!
- Thousands and thousands of bees live and work together in one hive!

A Cornucopia of Food that Goes, Glows, Grows, and Flows

During the harvest season we eat a great abundance and diversity of food. This is the healthiest food Mother Nature can provide! Do you know why? Can you think of an interesting way to set up a display of your beautiful harvest? Be sure to include a horn of plenty, called a cornucopia. Do you know any recipes to preserve the harvest from the Longhouse Garden through the Winter?

❧ **Which foods do you eat that Native Americans consumed?** Corn, beans, squash, sunflowers, honey, wild turkey, venison, rabbit, wild rice, acorns, walnuts, butternuts, beechnuts, hickory nuts, chestnuts, blueberries, cranberries, cherries, wild plums, pumpkins, herbs, potatoes, tomatoes, peppers, cocoa, maple syrup, vanilla beans, and game birds - like pheasants or ducks - are all Native American foods! Does this list sound like the ingredients of a Thanksgiving feast? Prior to the arrival of the Mayflower Pilgrims, nearly fifty percent of the world's plant foods were cultivated by Native American farmers in North, Central, and South America.

✍ **Can you draw a cornucopia full of these foods in your journal?** A cornucopia, or horn of plenty, is traditionally a goat's horn overflowing with fruit, flowers, and corn signifying prosperity. If you don't have a goat's horn on hand, than any cone shaped receptacle or ornament will do!

❧ **You can maintain high nutrient levels in the foods you eat by consuming native or locally grown fresh foods.** When foods are processed - boiled, canned or frozen - some of the nutrients are lost. When foods travel a long distance to supermarkets the nutrient values are often low. There are several reasons for this. Food that travels long distances must be picked before it is ripe or it will be bruised or mashed during transit. Ripe foods have had the proper amount of growing time that Mother Nature intended them to have, so they are full of sunshine, water and rich nutrients from the soil and air. Foods that do not grow to their full maturity have fewer of these food values in them.

❧ **Try the following taste test.** Taste some fresh foods as ripe as Mother Nature intended them to be, then taste some foods that you think are underripe or overripe. What do you think happens to food that sits around for a long time? Does it stay fresh? Which do you prefer? Throughout the season, sample the many seasonal native foods that grow in your area.

❧ **You might enjoy keeping track of the different foods you eat by starting a diet journal.** Record foods from lunches and snacks. What type of food do you like to eat most? Least? Try to identify the different food groups of each food you eat, such as grains, nuts and seeds, dairy, meat, fruits and vegetables. From this cornucopia of foods, can you tell which are native-grown foods, which are wild foods, and which foods are imported from other countries?

An easy way to remember the different categories of food are to think of whether the food makes you Go, Grow, Glow, or Flow. "Go" foods contain lots of sugars and starches that give you energy. "Grow" foods contain lots of proteins for growing bodies. "Glow" foods contain vitamins and minerals to keep you healthy. And, of course, "Flow" foods provide lots of liquid to keep the food moving through your body.

☛ ***Note**: for more information on this subject, please refer to 'The Go, Grow, Glow, and Flow Sisters Tell About Nutrition' on* page 152 *in "The First Farmers and Gardeners" journey.*

Want To Do More?

❧ **Which food groups contain a lot of protein?** What is protein? Which types of protein are healthier than others? How might combining food groups help to create a protein-balanced diet?

❧ **What is sugar? Fat? Fiber? Vitamins?** Which food groups contain a lot of sugar? A lot of fat? A lot of vitamins? A lot of fiber? Can you taste these qualities in the food you eat? If you have trouble answering these questions, look them up in a book, or ask someone who has "food wisdom."

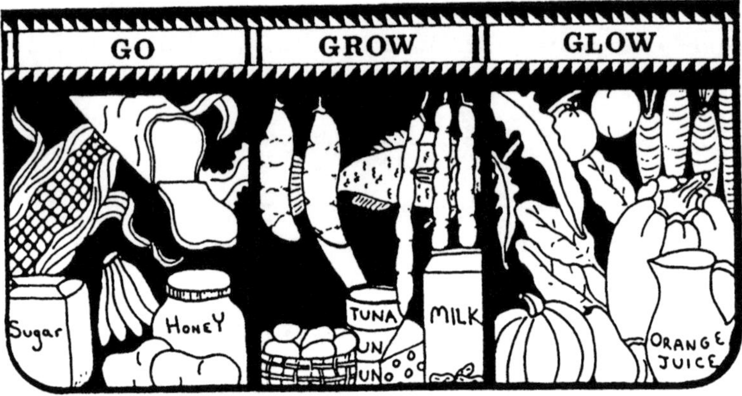

❧ **What is the difference between eating raw vegetables and cooked? Try this experiment:**

The Colorful Carrot Experiment

Boil some freshly harvested carrots. Look at the water remaining in the pot after cooking them. Do you see yellow water? Those are the A Vitamins boiled right out of your carrots! You need those A Vitamins to help you glow! Now steam a carrot. Steaming preserves vitamins, not to mention taste! What happens to the vitamins when you eat a carrot raw? Could this be why salads are so nutritious and tasty?

❧ **Why is each food group important?** What are some cautions for overeating too much of each food group? Can you eat too much fat? Too much sugar? What category of food does junk food fall into?

❧ **Think about your personal style of eating.** Do you eat from the different food groups? Is there anything you would like to change about your food choices? What do you drink? How much water do you drink in your daily diet? Develop a plan for changing one or two things in your diet. Try to stick to this plan for about a month. Maybe you can find a friend who wants to try the same idea. Buddy up to support each other. At the end of the month, reevaluate your plan.

Even More Curious?

❧ **Publish a collection of some of your favorite recipes for pumpkin pies, cookies, breads, and harvest snacks in a Three Sisters Cookbook.** The Three Sisters are favorite foods at Thanksgiving time. In your cookbook, acknowledge the Native food gifts, recipes, and traditions, as well as the traditions and recipes passed along by members of your own family or community. Consider giving cookbooks as gifts, or selling them to raise money for your upcoming garden projects.

Interesting recipes might include:

Apple Rings
Nut Butters
Pumpkin Tureen Soup Recipes
Boston Baked Beans
Sumac Lemonade
Journey or Johnny Cakes
Pumpkin Breads and Pies
Roasted Pumpkin Seeds
Corn Muffins

❧ **Harvested food can be preserved to make delicious treats all winter long.** You can dry apple rings or herbs, grind nuts into butters, and freeze or can applesauce. Add the following recipes to your cookbook and then, after the fun of making these recipes, eat these wonderful foods on a cold, winter's day!

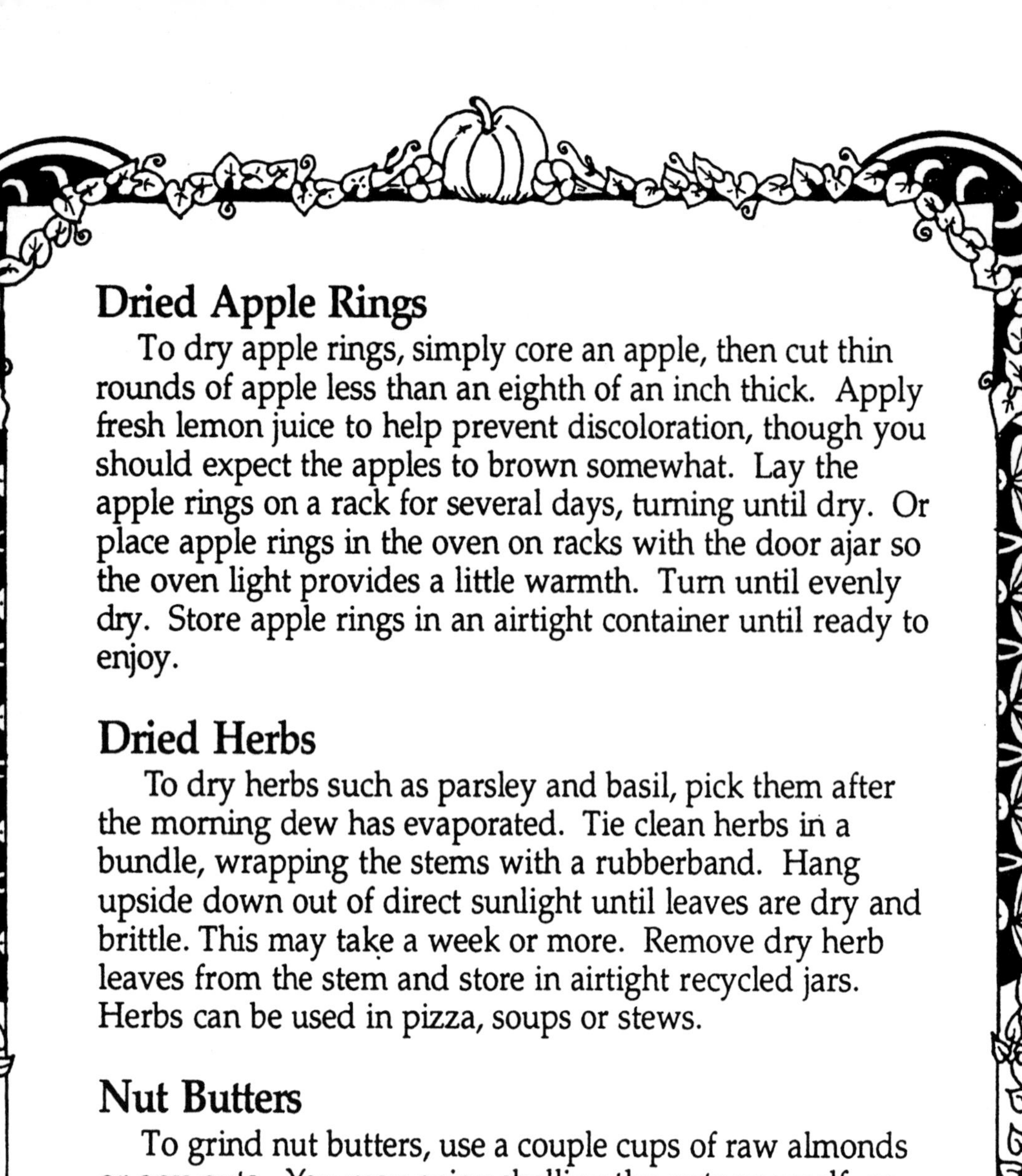

Dried Apple Rings

To dry apple rings, simply core an apple, then cut thin rounds of apple less than an eighth of an inch thick. Apply fresh lemon juice to help prevent discoloration, though you should expect the apples to brown somewhat. Lay the apple rings on a rack for several days, turning until dry. Or place apple rings in the oven on racks with the door ajar so the oven light provides a little warmth. Turn until evenly dry. Store apple rings in an airtight container until ready to enjoy.

Dried Herbs

To dry herbs such as parsley and basil, pick them after the morning dew has evaporated. Tie clean herbs in a bundle, wrapping the stems with a rubberband. Hang upside down out of direct sunlight until leaves are dry and brittle. This may take a week or more. Remove dry herb leaves from the stem and store in airtight recycled jars. Herbs can be used in pizza, soups or stews.

Nut Butters

To grind nut butters, use a couple cups of raw almonds or any nuts. You may enjoy shelling the nuts yourself, or buy already shelled nuts from the co-op in bulk. Place shelled nuts in a old fashioned vegetable grinder or a food processor. As you grind the nuts, they will form a butter or paste. Voila! Enjoy fresh nut butter on crackers or served as a carrot and celery dip. Store any leftovers in the fridge.

Applesauce

To make applesauce, peel and pare a couple pounds of apples you picked yourself. Cut into quarters. Steam in a pot with an inch of water in the bottom. Cook over low heat until the apples are soft. Mash apples, and you've got applesauce! Eat as is or sweeten with maple syrup and cinnamon. Freeze or can the leftovers.

WINTER

Winter ❧

Everybody wake up! Open your eyes! Stand up!
Be children of the light - strong, swift, and sure-of-foot.
Hurry, Clouds, from the four quarters of the universe.
Come, Big Snows,
that water will be abundant this summer.
Come, Ice, cover the fields,
that the seeds may grow into good crops.
All hearts be glad!

- Pueblo Song

THREE SISTERS: AN AGRI-CULTURE

The Three Sisters Native agricultural plantings of corn, beans, and squash contribute more than just food to Native communities. The Three Sisters provide an "agri-culture," a way of life rich with stories, ceremonies, gardening technology, customs, and etiquette. It has been practiced for hundreds of years!

❧ Here is a guided journey into the history and culture of Native food-gathering and gardening. You will discover some of the roles individuals play within the Native family and community. You will also discover that the spirit of the Three Sisters is alive and well in Winter.

"The Storytellers' Tales"

Imagine yourself a child of the Seneca, a people long known for being expert farmers and gardeners of the Woodlands. . . .

You are sitting at the fire circle in the bark-covered longhouse where you live. Seated all around you on straw mats woven from cattails are your grandparents, mother and father, sisters and brothers, aunts and uncles, cousins and friends. All of you have just finished eating, and now the storyteller, for whom the feast was lovingly prepared, begins to speak. As his voice rises like the smoke from the fire circle, you look about the longhouse. The long braids of corn drying along the walls have grown shorter during the course of the Winter. You think of the corn, bean, and meat stew you ate this evening. The recently harvested maple syrup that sweetened your meal is still sticky on your hands. You lick your fingers. The sweet taste reminds you that the end of Winter is drawing near. You begin to daydream of the sweetness of the approaching

CSP

Spring. But the storyteller's tale brings you back to reality. A thought suddenly occurs to you. This might be the final story of Winter! No more stories will be told around these fires till the first frosts in Autumn, when the corn is harvested.

❧ **In Native American traditions, the relatives on the mother's side of the family lived in the longhouse.** This extended family was called a "clan." Each family group within the clan had a fire pit or family hearth. The fire pit was used for preparing food, eating, drying clothes, or as a place for visiting or keeping warm. Look at a picture of the inside of a bark-covered longhouse. How did the community divide the space so that it was functional for everyone?

❧ **Do you think a multi-purpose, communal living space is a desirable way to live today?** Can you organize a small cooperative group and design a multi-purpose community dwelling? Include ideas for council meetings, food preparation, eating, clothing care, heating, playing, sleeping, growing food and so on. Remember to consider elders' as well as infants' and children's needs in your design and layout. Present your community dwelling design as an illustration, model, or diorama.

❧ **Furnishings for the longhouse came directly from the gifts of nature**, but the people needed to apply some creativity to these gifts to make them functional. Cattail mats provided comfort for those living in the longhouse. Braided corn made the interior of the longhouse beautiful. Can you design functional and ornamental furnishings that will meet your family needs? Can you adapt Native American food preservation techniques for storing the abundance from your harvest?

❧ **Can you also design a community house for your own maternal family?** Research your mother's family tree. Draw a maternal family tree that lists all her living relations. Then design a dwelling that expressly meets the needs of your maternal relations.

Want To Do More?

❧ **Traditionally, the storytelling season occurred between the first frost and the last frost.** This period of little daylight was made warm by sharing stories around the fire. When does the first and last frost occur where you live? How can you warm the cold, dark months in your community?

❧ **Hospitality was always plentiful in the Native community longhouse, even during the Winter months of scarcity and hardship.** A traveling storyteller or hunter was treated as an honored guest. The people generously welcomed him to the hearth and provided him with food and other comforts. It was, and still is, a tradition for the cook to prepare extra food at each meal in anticipation of an unexpected guest. The community stew pot symbolizes the idea of abundance rather than scarcity. It is a reminder of the ways in which the Great Spirit provides for the people.

What are your family and community practices regarding guests and hungry strangers? Is there anything you can do for the needy in your community? Prepare some harvest food for a community member or group.

Even More Curious?

❧ **Can you keep the spirit of the Three Sisters alive and well during Winter? Games are another good way to have fun during the Winter.**

As a way of keeping their spirits up during the harsh winter months, the Seneca played games and told stories around the fire. One favorite game was - and still is - the Bean Game. Turn the page to find out how to play this exciting game. . . .

The Bean Game

Eight elkhorn buttons and one hundred dried beans are needed for playing this game. The Seneca dye each button so that all the buttons have one color on one side, and another color on the other side. The players gather around a blanket. Fifty or more beans are placed in the "pot." These beans are like the coins in the "pot" of today's card games. Taking turns, each player tosses the eight buttons onto the blanket. If a player's tossed buttons show six of the same color, 2 points are given. Seven buttons of the same color equal 4 points, and eight buttons of the same color equal 20 points! A player receives one dry bean for each point earned. The first person to obtain fifty beans is the winner!

So get a blanket. Take one hundred beans out of the drying jar. Find something to substitute for the elkhorn buttons. Change the point system, if you like. Then find some friends who are willing to stay up all night to win beans!

CORNBREAD, FIRST BREAD OF THE AMERICAS

Cornbreads have fed Native American peoples for thousands of years. Some of the seed has been passed from generation to generation for over 3,000 years! Have you ever planted Indian corn or maize? Have you ever ground it? It is easy to make these traditional breads yourself!

❧ What recipe can you create that would resemble one of the first corn breads? What ingredients do you think you need? How will you prepare the cornbread? Write the recipe in your journal. Test it, then record your results. Maybe you'll need to make some recommendations in your journal for improving the bread the next time you make it!

For a tried-and-true recipe, try this one:

Cornbread

1 cup cornmeal
1 cup whole wheat flour
1/2 tsp. salt
2 tsp. baking powder
2-4 Tbs. melted butter or oil
1-4 Tbs. honey or maple syrup or molasses
1-2 eggs
1 cup milk

In a bowl, combine the wet ingredients. then mix in the dry ingredients. Pour into a greased 8-inch square pan and bake at 400° for about 20 minutes. Serve warm with butter.

● As you crack and grind the corn, observe, feel, and taste its different parts.

● As you grind seed into meal or flour, name the different parts of the corn seed. In your journal, record and illustrate the parts of a corn kernel as it passes from its seed to its flour stage.

Want To Do More?

❧ Try some of the following recipes using freshly ground cornmeal. Do you think cornbread has changed over time? How?

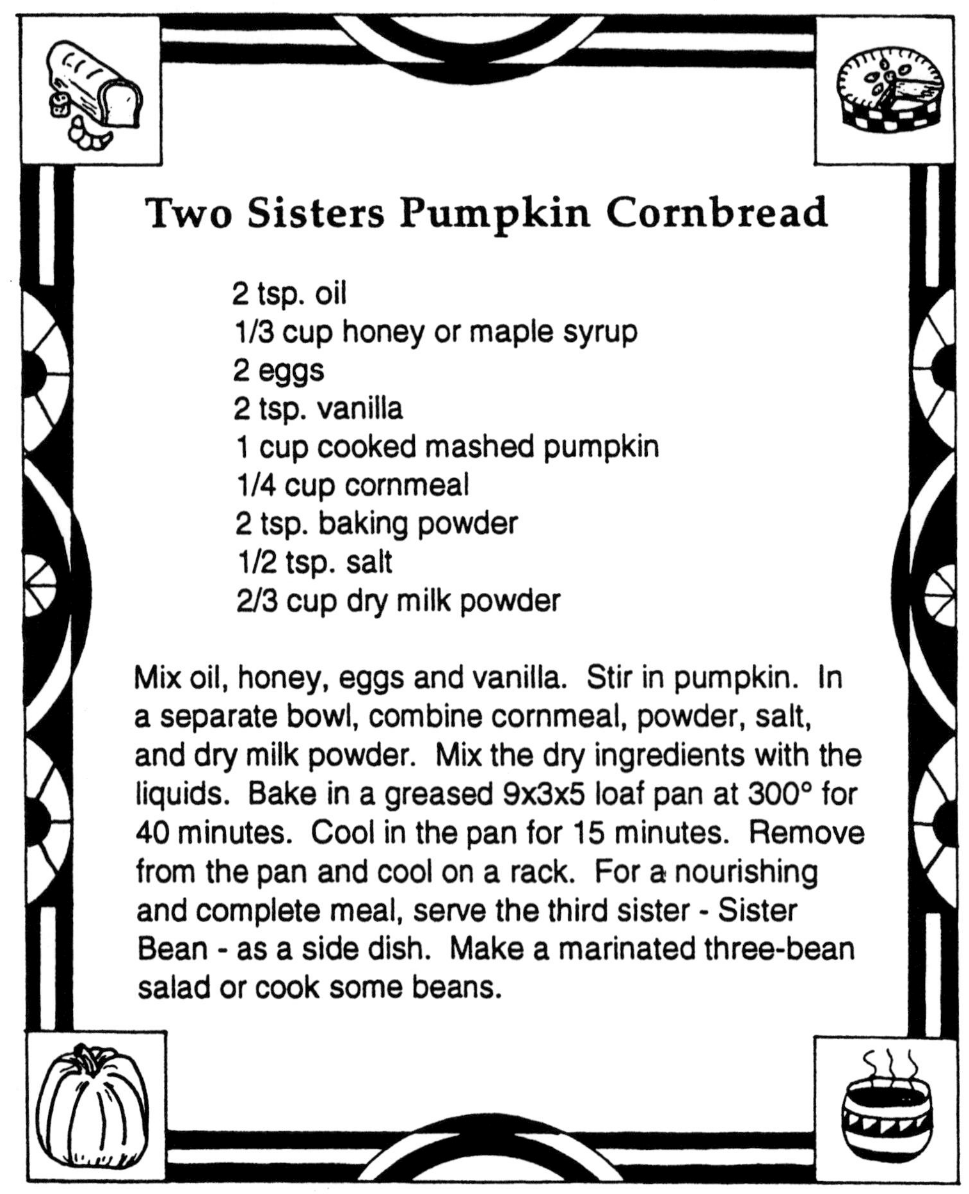

Two Sisters Pumpkin Cornbread

2 tsp. oil
1/3 cup honey or maple syrup
2 eggs
2 tsp. vanilla
1 cup cooked mashed pumpkin
1/4 cup cornmeal
2 tsp. baking powder
1/2 tsp. salt
2/3 cup dry milk powder

Mix oil, honey, eggs and vanilla. Stir in pumpkin. In a separate bowl, combine cornmeal, powder, salt, and dry milk powder. Mix the dry ingredients with the liquids. Bake in a greased 9x3x5 loaf pan at 300° for 40 minutes. Cool in the pan for 15 minutes. Remove from the pan and cool on a rack. For a nourishing and complete meal, serve the third sister - Sister Bean - as a side dish. Make a marinated three-bean salad or cook some beans.

Indian Corn Pone

Mix:
1 cup cornmeal
a dab of maple syrup or homey
one egg

Add:
2 Tbs. oil

Grease a heavy skillet. Spoon batter onto the skillet in four "pones." Brown both sides. Serve Indian Corn Pone hot with margarine, maple syrup, honey, or applesauce.

Even More Curious?

❧ The very first corn was grown in what is now known as Mexico. As indigenous peoples traded northward up the continent, the seeds of this ancient corn eventually found its way to the peoples of North America. Corn truly was, and continues to be, a gift from the native people of the Americas.

Can you create a mural time line showing the uses of corn as an important grain in America? How did the use of corn change over hundreds of years? What are some of the important uses of corn in your community? How do you use the gifts of corn in your life?

❧ You can read more about the history of corn in Aliki's book, *Corn Is Maize.* Another book, *The Discovery of the Americas,* by Betsy and Giulio Maestro, tells about the first people of America and the explorers who came to this land. Check the Bibliography at the end of this Guidebook for more stories and references.

❧ Continue the tradition of the Native people by giving a gift of cornbread, corn chowder or dried corn to a member of your community!

Three Sisters Round and Round Soup

Imagine yourself as a young Native child sitting around the campfire cooking with your grandmother. You smell the good soup as its cloud rises from the kettle. She notices that you are enjoying the good-smelling cloud, and as you stir the soup round and round, waiting patiently for it to be ready, she tells you a story.

"Round and Round Soup"

Ahh," she says, "smell carefully, my child. Can you smell the sky in the soup? It is in there, you know. For the sky is really the giver of this fine soup. Watch as the cloud rises from the soup kettle. Watch it as it journeys, my child. Where do you think it is going? It travels as invisibly as your breath, and gathers in the sky with others of its kind. Together they form a great cloud, gathering from all parts of the Earth Mother - streams, rivers, lakes, oceans - coming together in their meeting place in the sky. When the time is right, the clouds fall from their meeting place and nourish the Earth below by filling the corn, beans, squash, trees, and rivers.

"So, you see, each plant draws up the once-invisible ones into their roots, taking in some for their own nourishment and giving back to the sky that which is not needed. All the foods in the kettle are nourished by that cloud rising from the soup. And although all that is in the soup may not be tasted or seen, my child, it strengthens and nourishes us all the same.

"And so the cycle continues, round and round like the paddle that stirs the soup."

❧ Place some cups or jars outside at the beginning of a wet day and collect rainwater or snow to make this delicious soup!

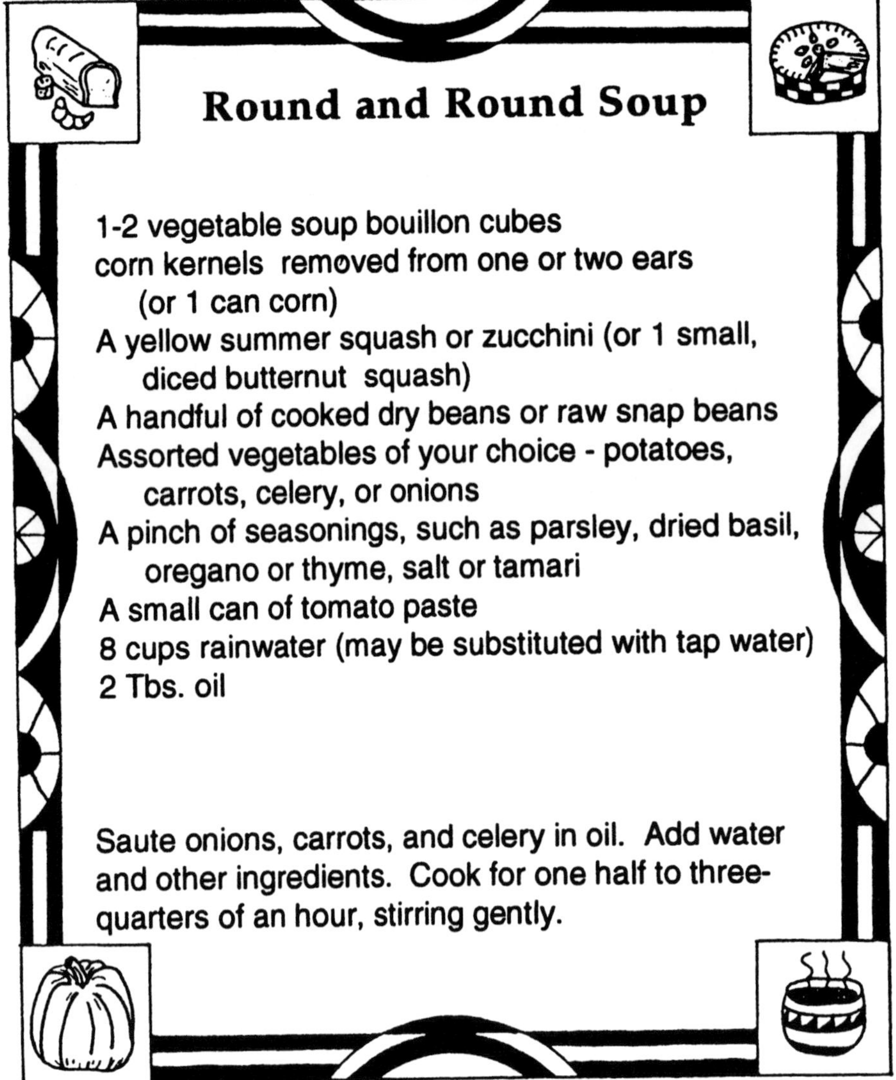

Round and Round Soup

1-2 vegetable soup bouillon cubes
corn kernels removed from one or two ears
(or 1 can corn)
A yellow summer squash or zucchini (or 1 small, diced butternut squash)
A handful of cooked dry beans or raw snap beans
Assorted vegetables of your choice - potatoes, carrots, celery, or onions
A pinch of seasonings, such as parsley, dried basil, oregano or thyme, salt or tamari
A small can of tomato paste
8 cups rainwater (may be substituted with tap water)
2 Tbs. oil

Saute onions, carrots, and celery in oil. Add water and other ingredients. Cook for one half to three-quarters of an hour, stirring gently.

As you stir the soup, remember the story Grandmother told. Tell it to a friend. . . .

Want To Do More?

❧ Make a pot of soup to donate to the local soup kitchen or emergency food shelf.

✍ Can you record and illustrate a cloud-to-soup cycle in your nature journal?

Even More Curious?

❧ Can you design an **experiment** to show parts of the water cycle, such as precipitation, evaporation, or condensation?

❧ You might try this **condensation activity**: Place a small, potted plant in a large-mouthed glass jar or terrarium. Water the plant before closing the glass container. Now you can observe a water cycle in motion!

❧ **Construct a rain gauge.** Observe and record precipitation for the month, season, or year.

✍ **What is the role of the Three Sisters in the water cycle?** Write about it or draw it in your nature journal.

How Do The Three Sisters Help You Go, Grow and Glow?

Did you know that the Three Sisters not only work well together in the garden, but also work cooperatively in your body?

❧ **Sister Corn** is rich in nutrients that are good for your body. What does cornmeal help your body do? Corn helps your body **Go**, as corn is full of energy food. Cornmeal is also rich in protein. Protein helps your body **Grow** and repair itself. And - like most yellow foods - Sister Corn contains Vitamin A, which helps your skin **Glow**. Thanks to Sister Corn, you get **Go, Grow and Glow power** all in one convenient package! No wonder corn was called the "giver of life" by the ancient peoples! Her power was felt long before nutritionists discovered her good qualities.

Is corn among the ingredients in the foods you eat? When you prepare your own meals, you are aware of the ingredients that go into it. For prepackaged foods, though, read the labels to discover exactly what is hidden inside. You might discover several kinds of ingredients made from corn - corn syrup, corn starch, corn oil or cornmeal!

 For a week, keep a Go, Grow, Glow journal, listing all the corn food products you eat. Which corn food products help you Go? Which ones help you Grow? Glow?

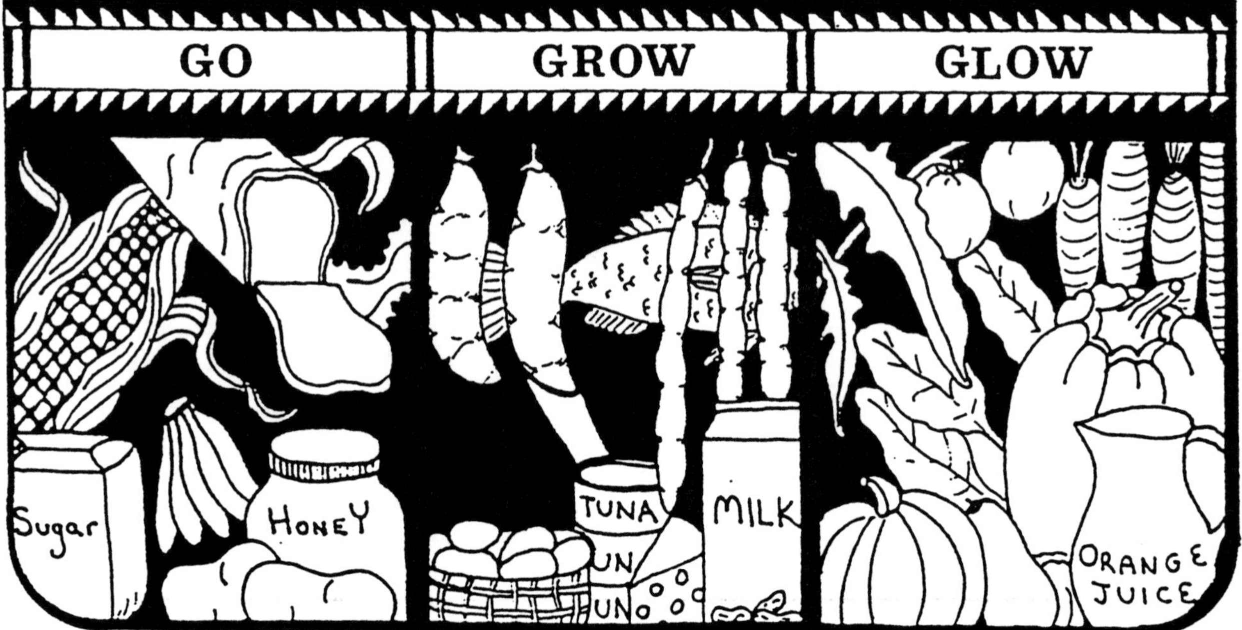

❧ **Sister Bean** is a great companion to Sister Corn in the garden. But would you believe she is a real sister in your body, too? Two kinds of vegetable proteins eaten together provide the necessary ingredients that replace animal protein. Beans are an excellent source of vegetable protein. Does Sister Bean help you to Go, Grow or Glow? Whether they are in the garden or in your body, Sisters Corn and Bean make quite a team!

In your Go, Grow, Glow journal, record all the bean products you eat during a week.

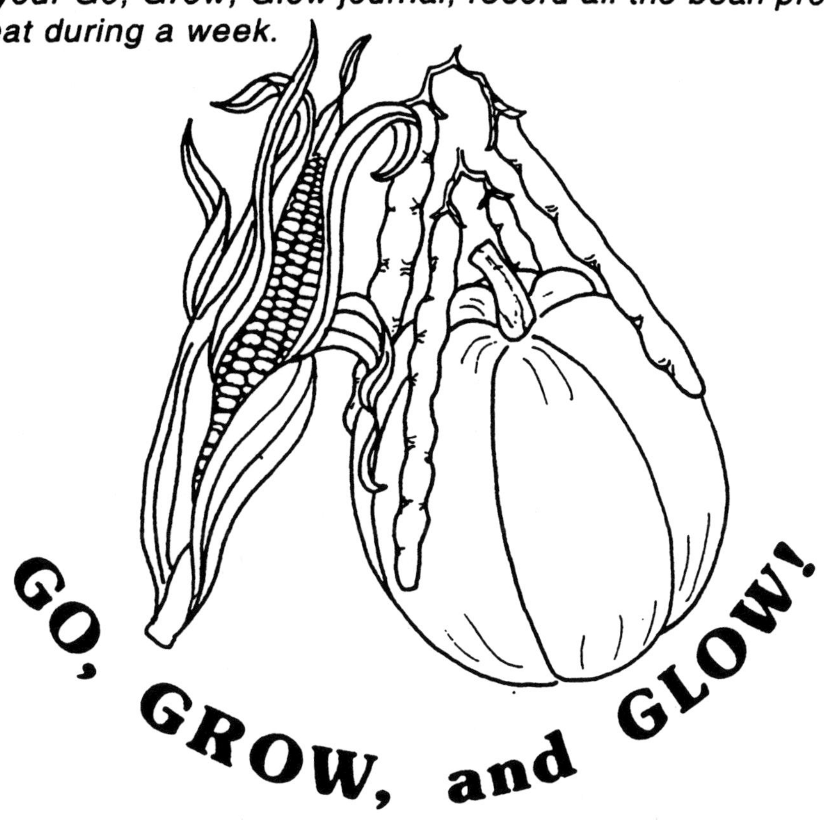

❧ **Sister Squash - or Pumpkin -** glows on Halloween night, and does a similar job for your body. Sister Squash's color gives a clue to the work she can do. Orange and yellow foods contain a lot of Vitamin A. Vitamin A keeps your skin, hair and the rest of your body glowing healthy bright. Do you think you eat enough "Glow" foods?

In your Go, Grow, Glow journal, illustrate your meal and snack choices that contain Sister Squash.

Want To Do More?

❧ **Think about your diet. Which foods in it have qualities that contribute to good health?** Which of the following two foods contain more quality nutrients: "traditional foods" or "fast foods"?

Traditional plant foods do not contribute to the high level of heart disease that exists in our country. Studies show that Native Americans who follow traditional diets rarely suffer heart disease. But Native Americans who consume fast foods - either because they cannot afford high quality foods or because they are unaware of the risks - are prone to heart disease - as we all are. This is because non-traditional diets, such as fast foods, are high in fat and sugar. These diets cause diabetes and general poor health, as well as heart disease.

❧ **Here is a snack food suggestion** that combines the high quality of traditional foods with the trendy quality of fast foods!

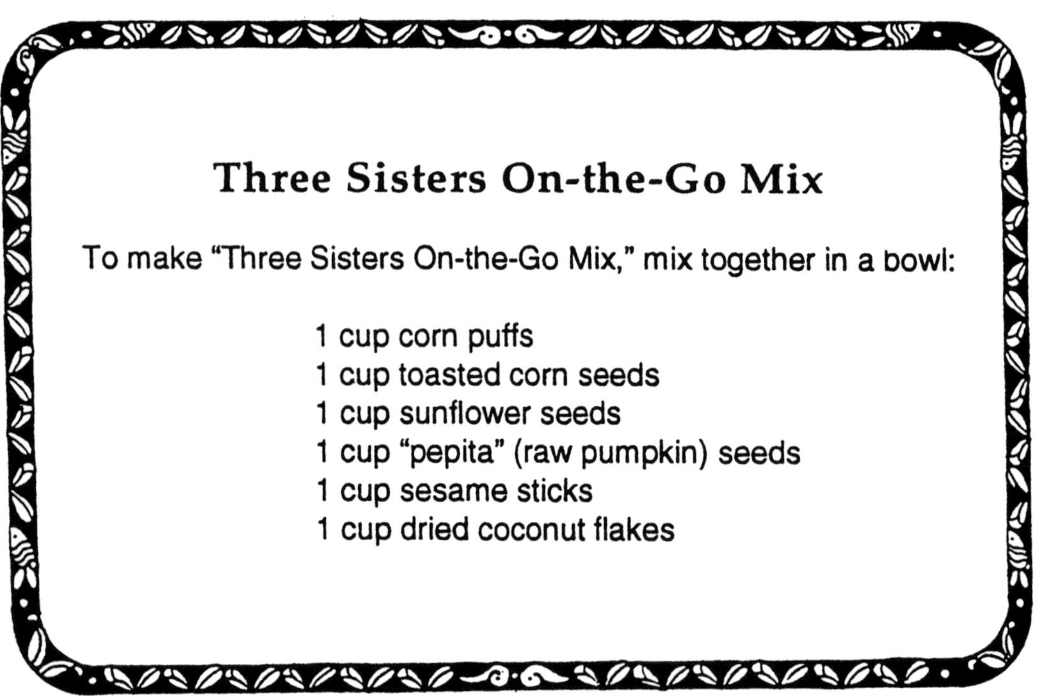

Three Sisters On-the-Go Mix

To make "Three Sisters On-the-Go Mix," mix together in a bowl:

1 cup corn puffs
1 cup toasted corn seeds
1 cup sunflower seeds
1 cup "pepita" (raw pumpkin) seeds
1 cup sesame sticks
1 cup dried coconut flakes

An Indoor Garden Center

Instead of simply dreaming of your Three Sisters garden, you can be growing plants indoors all Winter long! An Indoor Garden Center is an opportunity for experimenting, documenting, measuring, and growing food to maturity indoors!

❧ This is a wonderful opportunity to invite community members to assist you in building an Indoor Garden Center. After the basic structure is built, can you use your imagination to decorate your Indoor Garden Center to look like a Native American longhouse garden? Bark, leaves, corn husks, cattails, dried flowers, can set the stage, while models of animals, wickiups, longhouses, and other features of a landscape can bring it to life.

☛ **Note:** Please refer to 'Indoor Winter Garden' and 'Three Sisters Plant Adventures in the Indoor Garden' located in the "First Farmers and Gardeners" journey, pages 127-139 for months of indoor gardening tips, plans, and adventures all winter long.

♠ You can germinate last year's harvested seeds in the Indoor Garden Center, or you can purchase new seeds. Vegetable and flower seedlings can be planted in recycled containers containing about three inches of germinating mix. Sunflowers and pumpkins grow better undisturbed, so put them in six- to eight-inch tall recycled milk containers.

Growing Native Foods in the Indoor Garden

For an Indoor Garden Harvest Salad, grow your vegetables in January and harvest them in March or early April!

❧ **Bush beans, cucumbers, and cherry tomatoes are relatives of ancient foods that were harvested and cultivated by Native peoples.** Sow some seeds that may have been passed down through the generations by previous Longhouse gardeners or other Native peoples. Plant only those seed varieties that do well in container gardens, such as bush beans and the great-great ancestor of the tomato, Red Currant Tomato. Add lettuce, basil, carrots, radishes, and nasturtiums to these plantings.

❧ **Some catalog companies list special plants for small gardens.** Some recommended container varieties are available from Shepherd Seeds. In their "Baby Vegetable Collection," they offer miniature carrots, beets, scallop squash, onions, lettuce, and bush beans. Grow them for a complete salad!

❧ **Sow container variety seeds in six-inch pots** filled with a moist germinating mix. You can make your own organic germinating mix. Simply add one part each of peat, compost, pearlite, bone meal, worm castings (optional), and vermiculite.

❧ **For a little sisterly companionship in each pot, grow a bush or pole bean plant, a radish, or a carrot and a lettuce plant.** The bean plant, as it blossoms, will provide nitrogen to the other plants. If you plant pole beans, tie a string to the ceiling, or let the plant climb and twine around the Indoor Garden Center. The radish and carrot will seek a deep growing space. Shallow lettuce roots will not compete with the carrot. Each pot can be treated like a mound of Three Sisters.

You must provide all the nutrients for each container, just as you provide nutrients for each mound planting. You cannot bury fish bones in each pot as you would in a mound, but you can feed your plant with liquid seaweed or fish emulsion. Water your pots before the soil gets too dry, and mist each plant with a foliar growth solution each week.

❧ **Before you begin planting, can you think of what a germinating seed needs?** To help you find some answers, try the following experiment:

The Baby Bean Experiment

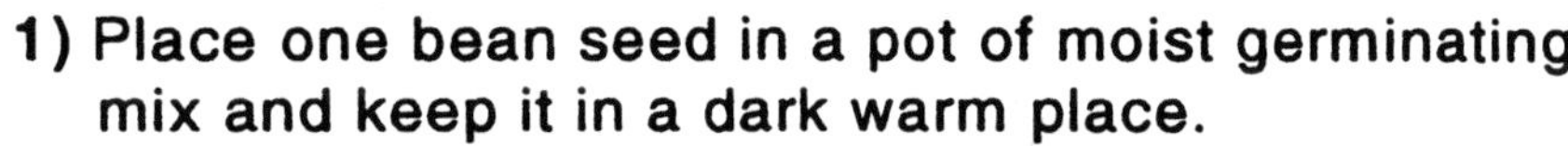

1) Place one bean seed in a pot of moist germinating mix and keep it in a dark warm place.

2) Place another seed in a pot of moist germinating mix and place it in the refrigerator.

Keep these seeds watered.

3) Place another seed in a pot without a germinating mix or moisture.

4) Observe what happens. What does a germinating seed need?

Math Nature's Way

❧ For the next two months, watch the plants in your Indoor Garden Center and try to answer these questions:

- How many days does it take each plant to germinate?
- Can you chart and compare the growth of the different kinds of plants?
- Can you chart and graph different plant varieties according to their height in inches, centimeters, or feet?
- What is the weight of plants before - and after - watering?
- What is the weight of each plant's harvest?
- What is the volume of water given to each plant as measured in cups, pints, quarts, liters, or gallons throughout the growing season?

Want To Do More?

❧ Start your seeds indoors:

♠ In March or early April you can sow herbs, sunflowers, and flower transplants in the Indoor Garden Center. These plants can be transferred to your outdoor Three Sisters garden or used as gifts for Mother's and Father's Day.

♠ Bush beans for gift-giving can be grown in six-inch pots and used as windowsill plants. When the beans mature, eat them right out of the pot! Be sure to fertilize bush beans monthly. Add liquid fish emulsion, seaweed, or organic plant food while the beans live in their pot on the windowsill.

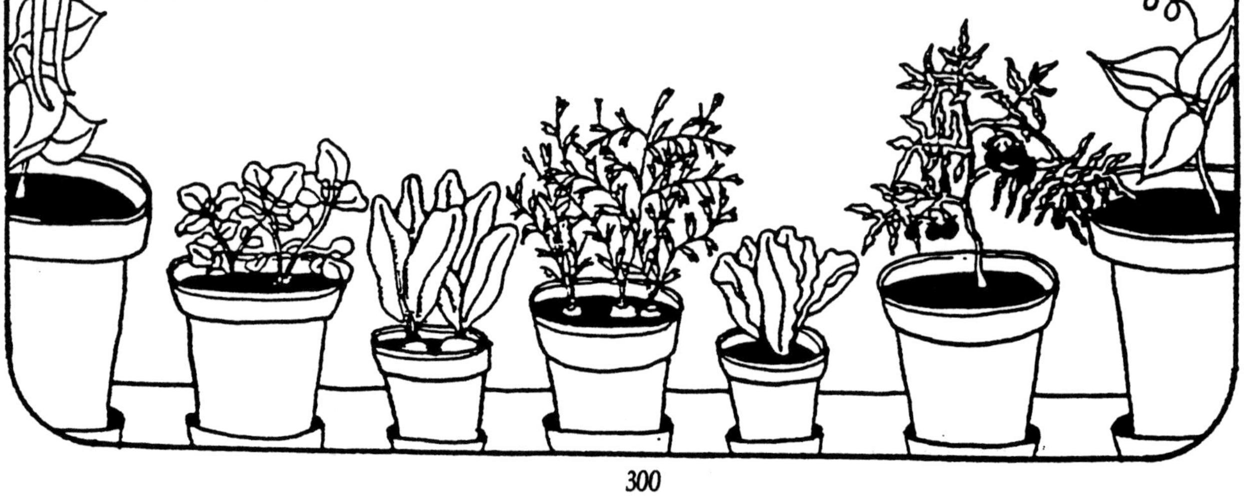

Sweeten Up the Winter Blues

How about a "Sweeten up the Winter Breakfast" to break the cabin fever syndrome that arrives right around sugaring season?

❧ Native winter breakfasts among the Iroquois sometimes consisted of "snowfood" prepared from popcorn and hot maple syrup. Thank the good Earth that there was something to relieve the long winter season! Try some snowfood. Which is more enjoyable - snowfood or today's breakfast cereals?

❧ Make the following recipes and "Sweeten Up Your Winter Blues."

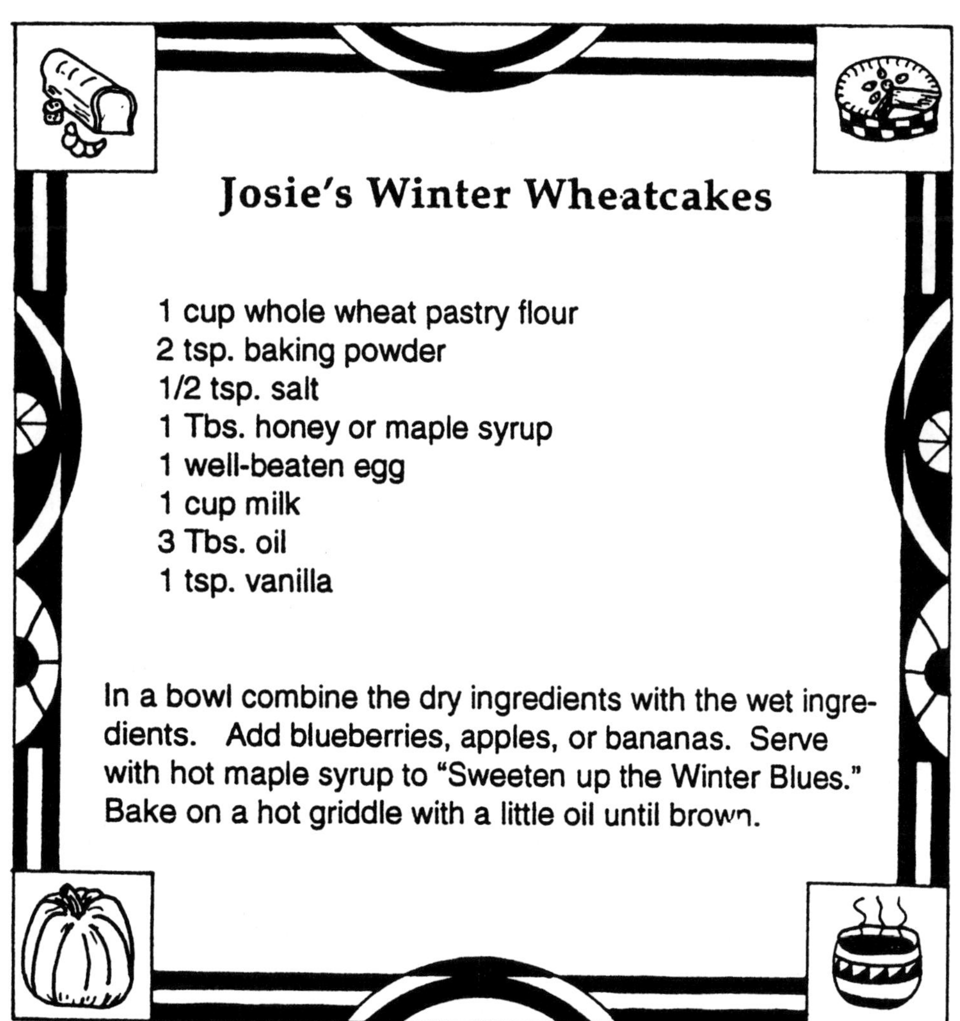

Josie's Winter Wheatcakes

1 cup whole wheat pastry flour
2 tsp. baking powder
1/2 tsp. salt
1 Tbs. honey or maple syrup
1 well-beaten egg
1 cup milk
3 Tbs. oil
1 tsp. vanilla

In a bowl combine the dry ingredients with the wet ingredients. Add blueberries, apples, or bananas. Serve with hot maple syrup to "Sweeten up the Winter Blues." Bake on a hot griddle with a little oil until brown.

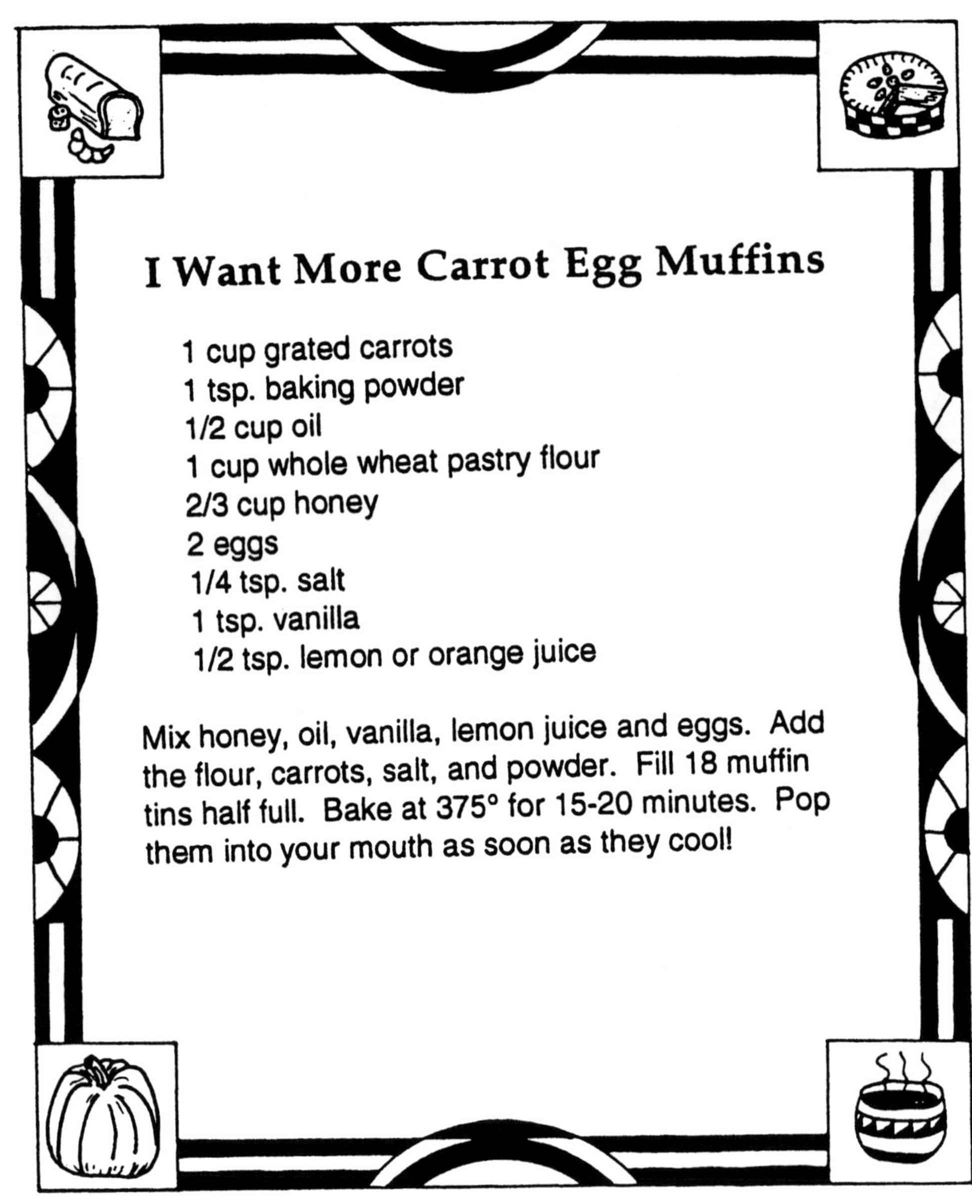

I Want More Carrot Egg Muffins

1 cup grated carrots
1 tsp. baking powder
1/2 cup oil
1 cup whole wheat pastry flour
2/3 cup honey
2 eggs
1/4 tsp. salt
1 tsp. vanilla
1/2 tsp. lemon or orange juice

Mix honey, oil, vanilla, lemon juice and eggs. Add the flour, carrots, salt, and powder. Fill 18 muffin tins half full. Bake at 375° for 15-20 minutes. Pop them into your mouth as soon as they cool!

❧ Make a "Sweeten up the Winter Blues" cookbook with graphic illustrations of ingredients and simple recipe directions.

Want To Do More?

❧ You might enjoy **experimenting with recipes** that use different sweeteners such as honey, maple syrup, or apple juice. Prepare samples of these foods for a snack or a nutritious breakfast. Compare the tastes. Try varying amounts of sweeteners and see how they compare. Can you recognize the different sweeteners used in each recipe? Which recipes do you think are the healthiest choices you can make?

❧ Winter can be a lonely, difficult season. Cheer it up with a **"Be a Friendly Neighbor Project."** You might enjoy planning a **"Sweeten Up the Winter Breakfast"** for your class, neighbors, or local shut-ins. Plan a **"Sweeten Up the Winter Food Drive"** for your local food shelf. Invite people to bake and make donations to an event of either kind. Include recipes with these goodies.

Even More Curious?

❧ Many breakfast cereals today still use corn and sweeteners as ingredients. **Compare the ingredients, nutritional contents, and flavors of several cereal brands**. Which contain the most grain, sugar, non-food additives, and fats? What wise food breakfast choices would you like to make?

❧ **What is the nutritional value of maple syrup?** Honey? Sugar? Corn syrup? Honey, corn syrup, fruit juice concentrates, and sugar are sweeteners contained in breakfast foods like muffins, breads, and pancakes. Compare these sweeteners for differences in nutritional values. Are there any vitamins, protein, and fats in the sweet products you eat?

❧ Traditionally, merrymaking, storytelling, and social activities in Native societies fill the winter months. Community strength keeps the people's spirit playful. In the stillness of Winter, look within yourself and reflect upon your own heart. The human potential can be observed with a renewed clarity at this time - a clarity which sometimes is possible only during the crystalline silence of Winter.

SPRING

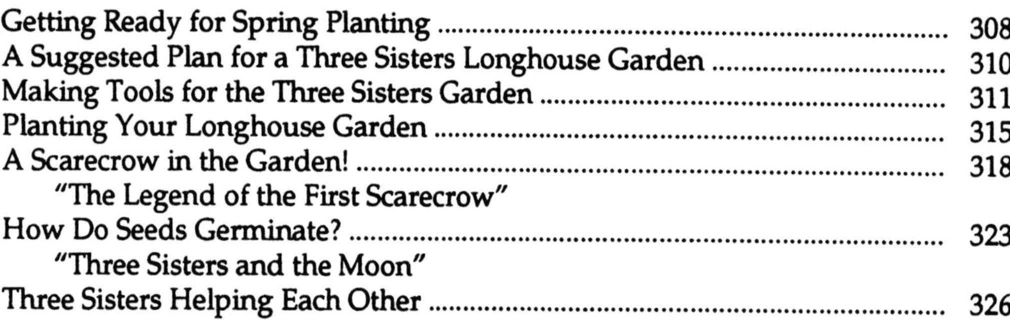

Spring ❧

Walk softly upon the Earth Mother in Spring, for she is pregnant with Life.

- unknown

Getting Ready for Spring Planting

May Day through Memorial Day is a good time to make your dream garden a reality. Plan a garden design, and prepare seeds from last year's crops for this year's sowing.

❧ Mounds are a traditional way of caring for the Three Sisters in Native gardens. Generally, mounds are one foot high, 3 feet in diameter, and should be spaced three feet apart from one another. Caring for your garden is like nurturing a mother-to-be. Feed and nourish her with strengthening foods, sing her growing songs and wish her well. Sow seeds, then weed and tend her till her belly bursts with life-giving foods.

Native mound gardens are the first known examples of raised-bed gardening. Mound-gardening concentrates soil amendments in the growing area only, conserving resources by not feeding walking paths or areas between the rows. Mound gardens hold soil around the stems of growing plants, giving them a strong foundation. The deep, loosened soil in mounds also allows for combinations of complimentary plants to grow together. Can you recreate a traditional Native American Three Sisters garden by growing your plants in mounds?

Math, Nature's Way

❧ **How can you plan and measure the arrangement of the mounds?** In traditional Native American times, measurements were not made with rulers or yardsticks. How might a foot-length have been measured hundreds of years ago? In your community, perhaps there is an elder with a "foot" to guide you in measuring your one-foot high, three-foot wide mounds. To make a circle three feet wide, connect two sticks with a foot-and-a-half long string tied in the middle of each stick. Place one stick in the center of the mound-to-be, and draw the string tight with the other stick. Now trace the outer limits of the three-foot wide mound by rotating the outer stick in a circle around the center stick.

❧ **How can you measure a three-foot distance between your mounds?** There are many ways. A three-foot distance can be measured in a "pace." Is there an elder person whose pace measures approximately three feet? Use this pace measurement for spacing the mounds three feet apart.

❧ How do you prepare your Three Sisters seeds for planting?

First of all, check garden soils to be sure they are dry and ready to receive your seeds. Also, check the frost dates to determine which seeds can be planted.

♠ **Sister Corn's seeds** must be sown after the last frost, but two to three weeks prior to planting beans, squash, or pumpkins. This gives the corn ample time to become strong before supporting the beans and competing with squash plants.

If the corn-growing season is short where you live, you may want to start some seeds inside. Six weeks prior to planting day, plant some of the corn seeds in individual peat pots in the Indoor Garden Center. Peat pots lessen transplant shock and root damage, and promise a higher survival rate for corn, which is not ordinarily transplanted. Since corn is not fond of transplanting, you should expect a 25% loss after transplanting it into the garden. To avoid a disappointing harvest, plan accordingly.

Remove last year's dried corn kernels from the cobs. You can do this by using your thumb to flick kernels from the cob. The night before sowing the seed, soak the kernels in spring water. What will this soaking process do? It softens the toughened, outer part of the kernel, giving it a helpful boost in the germinating process. If performed with mindfulness, gratitude, and care, this act also prepares the seed-sower for the ceremony of planting.

♠ **Sister Bean and Sister Squash** can wait to be planted until after the last frost - and after Sister Corn is several inches tall. Sister Squash's seeds are tender, however, and do not need to be soaked. Sister Bean likes to have her seeds soaked the night before planting to soften them.

A Suggested Plan for a

THREE SISTERS GARDEN

C: corn for drying
2B = 2 pole beans to climb corn stalks
S : squash trained to ramble

Pc : Popcorn
B : Bushbean

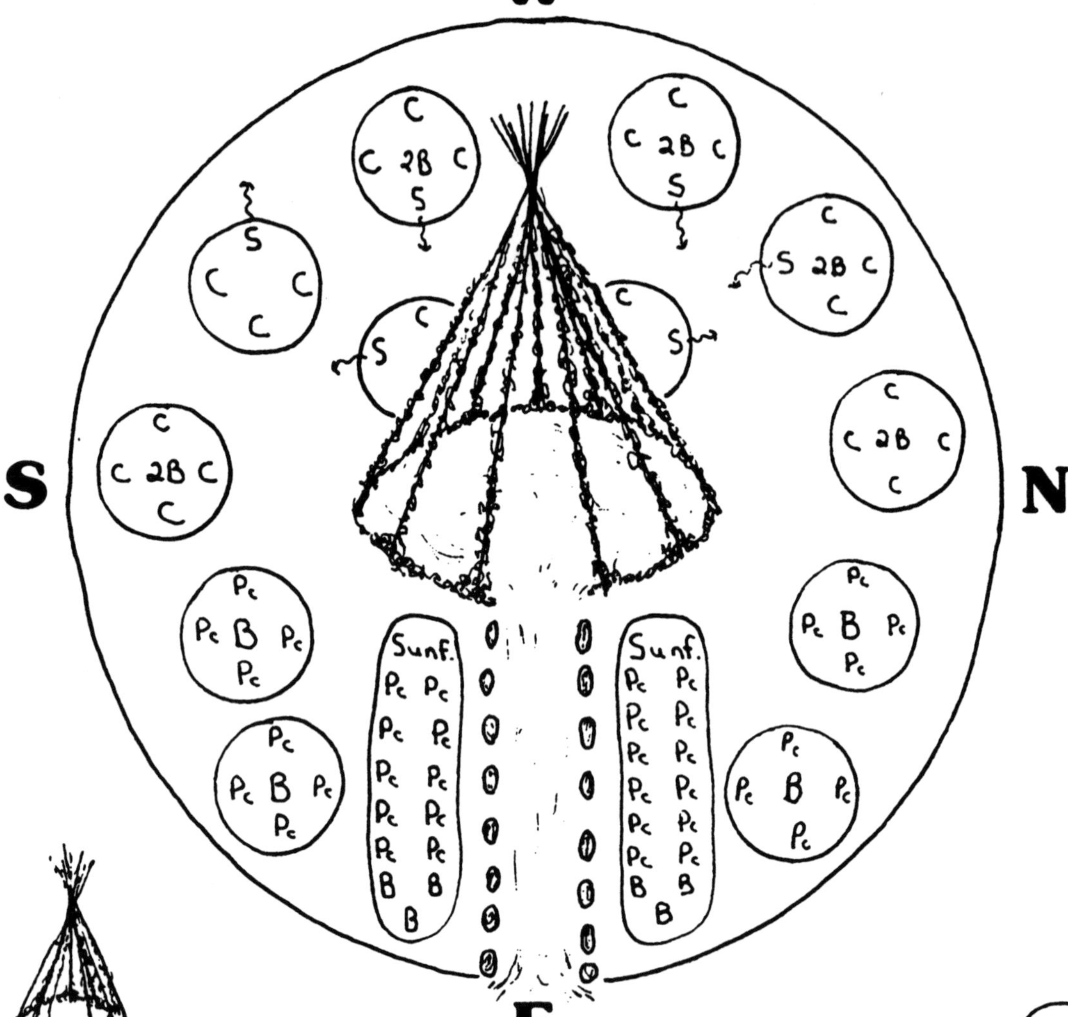

6'-12" diameter wickiup traditionally opens to the EAST. (fits 10-20 children)

mulched path with stone border leads to wickiup entrance

Sunf. = Sunflower
Pc = Popcorn
B = Bushbean

Making Tools for the Three Sisters Garden

Is this the first time you have been a Three Sisters gardener? As you know, the first farmers of this land were Three Sisters gardeners. Tools used thousands of years ago by those farmers still work today. Make your own simple tools and a birch bark cup for a thirst-quenching drink of water.

❧ **What tools do you think the first farmers and gardeners of a thousand years ago used to plant corn?** Experiment with different natural objects to see how well they perform in the soil.

- What natural object would you use for removing unwanted wild plants?
- What object would be best for carrying water?
- Can you find an object that would be good for loosening the soil?
- What kind of tool can you make for sowing seeds?

❧ **If weeds or wildflowers creep in, how can they be removed?** If Sister Squash does her job well, you will not need to do much weeding in the garden. But before she is fully grown she will probably need your help. Can you think of a way to attach a natural digging or scratching implement to the end of a stick so that it works as well as a hoe? Try to make a deer antler rake, as described in the story on the next page. Or make a clam-shell hoe, or a deer shoulder blade hoe, both of which are familiar to the Northeast Natives. How can you attach a deer shoulder blade or clam shell to a stick? Don't forget that your hands make fine tools, too. Use them to hand-pick weeds. If it is hard to pull out a weed, use a clam shell to help loosen the weed's roots first. Weeds help make fertile compost, so toss them into your compost pile.

❧ The following story, told by Wolf Chief of the Hidatsa people of North Dakota, tells how the first gardeners of this country learned to use rakes.

Old Magic Woman's Rake

Long ago, Old Magic Woman lived by a little lake. Next to her lodge was her garden. The garden was tended by male deer who made their home in the nearby forest. The bucks used their horns to rake up the weeds that grew in the garden.

When the deer began shedding their antlers for the first time, Old Magic Woman gathered them up and fastened them to sticks and used them to work in her garden. Her grandson saw that these rakes were a good thing, so he began teaching the people how to make deer antler rakes.

Eventually the people began making rakes from ash wood. The rake tines resembled deer antlers. Some deer antlers had six tines, other had seven. So to this day, ash rakes are made with six or seven tines."

❧ Native people have been growing Three Sisters gardens for a long time. They burned the fields to clear them of unwanted plants. The ashes covering the ground sweetened the soil. **What tool would be useful for starting a fire?** If you guessed rubbing two sticks together, give it a try! Place dried leaves or moss on a flat rock. Holding one stick in place on the moss or leaves, rub two sticks together for as long as possible. It takes a good deal of practice to start a fire this way, but if you succeed it will be a rewarding experience. If you are unable to make a spark, carefully feel the place where you have been rubbing. Can you imagine this spot becoming so hot it begins to burn? Today, some people still use the ancient bow and drill to spark a fire - but patience is required to accomplish this feat!

❧ **How might Three Sisters gardeners loosen the soil for planting?** A long time ago digging sticks, antlers, animal bones, clam shells, and sharp, three-sided rocks were used. A digging stick is easy to find. Look for a strong branch or limb. Sharpen one end of the limb so it can be driven into the ground. This will easily loosen the soil, yet you will probably notice that it does not work as well as modern day tools.

You can make your own Native style **digging stick** by gathering a fallen stick from the forest floor. An elder can carve designs on your digging stick.

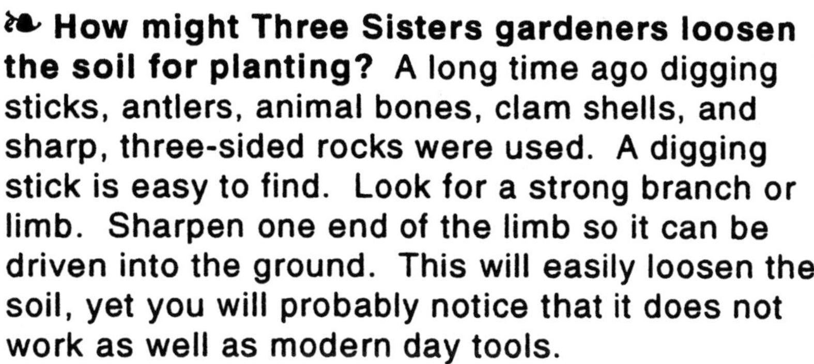

❧ **Planting sticks** help the seed find its way into the prepared garden soil. To make a planting stick, gather strong branches from the forest floor. Find a thin, strong branch the right width for poking seed-size holes in the ground. If the branch allows you to bend over in a comfortable position, then it is the proper length for you - after all, you do not want to get so tired you cannot plant all your seeds! Make your planting stick special by wrapping colored yarns around the middle of it in a spiraling or God's-eye pattern. You can even dangle feathers or beads from the handle. Some garden supply shops sell planting tools called dibbles, which are made of metal and wood. But they are not as exciting as making your own!

❧ **A Possession stick** will enable you to designate your garden space in a traditional Native way. Possession sticks were often used to designate wood pile caches in a village. Forage for sticks on the forest floor, then add ornamental details like colored yarn, feathers - or whatever moves you. Now you have your own possession stick to mark your own plot!

❧ **Are you thirsty after all this work?** To quench your thirst on a hot gardening day, make a birch-bark cup!

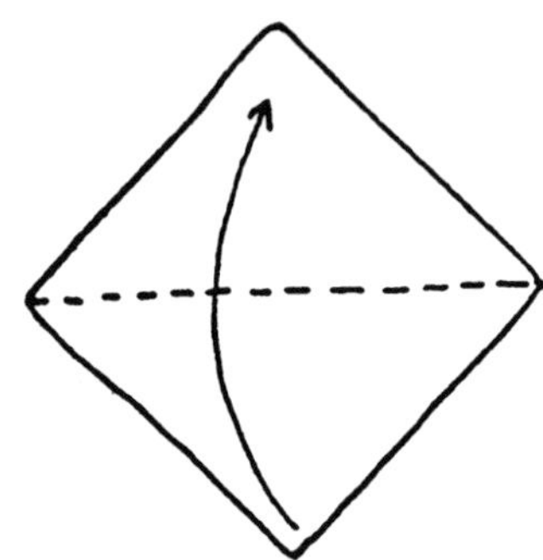

A Birch-Bark Cup

1) Fold an 8" x 8" piece of soaked and softened birch-bark in half to form a triangle.

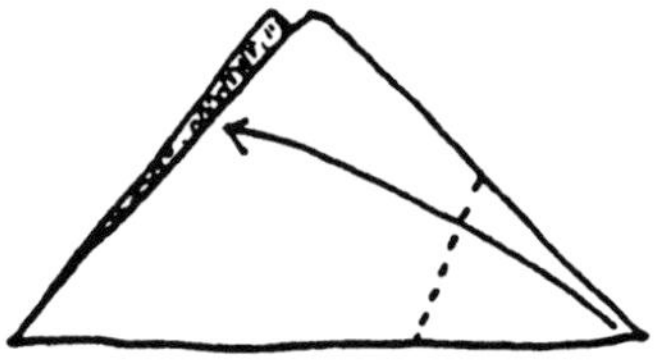

2) Fold the right corner to meet the left edge.

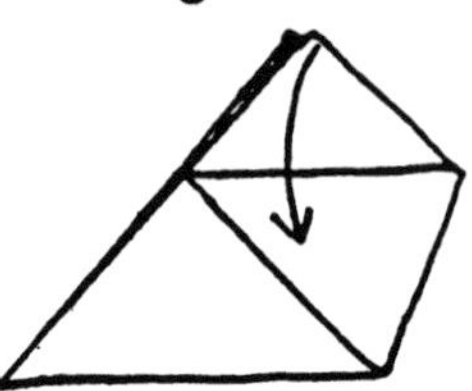

3) Bring the front top triangle down over the front flap.

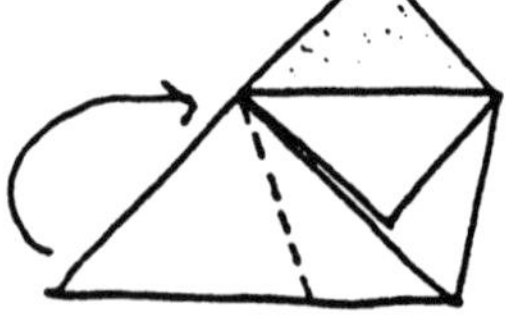

4) Fold the left corner to the *back* to meet the right edge.

5) Fold the remaining top triangle back down over the back flap.

6) Squeeze edges together to form a cup. Let harden in this position.

Planting Your Longhouse Garden

Growing a successful garden is an important process for any new or old Three Sisters gardener. Gather your Three Sisters and Brothers gardening partners for this exciting moment and plan a schedule for caring for your garden. For inspiration, look at the following suggestions regarding Three Sisters gardening practices.

❧ Break up into groups of Three Sisters and Brothers gardeners, three persons to a group. Decide which roles and tasks you would like to perform. Traditionally, the men prepared the fields for gardening after the sugaring season was finished. Crop residues from the prior year were burned, and the ashes used to sweeten the soil. Often, fields lay fallow, resting for a year so that the Earth could replenish herself. If a new field were needed the men would work with their axes, felling trees and burning them to clear a growing space.

The women's tasks in the garden mirrored their role of bearing and bringing forth life. They organized the mound preparations, the planting, hoeing, weeding, and harvest bees. They weeded and hoed while the children chased the crows and hungry deer from the gardens. They staggered the sowings so that all the food would not ripen at once. If the women's gardening season was successful, the abundant harvest enabled them to feed the entire village.

❧ **If you decide to follow Native American practices, plant four, six, or seven corn**

seeds per mound. These numbers reflect the directions, or life forces, which sustain the people. Four seeds represent North, East, South, and West. Six seeds represent North, East, South, West, Earth, and Sky. Seven seeds represent North, East, South, West, Earth, Sky, and Oneself, the child of all these elements. Since four corn plants work best in a two-foot mound, thin to four plants after several weeks growth by carefully pinching off the smallest plants. Never remove the entire corn plant because doing so may damage the young roots of its neighboring sisters.

Corn will not grow true if two different varieties mature in your garden at the same time. To be on the safe side, choose two varieties that mature weeks apart from one another. For example, choose a drying corn of 100 days and a popcorn of 85 days. Pollination by wind works best when corn is planted in blocks in the garden.

❧ **In two weeks, plan to sow two or three seeds of the pole bean around the emerging corn**, approximately three inches away from the corn plants and in the same mound. Sow bean seeds at a depth equal to the top knuckle of your thumb. Plant pole beans around the wickiup. Strings tied horizontally at one-foot intervals around the wickiup poles will serve as a trellis for Sister Bean. Flowering bean plants provide a nourishing nitrogen, which corn plants readily exhaust from the soil.

❧ Around the outer rim of the mound and at the same depth as the beans, **sow several squash and pumpkin seeds or seedlings**. Or - as you did with the corn - prepare squash in peat pots for transplanting. Once the squash seedlings are firmly established, thin them to two per mound. Thinnings can be placed in the compost or gently removed and transplanted to another garden.

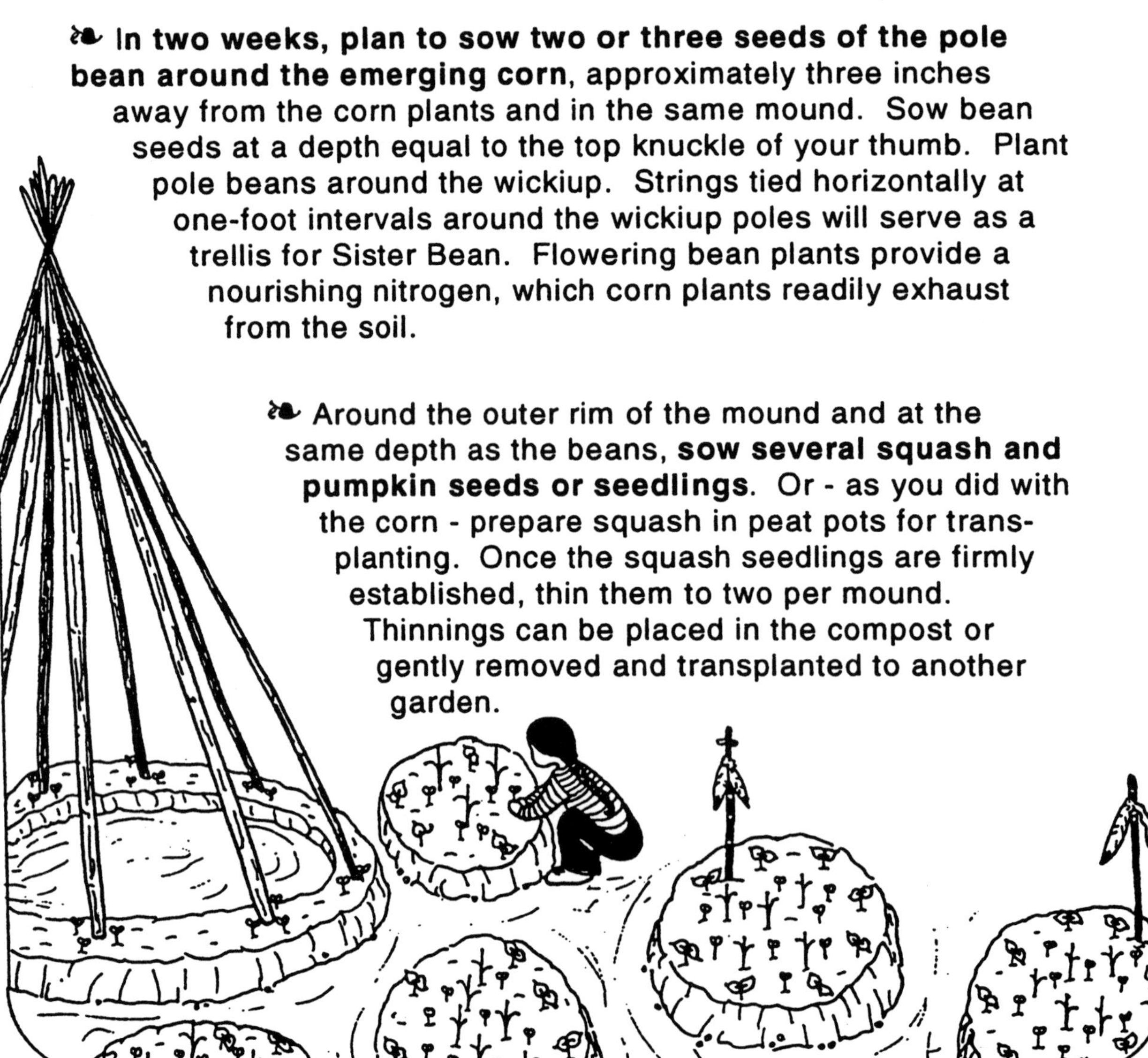

❧ **Embellish your Three Sisters with other plants of your choice** - sunflowers, gourds, lettuce, quick-growing radishes, and flowers. Cornflowers, marigolds, and zinnias attract pollinators to your Three Sisters garden.

❧ **Feasting and singing is a welcome custom during the planting ceremonies.** Traditionally, the women were the seed-sowers and tenders of the gardens, responsible for food acquisition and preparation. The men embellished the meal with food from the hunt. Today, both men and women tend the garden - and hunt, too! As a reward for your hard work, prepare some cornbread or popcorn sprinkled with margarine and nutritional yeast. Sing to the Earth, to the Sky, to the plants. Sing to each other!

This fine gardening tradition was the basis for the Iroquois nations', especially the Seneca's, large orchards and field crops. These Native American farms became recognized and admired by the European settlers as the breadbasket of the Northeast.

A Scarecrow in the Garden!

In Native American communities, it was the children's task to scare away marauding crows during the Dry Grass Moon in Summer, when ears of corn were ripening inside their protective husks. Corn was a staple of Native American diets, and it was crucial that none of the harvest be damaged or lost to the hungry winged ones. This tradition has existed in cornfields throughout the Americas for thousands of years.

❧ Today, the children have been replaced by scarecrows and family dogs. Scarecrows can be found in any type of garden. Have you have ever wondered how the first scarecrow came to the cornfields? Listen to the following story, created from our author's imagination.

"The Legend of the First Scarecrow"

It was a hot summer afternoon, and the waxing Harvest Moon was nearly full. Two more days and it would be time to harvest the succulent corn that grew on the tall stalks.

The children assigned to guard the corn were bored. They played games between the rows, their eyes and ears alert for the pesky black birds that cawed in the distance. But no crows had flown into the garden since the sun was four hands above the horizon, and now the red disc was sinking in the west.

Still, it was very hot. The restless children longed for a cooling breeze, for a swim in the creek. Little Bear was saying, "Nothing fun ever happens around here," when a strangely dressed figure approached them. He was very odd, indeed - he could walk and talk, yet he was clothed in rags and appeared to be stuffed with straw! He greeted the children with a jaunty smile as he hurdled the garden fence. Even more amazing, he picked five ears of corn and began to juggle them before the startled children could stop him. Seeing their astonished faces, he stopped jug-

gling for a moment and introduced himself.

"Greetings, my friends. I mean no harm. I am a good friend of Corn Spirit, who presides over this corn. You might say I am the corn's guardian spirit, for it is my task to travel from village to village to ensure a successful corn harvest."

The stranger then plucked a sixth ear of corn from the stalk and added it to his juggling game. After a few minutes of this he handed an ear to each child.

"These ears are ready to eat," he said.

He sat down with them to enjoy the fresh, sun-warmed corn. The sweet kernels melted in the children's mouths. When their bellies were full and their thirst quenched, they began to question the stranger.

"How long will you be with us?" Starflower asked.

"What is your name?" Runs With the Wind asked. "And where did you come from?"

Little Bear pulled at some straw sticking out of the stranger's cuffs as he wondered aloud, "Why do you have straw sticking out of your clothes?"

The stranger laughed and began to tell his story.

"My name," said the stuffed, ragged man, "is Talks With Winged Ones. I visit gardens just before the harvest. There I talk with the birds and try to persuade them to stay away from the corn until the harvest is in. In return for this favor, I promise the birds that they will never go hungry. As for this straw - well, that is what I am made of! If you look closely you will see that my head is a large pumpkin, my eyes are crab apples, my teeth are made of corn, and my hair is made of corn silk."

Indeed, when Talks With Winged Ones smiled, he exposed rows of multi-colored corn teeth, and his eyes shone like polished apples. Then the children noticed that his feet were actually ears of corn! And that was not all - his hands were small squashes, and his long green fingers were beans.

Still smiling, Talks With Winged Ones leaned over and

whispered to the circle of children at his feet. "Shhhh! Tonight I will hold council with the crows, and tomorrow I will leave shortly after sunrise. But do not fear - during the next seven suns the corn will be protected from the birds. It will ripen as it should, and you will be able to sneak away and play in the river. But let this be a secret between us!" His smile broadened. "At daybreak tomorrow, you will notice a surprise when you arrive in the garden."

The next morning, the children ran to the garden, eager to discover the surprise the stranger had mentioned. To their astonishment, they found him hanging on a post in the middle of the garden! He looked awfully uncomfortable. Thinking the crows had played a mean trick on their friend, they decided to rescue him. But as they struggled to lift him off the post, they realized they had been fooled. This was not Talks with Winged Ones, but a stuffed, floppy look-alike! And yet the look-alike worked wonderfully - for the crows did not appear at all that day.

To their delight, the children were able to abandon their duty and swim in the river during the hottest part of the day. They also took walks in the shady forest to collect nuts, roots, and tubers to eat. The children did not see the crows again until after the harvest, when the shiny black birds returned to the garden to scavenge the remains scattered upon the earth.

To the children's delight, the guardian of the corn appeared seven suns before the harvest every Summer thereafter. By the light of the waxing Harvest Moon, he held council with the crows. At daybreak he was gone, leaving his twin hanging from a post in the middle of the garden.

As time went on, the children realized they no longer had to guard the corn at all. All they had to do was make a floppy twin - and the crows would stay away from the corn.

And that is how the scarecrow came to be! *Ho!*

❧ If you do not have time to act as a scarecrow for your Three Sisters garden, design something to do the job for you. But remember - once Sister Squash begins to grow, she will do her share to discourage four-legged visitors!

What can you do to deter birds from your garden?

Make a Scarecrow!

1) Lash two sticks together in the shape of a T.

2) Stuff an old grain sack with old clothes, rags, leaves, or plastic bags. Attach the sack to the top of the T as a head.

3) Tie bundles of feathers together. Dangle streamers of old fabric and the bundles of feathers from the crosspiece. Using a variety of recyclable materials, create a personality for your scarecrow.

4) Bury the scarecrow pole in a six- to eight-inch hole so that the wind will not blow it over.

How Do Seeds Germinate?

Seeds germinate below the ground, incubating in the darkness of the Earth. They simply require the right amount of warmth and moisture and a place for the roots to grow to call home. There are other things, of course, which will enhance plant growth, as the following story, written by our authors, explains.

"Three Sisters and the Moon"

Grandmother called to the children sleeping beneath the starlit sky. "Come from your beds, my chil dren, Grandmother Moon calls the seeds to rise."

The children did not fully understand their grandmother's words, yet her voice seemed full of magic. Quietly, in the hush of the moon's bright glow, they walked beneath the shadows of tree and cloud to the field, where a short time ago they had planted the Three Sisters. At the garden's edge Grandmother spoke softly to the Earth. She spoke with a kindness in her heart that was so full it seemed to reach out and touch the children as well. Glancing at one another, the children wondered what was about to happen.

Leaving her shoes at the garden's edge, Grandmother entered the garden. Grandmother often walked with bare feet because she liked touching the Earth Mother. She said she could receive Earth's messages and feel Her strength when she walked in this manner. The children removed their shoes and silently followed. Grandmother bent toward the mounds and sang a growing song to the seeds cradled deep in the belly of the Earth. As the children gathered around the mounds, they were surprised to see the green, feather-like corn stalks shimmering beneath Grandmother Moon's light. They were even more astonished to see that some bean seeds, enclosed in oval green cases, had risen from the Earth. These seeds reflected Grandmother Moon's light, resembling her round face.

All things seemed to mirror the moon on this night. Grandmother seemed as wise as Grandmother Moon herself, the soft light glowing around her bent body as she sang to the cradled seeds.

Walking home from the garden that evening, the children whispered to their grandmother, "How did you know the green children would be there to hear your song, Grandmother?"

Grandmother then told them what the Moon had told her long ago. "In the fullest light of the Moon's face dwells a power of Sun and Moon and Water, which calls to the spirit of the Earth. This power beckons the plants to rise to the light of the Sun, to grow full-heartedly upon the face of their Mother Earth. It is in this time of the fullest moonlight that the spirits of Earth and Sky and Water rise up and dance together. Those who wish to strengthen their own growing power may dance and sing with the green children as the plants greet the light of the world. Together you can dance your growing dance, sing your growing songs. And so it is, my children."

The children fell back to sleep as Grandmother hummed a growing song beneath the light of the moon.

❧ The ancient method of planting according to the moon's phases is still practiced today.

The gravitational pull of the moon, which causes high tides, also affects water levels in growing plants. Seeds planted during the new moon can absorb more water from the soil because as the moon "waxes," or grows full, the moon's gravity pulls the water to the surface. But as the full moon "wanes," or begins to decline, so does the force of its gravitational pull. Now the Earth's gravity increases, and the water sinks deeper into the soil.

Root and foliar growth also wax or wane with the moon's rhythms. As the new moon grows to its full phase, the increased light stimulates leaf growth. Root growth is just the opposite - as the full moon declines, root growth increases. Can you guess why root growth increases with the moon's decline?

❧ Would you like to plant your crops according to the lunar calendar? By conducting an experiment, you can discover firsthand how the moon influences seed germination.

A Moonlight Experiment

1) Plant some vegetables according to the lunar calendar so that they will germinate during the new moon. Germination rates can be determined by checking seed catalogues or seed packets.

2) Plant additional vegetables of the same variety so that they will germinate during the full moon or during its other phases.

3) Chart and compare the results in your journal. According to your experiment, how does the moon influence plant life?

❧ How might the moon influence animal or human activities? What are some benefits of being a lunar gardener?

Three Sisters Helping Each Other

How can we garden in the same spirit of cooperation as the Three Sisters?

❧ You may have noticed that many plants and animals have special methods or systems of cooperation, whereby one plant or animal actually aids another, and vice versa. This cooperative, natural process is known as "**symbiosis.**" The Three Sisters have a symbiotic relationship.

❧ You can think of the Three Sisters as **companions** in the garden - and they truly are! Look at the Three Sisters growing alongside one another. How do you see them helping each other? Notice how **Sister Corn's** strength increases as she steadily reaches for the sky. Does she act as a trellis, a support for Sister Bean?

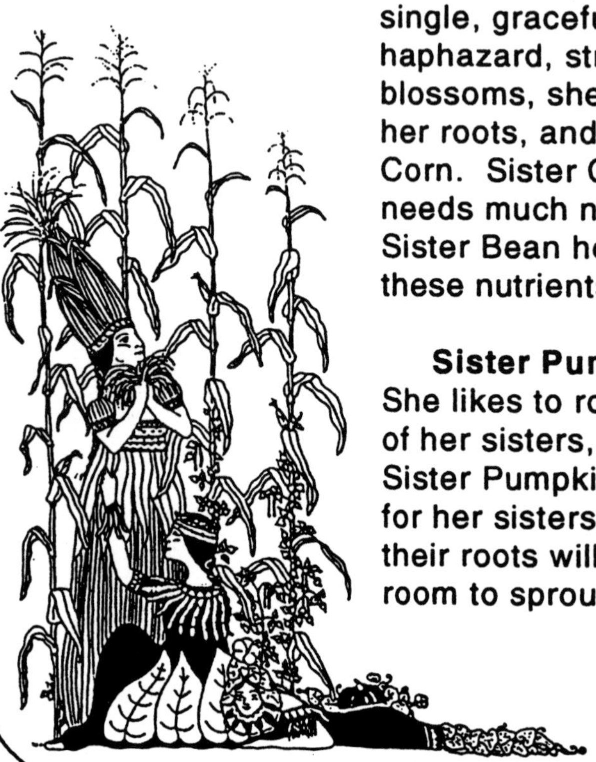

As **Sister Bean** winds her way up and around Sister Corn, notice how she rises in a single, graceful rhythmical spiral, rather than a haphazard, strangling mess. As Sister Bean blossoms, she draws nitrogen from the air into her roots, and actually feeds the roots of Sister Corn. Sister Corn is a hungry feeder, and needs much nourishment from the soil to grow. Sister Bean helps her Sister by replenishing these nutrients.

Sister Pumpkin has a wandering nature. She likes to roam and ramble around the feet of her sisters, who take up little room. As Sister Pumpkin wanders, she provides shade for her sisters, trapping the earth's moisture so their roots will not dry out. Weeds hardly find room to sprout as she covers the Earth with her carpet of leaves! The prickly spines on her stem and leaves are unfriendly to raccoon or deer, who might otherwise enjoy feasting here. The living mulch she provides is of great benefit to her sisters.

What additional flowers and herbs work in symbiotic relationship with the Three Sisters?

❧ **List all the jobs you and your sister and brother gardeners can share, and make a calendar of when to do them throughout the gardening season.** These jobs might include seed-sowing, feeding seedlings, watering, thinning seedlings, scaring away crows, weeding, or mulching. You might find it fun to imitate the Three Sisters' spirit of cooperation by dividing gardeners into groups of Three Sisters gardeners and Three Brothers gardeners. Let the Three Sisters' wisdom inspire you as you plan and care for your Longhouse Garden.

SUMMER

Summer ❧

Among the flowers I am moving reverently.
Among the flowers I am singing, dancing.
Berries ripen,
Fruits ripen.

- old Seneca chant

WELCOME TO SUMMER: TENDING YOUR THREE SISTERS GARDEN

Summer contains many joys, not the least of which is watching your Three Sisters grow! Now is the time when Sister Corn, Sister Bean and Sister Squash stretch and grow and finally burst into flower and fruit. The garden is growing before your very eyes!

❧ In Summer, your Three Sisters need more care than at any other time of year - they hope you will not forget about them! This presents an opportunity for you to practice a "caretaker mind" toward your Three Sisters.

A "caretaker mind" is an attitude of generosity and caring. If you carry the right attitude in your heart while doing garden chores, you will feel it grow within you. Try to establish gardening practices that contribute to the overall good feeling of a "caretaker mind." Can you create guidelines that will help you enjoy your garden tasks?

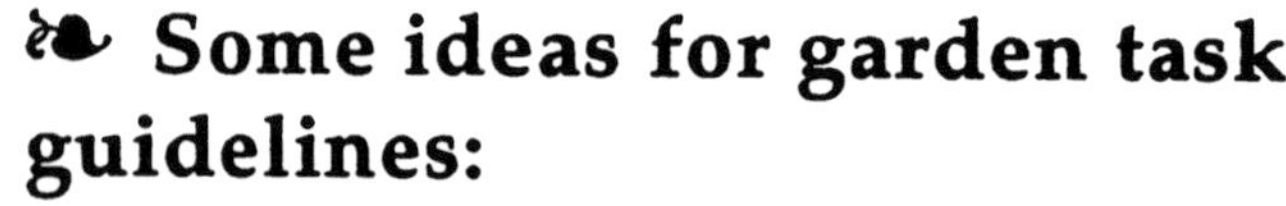

❧ Some ideas for garden task guidelines:

♠ **Study the area in and around your garden every day.** The entire Earth is a garden, or habitat. It provides order, balance, and life for many creatures. To increase your awareness of the earth as a garden, reflect regularly on your environment. How does the adjoining lawn or grove of trees, raincloud or sunlight nourish your garden? Take the time to appreciate how all these elements cooperate in providing life for you and your garden partners - like toad and dragonfly, mouse and earthworm, bluebird and sparrow. Before beginning your day's work, make a brief tour of the garden. Drink in the colors, shapes, fragrances, and harmonies that exist there.

♠ **Do your gardening during the cool, early morning or late afternoon hours.** Take a tip from birds and insects, who are more active during the cool part of the day. Spending time in the garden with these natural partners is an added bonus. Bird and insect activity will provide you with a general sense of the garden's health, as well as adding song to your day. Take note of the elements of your garden that work well together, and appreciate this wonderful plan. If you see areas that need attention, make a mental note to offer some assistance. Try to avoid a "conquer and control" attitude towards garden problems. Instead, ask your garden: "What Earth-friendly assistance do you need?"

♠ **If you find certain garden tasks strenuous, do them only for short periods of time.** For example, spading or hoeing can cause blisters and backache - a challenge for developing a "caretaker mind"! Rotate these chores with a garden partner, or do the task for short periods of time. A gentle, stretching warm-up is fun to do alongside your garden. (See the yoga stretches in *Be A Frog, A Bird, or A Tree* by Rachel Carr listed in the Bibliography.)

♠ **On a hot, sunny day, the cool earth beneath your feet can refresh you!** Try gardening barefoot, unless you are using tools which demand foot protection. Does being barefoot cause you to move in a gentle manner? Gardening barefoot is certain to strengthen an attitude of "caretaker mind."

♠ **Provide gardens with adequate water.** Wilting plants are indications of water depletion - they need immediate attention! Gardens should be watered in the early morning. Plants are very thirsty at that time, for they do most of their growing in the morning. Also, little water evaporation takes place in the early morning hours, so the soil gets a good soaking. Mulching your garden in late Spring, after the soil has warmed up, is a good soil conservation practice. Practice water conservation by collecting rainwater in rain barrels. This is a wise practice in areas of low rainfall or drought. Use the rainwater for all your gardening needs.

♠ **If you garden during the heat of the day, wear sunscreen and a hat.** Bring along a cool jug of water or lemonade. Moisten a bandana with water and tie it around your neck or forehead to keep your body cool. Whistle your favorite garden song, and quit working when you get tired. Singing will help you to maintain a "caretaker mind"! (If you do not know any good gardening tunes, see the one called "The Earth Is My Mother" on page 8 of this activity.)

❧ **Don't let weeds challenge your "caretaker mind."** The best time to weed is after a soaking rainfall, when the ground has drained and the plants have dried. Remember, a weed is a wild relative of your Three Sisters. Take a moment to determine whether the weed plays a role in maintaining your garden's health. Is it a legume, which provides nitrogen to the soil? Is it a living mulch, preventing other unwanted plants from taking root? Is it a single, beautiful weed that attracts butterflies, bees, or your admiration? But if the weed is "out of place," remove it. Don't be surprised if you find yourself admiring its incredible root system - especially if you must struggle to remove it from its home! Place it in the compost. That way it will contribute to the garden's cycle. Using weeds as compost insures that they bring their qualities to the garden - giving the soil the nutrients it likely needs - without taking up standing room.

❧ **Plan regular visits to your garden to observe quiet moments or conduct mini-celebrations.** If you have a special place to sit in your garden, go there to draw, listen, daydream - or snack on the first wild strawberries of the season! Don't miss the opportunity to take a monthly walk in your garden beneath the full moon. Numerous nocturnal events in a garden, such as a full moon or a star dazzled sky, provide a kind of magic you will never forget.

Want To Do More?

❧ **What happens when an ear of corn falls to the earth and germinates?** Ancient peoples discovered that when an ear of corn fell to the earth, seeds competed for space and nourishment. Observe this phenomenon for yourself in the following experiment:

The Too-Many-Seeds Experiment

1) Remove the husks and silk from an ear of corn, but let the kernels remain intact on the cob. (If you do not have an ear of corn, use the seed head of a wheat plant in the experiment.)

2) Plant part of the ear of corn, keeping it well watered.

3) Observe what happens to the closely spaced kernels.

What must be done to assist the corn so that it is properly planted?

❧ **By interacting with and tending the Three Sisters, you can develop a feeling of connectedness with the plant world**. Such an experience instills in a person a responsible, caring attitude towards life. Ancient peoples developed a similar partnership with the Three Sisters, especially corn, which insured that the crops would nourish future generations. Today, corn is still celebrated as one of the major food crops of the world. Through your experiences in your Three Sisters garden, you can join with Native cultures in celebrating corn, beans, and squash as partners in life.

❧ **Singing a song is always a good way to celebrate!** This song is perfect for thoughts of caretaker mind.

"The Earth Is My Mother"

The Earth is my Mother, she's good to
me,
She gives me everything that I ever
need.
The food on the table, the clothes I wear,
The sun and the water and the clean
fresh air.
There is just one thing she asks of me,
I treat her as kindly as she treats me!
I treat her as kindly as she treats me!

\- Carol Johnson

The Earth Is My Mother
Carol Johnson
D
1. The earth is my moth-er, the earth is my moth-er, She's
2. Her ways are gen-tle, her ways are gen-tle, Her
Em G
good to me, she's good to me. She gives me ev' - ry -
life is strong, her life is strong. Liv - in' in
D A7 D G
thing that I ev - er need. She gives me ev' - ry -
tune like a beau - ti - ful song. Liv - in' in
D A7 D
thing that I ev - er need. Food on the
tune like a beau - ti - ful song. There's just one
Em
ta - ble, food on the ta - ble, the clothes I wear, the
thing, there's just one thing she asks of me, she
G D
clothes I wear, the sun and the wa - ter and the
asks of me, I treat her as kind - ly as
A7 D G D
cool fresh air, the sun and the wa - ter and the
she treats me. I treat her as kind - ly as
A7 D D F♯m G
cool fresh air. The earth is our moth-er and our best friend
she treats me.
D G A7 D
too, the great pro - vid - er for me and you. The
Copyright © 1981 Noeldner Music (BMI) P.O. Box 6351, Grand Rapids, MI 49516. Used by Permission.

Sister Corn

Journey With Sister Corn

The individual journeys you will take with the Three Sisters are wonderful guides for reviewing seasonal plant development. You might find them useful in Autumn, just prior to harvest. Drawings of the stages of growth can be recorded in nature journals. In this way you can document the adventures of the Three Sisters.

❧ Come along on a journey with Sister Corn as she grows through the Spring, Summer, and Autumn. If you wish, reproduce the following description and hang it on your garden bulletin board.

Sister Corn begins her journey in the darkness of Mother Earth. She emerges from her dark home when the earth is warmed by the spring sun and moistened by the spring rains. As the kernel appears, it sends a root deep into the earthen home that gave her life.

A green feather shoots up from this kernel. The feather greets the spring sky above the belly-shaped mound encircling her. Day after day, bathed in sunlight and raindrops, Sister Corn Feather rises as a green child upon the Mother Earth. Watch her as she grows taller and stronger. Watch her leaves bend back towards the Earth, much as a young child's arm gropes for its mother's hand.

Throughout the Summer, Sister Corn grows taller and taller. She seems to seek the sky, to reach for it. She is crowned by a tassel, which shimmers in the wind. Soon golden pollen beads appear, covering the tassel crown with their richness. These golden pollen jewels cling to the tassel, the father, which harbors them until the winds carry them below to the mother silk.

Feel the soft, moist, bright silk, which dangles from the small husk of the mother parts. The golden pollen travels along these silky threads to reside within the husk. Do you see the small protective husk which surrounds the silky threads? Here the mother and father energy combine to form the milky seeds.

After a long, healthy growing season, fed by nutrients from the earth and sky, the young, milky seeds grow fuller. Gently squeeze the cob. You can feel the milky seeds spring under your touch as the cob grows larger each week. Traditionally, when the milky seeds are full and cover the cob with their abundance, it is time for the Green Corn Ceremony. Express your thankfulness to Sister Corn, then enjoy a raw ear of "green corn." It is sweet and milky, not dry or as ripe as the cornmeal kernel you will grind at harvest time.

When the milky seeds are fully mature, the silky threads dry to a rich brown color. According to tradition, this signals the upcoming harvest. After the harvest, another ceremony of thankfulness takes place, this one lasting three days.

❧ Opening the fully dry husks is a moment to treasure! Hidden within each one are the jewels of the harvest, for no two ears are the same in their beauty. When you remove the silks and peel back the husks, look at the perfect organization of each seed on the cob. Not long ago a golden bead of pollen traveled from the father part of Sister Corn to the silky mother part, signaling the formation of these seeds.

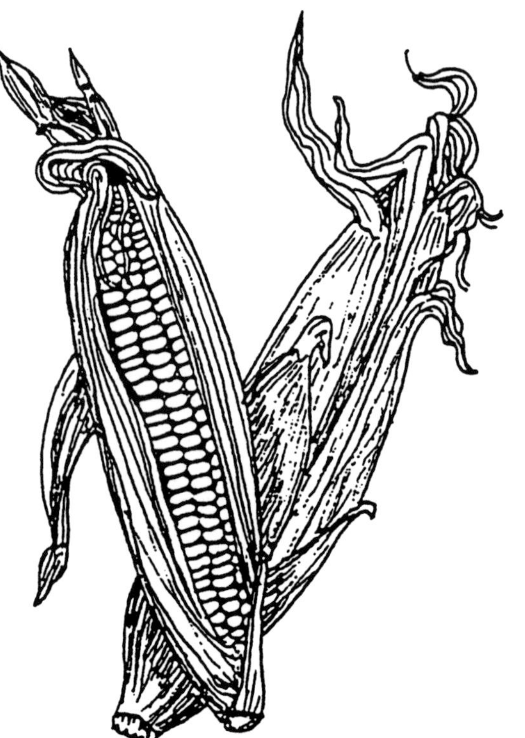

❧ The husks protected and cradled each forming seed as it grew to this fullness. Silks and husks can be dried and used to make beautiful crafts, or composted to enrich the mounds next growing season.

❧ The seeds can provide food for you today. Or they can become your seeds for tomorrow, for they are ready to begin their journey back into the Mother Earth, where they will be cradled in darkness as the cycle of life begins anew.

Math, Nature's Way

❧ Corn had a high value for the ancient peoples of the world, just as it does for many contemporary Native cultures. How could you use corn to establish a trade or barter system?

❧ Appreciate corn for its own inherent order and patterns. What can you learn from a simple ear of corn? How many rows are there on an ear? Are the kernels arranged in a special way so that they fit together

Sister Bean

Journey With Sister Bean

Imagine a journey with Sister Bean as she grows through the Spring, Summer, and Autumn. If you wish, reproduce the following journey and hang it on your garden bulletin board.

Sister Bean emerges from Mother Earth's deep, dark cradle with a strength that may surprise you. If you watch closely, you will see Sister Bean raising the earth up and out of the way as she lifts her strong, fleshy bean head into the light of Spring. Later, the bean head assumes a position below the plant's tender leaves, which lead the way higher and higher around Sister Corn.

Do the first leaves lead the way to the top of the bean vine, with other leaves filling in below them? Or do sets of leaves grow above the older leaves, racing skyward as they spiral around Sister Corn?

How does Sister Bean reach skyward? Do you see the vine spiraling, reaching for something to coil itself around? Like a dancer, the bean vine circles smoothly without losing her direction, eventually weaving her way up Sister Corn. Observe the direction in which Sister Bean weaves and spirals. What else in Nature have you observed that spirals or moves in this dance of the directions? Can you find out what creates this harmonic dance?

If Sister Bean seems to need a guiding hand to attach herself to a wickiup string or trellis, take part in a helping relationship by assisting her in her dance. In which direction will you move together?

Sister Bean has the amazing power to nourish her hungry Sister Corn. Her roots lie deep beneath the earth. Lightning and rain, bearing gifts from the sky, carry nutrients down to nourish these roots. Later, Sister Bean releases the nutrients and shares them with other sisters, especially hungry Sister Corn. Naturally, you will want to look at her incredible roots! But do not disturb Sister Bean while she is growing. Instead, remember to look at them at the end of the garden season when you carry Sister Bean to the compost. Search for tiny nodules, or bumps, on her roots. Here lies the amazing adaptation which allows Sister Bean to be of assistance, in a symbiotic or helping way, to her other sisters. These nodules or bumps allow her to release nitrogen into the soil.

Because the flowers of Sister Bean are not ordinary, they are worth a close-up look. Do you see parts of the flower that seem inflated? Do they look a bit like pillows? Do you see the pistil and stamen, the male and female parts of the flower? Watch for the pollinators who come to Sister Bean. What do they do? How do the flowers change from day to day?

Before long, the slender beginnings of Sister Bean dangle from the blossoms. Watch each week as these slender threads fill out and become a fleshy pod, which may curve gently like a canoe. The pods seem to dangle and sway in the breeze, moving to Sister Bean's spiral dance. As they fill out, you might wonder about the strange bulging shapes which seem to be bursting within the pods. Each pod is a treasure box that holds the secret gifts of Sister Bean, not to be revealed until the season of the Great Give Away.

Your patience will be rewarded, for when the first frost approaches and the pods seem about to burst open, the time of the Great Give Away has arrived! As you open each treasure box pod, you will find beautiful, jewel-like shapes. Add

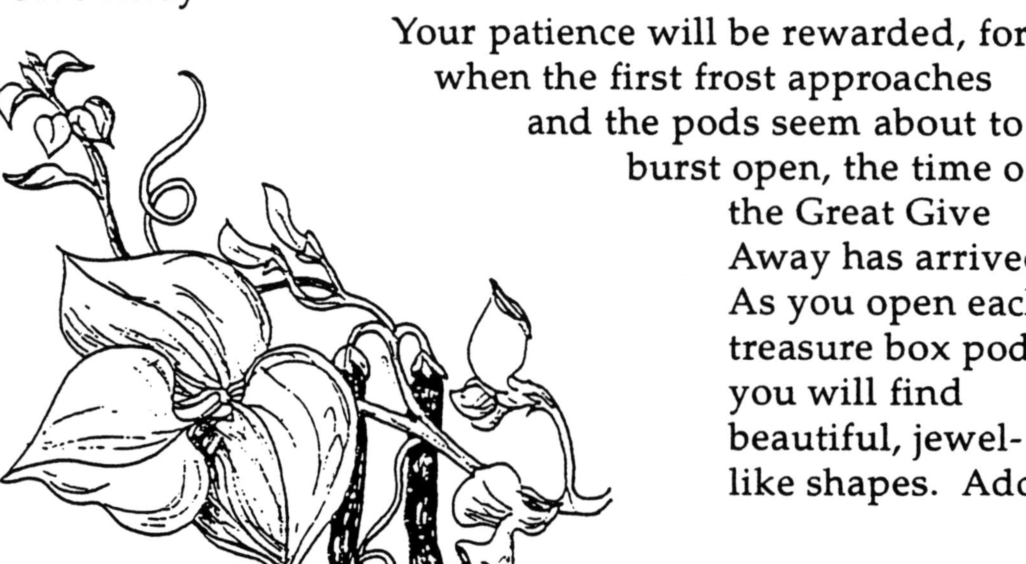

these jewels to a soup or stew, or keep them for yet another generation of Three Sisters.

> ☛ ***Note:*** *The Bean Sister described here is a climbing bean, such as the Scarlet Runner Bean. Other varieties of climbing or bush beans have similar, yet unique, qualities. If you wish, grow one of the other varieties, and adapt the nature study accordingly.*

Sister Squash
CSP

JOURNEY WITH SISTER SQUASH

This journey with Sister Squash follows her as she grows through the Spring, Summer, and Autumn. If you wish, reproduce the journey and hang it on your garden bulletin board.

As in the growing cycle of her two sisters, Sister Squash lies quietly for a time in the belly-shaped, earthen mound. Her roots reach deep at first, then green, juicy, baby leaves sprout. Sometimes the baby leaves wear the seed for a cap. But soon Sister Squash's large, quick-growing leaves shed the seed cap and her true leaves appear just above her baby leaves.

Look carefully at these true leaves, for they differ from the baby cotyledon that originally emerged from the earth. Do you see a lobed leaf with strong veins? Are the colors above and below the leaf the same? Sister Squash's task of defending her two sisters from raccoons and deer begins right away. If you look carefully around her stem and leaf, you will find the prickly protection she provides.

The first true leaves and those that follow grow upon a vining stalk. Soon a tendril curls and coils from this stalk, ready to reach out and support Sister Squash if she needs to climb a fence or bush.

Observe the golden flowers when they bloom. There are mother and father flowers. Both types of flowers have five starry, bell-shaped lobes. Each morning a star-shaped flower holds its blossom up to the morning star, the sun. After the morning star has poured down its light for awhile, the star shape becomes more like a vessel - as if the golden squash flower is trying to capture and hold every beam the morning star sends its way. Both the mother and father flowers greet the morning star, but if you look closely you will see that the two flowers are not exactly the same.

Can you tell the difference between the male and female flowers? The mother blossom, or female, is the one with the small, round green globe behind the blossom. This green globe will later develop into a pumpkin if it receives the pollen produced in the father, or male, blossom. Look into the male blossom and you will see golden pollen clustered on the long stamen. Can you smell the nectar the bees are searching for? Look at your nose - you are wearing some of Sister Squash's male flower pollen! How does the pollen travel from the female flowers to the male flowers? A bit of quiet observation might reveal the answer.

Watch what happens to the green globe as Summer passes. You might have to search below Sister Pumpkin's prickly leaves, which spread like a carpet across the feet of her other sisters, to find the globe. The ground beneath these umbrella-like leaves is moist because the sun cannot strike the earth. On the outside of the globe, you will see a glossy young skin. This skin will change color and become leather-like as the Summer progresses. What you cannot see is that inside the growing globe the seeds are cradled in a stringy hammock of squash flesh and are growing larger each day.

Even a beginner Three Sisters gardener can tell when Sister Pumpkin is ripe. Thump the pumpkin with your knuckles and listen to its earthy, drum-like sound. A very ripe pumpkin may lose its stem when you try to pick it up by its natural handle. If it does, you will discover a wonderful surprise. Do you see the shape of a five-pointed star? This was once the blossom that greeted the morning star!

THREE SISTERS GUIDE TO ORGANIC INSECT REMEDIES

Six-leggeds are a natural part of the circle of life. A healthy garden can occasionally withstand six-legged visitors, but the best way to prevent damage is to tackle any problems with the insects when they are first sighted.

❧ Here are some tips for Three Sisters gardeners regarding six-legged neighbors.

♠ **Healthy soil in the Three Sisters mounds creates a healthy garden.** And a healthy garden will usually discourage whole nations of six-legged visitors!

♠ **Remember to stay out of wet gardens!** Diseases may be spread unknowingly by gardeners when they tend the Three Sisters. This is especially true on wet days. Much as a bee deposits pollen, diseases can be transmitted by wet shoes, sleeves, and pant cuffs. Diseases invite six-leggeds to feast in your garden.

♠ **Weeds are wildflowers** that sometimes have a place in a cultivated garden. Some weeds are edible. Some weeds are natural groundcovers that prevent more invasive weeds from taking root as well as retain moisture in the garden. But sometimes they can become shelters for harmful six-leggeds. Care should be applied when making a decision about whether a weed is helpful or not.

♠ **Marigolds and nasturtiums** planted around the Three Sisters will repel six-leggeds.

♠ **If you see insects,** catch some in a magnifier box and try to identify them. Many insects benefit the garden and should be

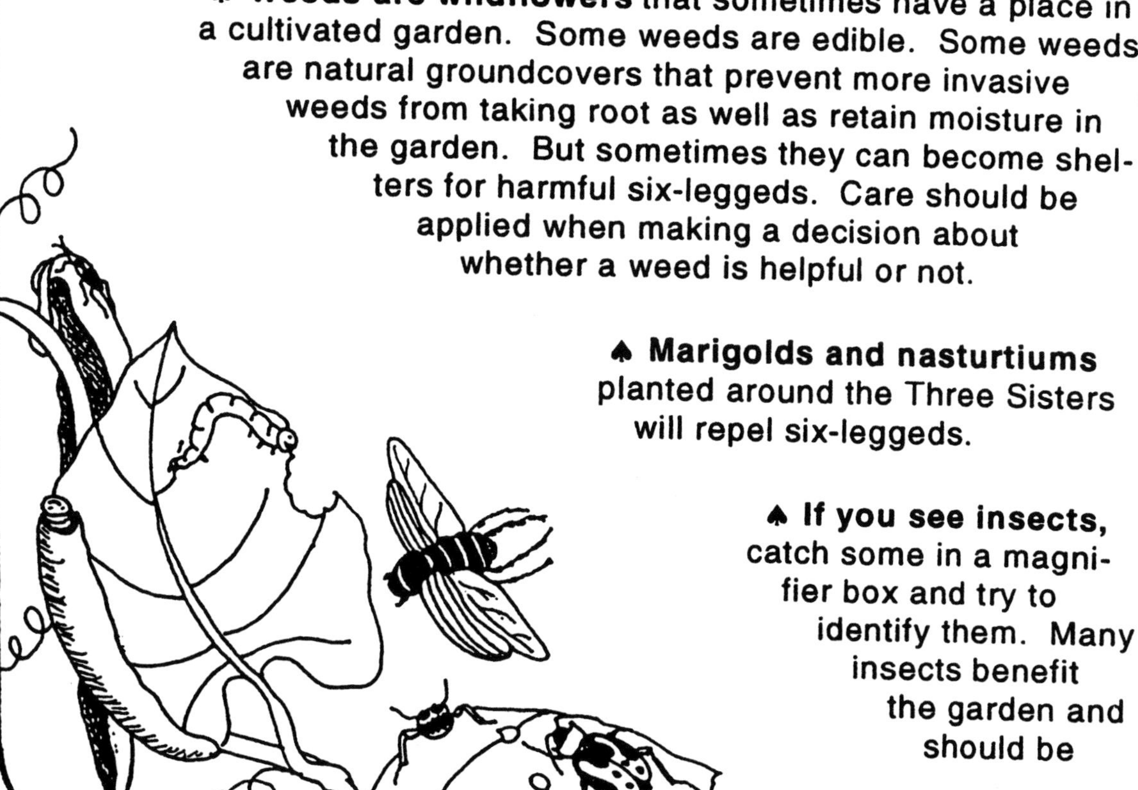

encouraged to take up summer-long residence among the Three Sisters. Some beneficial insects are ladybugs, praying mantises, bees, butterflies, ground beetles, lacewings, and wasps.

♠ **If you discover insects eating your Three Sisters,** blast them off with hose water. Or hand-pick them off and drop them into a bucket of water (don't forget to say "Sorry"!).

♠ **Brew up some spicy, smelly tea and apply it to your plants.** Most likely the insects will decide they would rather dine elsewhere. Here is a simple recipe for making a gallon of insect-deterrent tea:

Beastly Bug Tea

Blend a bulb of garlic,
one onion,
one hot pepper and
a gallon of water.
Strain the liquid, then spray or sprinkle it on your
Three Sisters.

❧ Reproduce the following "Three Sisters Organic Insect Remedies" and hang it on your garden bulletin board or garden shed door.

Remedies for Pesky Insects

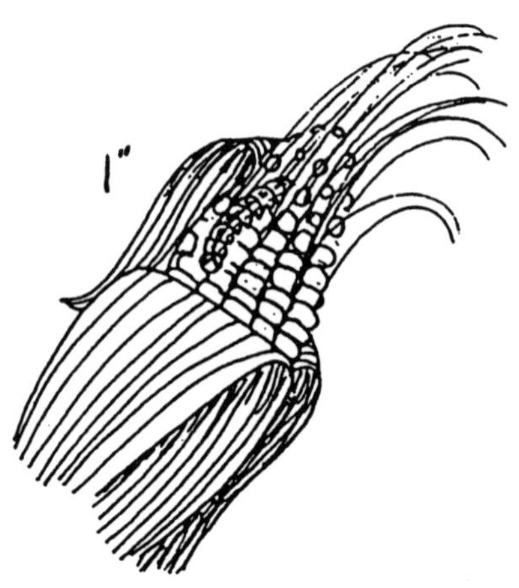

❧ Six-legged visitors to Sister Corn include **Corn Earworm.** This striped caterpillar is light yellow or green or brown, and has a yellow head. Corn Earworm takes up shelter inside the ear of corn, where it munches contentedly on the tender kernels. Once it is inside the ear, you will not notice its presence until you husk a juicy ear for yourself. But don't worry - you won't eat a Corn Earworm by mistake! They are easy to see. And they usually leave plenty of kernels for you to eat. Remove Corn Earworms and spent kernels by cutting them away with a knife. If you find a lot of Corn Earworms, spray the spicy insect-deterrent tea onto the brown silks of each ear of corn.

❧ Six-legged visitors to Sister Bean include the **Mexican Bean Beetle.** These beetles are the size of your fingertip. Some people think that Mexican Bean Beetles resemble Ladybeetle - also known as Ladybug - because their bodies are covered with black dots. Upon closer inspection, however, you will see that Mexican Bean Beetle has a yellow- to coppery-brown shell. Look on the underside of Sister Bean's leaves for clusters of tiny, pinpoint-size yellow eggs. These eggs can be crushed by running your thumb over them. This will prevent future generations of Mexican Bean Beetles from inhabiting your garden. Mature Mexican Bean Beetles quickly fly off when you approach them. If Mexican Bean Beetles begin to reduce Sister Bean's lovely, lush green leaves to skeletons, get rid of them with the garlic, insect-deterrent tea.

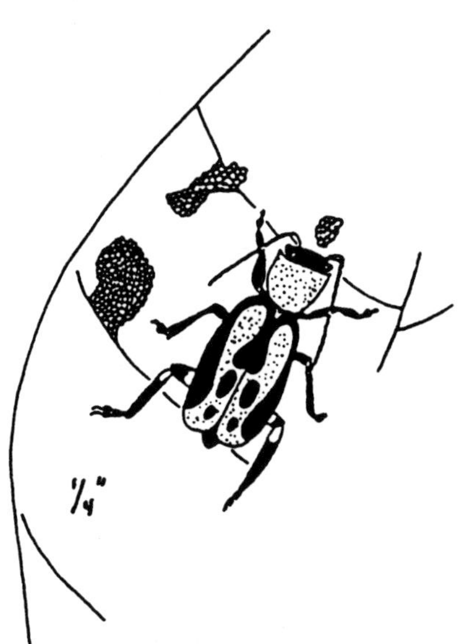

Two families of six-legged visitors may hide beneath Sister Squash's large, prickly leaves:

❧ **Squash Borer** is a white worm with a brown head. One way to tell whether Squash Borer is active is to look for wilting vines. These worms hide within Sister Squash's stem, so check near the base of her stem for yellow deposits that resemble sawdust. If you want to get rid of Squash Borer, carefully slit the stem and take the worm out. If you want to strengthen Sister Squash afterwards, look for a joint in her stem. Cover this joint with damp soil or mulch, and encourage Sister Squash to root there.

❧ **Squash Bug** loves to wander along the underside of Sister Squash's leaves, or to rest in the cool, moist canopy provided by those leaves. Oftentimes you will find a group of Squash Bugs gathered beneath the canopy, clustered around the mound near the plant's stem. Look for a triangular-shaped shield on the bug's upper back. All "true bug" family members can be identified by this triangular shield. Since Squash Bugs spread disease, hand-pick them from the plant. You will have to be fast, though, because these gray-to-brown Squash Bugs can move quickly! One way to deter Squash Bugs is to spread wood ashes around Sister Squash. If the plant is seriously damaged, bury Sister Squash's vine every few feet. This will help the plant re-root itself, which will prevent it from dying.

☛ ***Remember:*** using chemicals to control insects is not in the best interest of your Three Sisters, the earth, or your diet! Besides, it is rare to lose an entire crop to insects. If you do lose an entire crop, it may better to offer that crop up to "experience," and the following year take better precautionary measures to insure the health and vitality of your garden.

Summer Care for the Longhouse Garden

Gardening throughout the summer months requires organization to insure a successful harvest.

❧ **Who will care for the Three Sisters during the summer months?** Organize parents and elders to support you in caring for your garden during the Summer.

❧ **Weekly maintenance and a check list of garden tasks can be displayed on a community bulletin board or in a tool shed.** Reproduce the garden outline on the following pages as a way of insuring that your Three Sisters garden is cared for during the Summer.

Be sure to include some cooperative games, in the spirit of the Three Sisters, when you gather for gardening tasks!

❧ The story of the Three Sisters will always continue. The unexpected magic of the seasons and cycles will always bring your journey full circle. The story is in the seed you sow. Our story to bring us full circle is "The Legend of Indian Summer." What will your story be?

Summer Garden Sign-up Calendar

❧ Gardening throughout the summer months requires a bit of organizing to insure a successful harvest. Who will care for the Three Sisters during the summer months?

	First Week	Second Week	Third Week	Fourth Week
Water				
Weed				
Mulch				
Fertilize				
Thin Seedlings				
Insect Remedies				

JUNE

Summer Garden Sign-up Calendar

❧ Gardening throughout the summer months requires a bit of organizing to insure a successful harvest. Who will care for the Three Sisters during the summer months?

	First Week	Second Week	Third Week	Fourth Week
Water				
Weed				
Mulch				
Fertilize				
Thin Seedlings				
Insect Remedies				

JULY

Summer Garden Sign-up Calendar

❧ Gardening throughout the summer months requires a bit of organizing to insure a successful harvest. Who will care for the Three Sisters during the summer months?

	First Week	Second Week	Third Week	Fourth Week
Water				
Weed				
Mulch				
Fertilize				
Thin Seedlings				
Insect Remedies				

AUGUST

How Indian Summer Came To Be

Although Summer is drawing to a close, every year there is a special reprieve called Indian Summer. The following story of the seasons, written by our authors, describes nature's way of waving a final farewell. Listen, and you will discover why Summer returns to issue a brief, gentle good-bye before the earth settles into a long, deep rest - a rest she sorely needs before beginning yet another season in the Three Sisters garden.

"The Legend of Indian Summer"

When the Earth was young, there were only two seasons: Winter and Summer. Eventually Spring and Fall came along to ease the transition between the two. The new seasons made it easier for the plants and creatures to adjust. Fall gave them time to prepare for the cold, snowy months, while Spring allowed them to wake up from Winter's long sleep.

And then an odd thing happened. Winter fell in love with Spring, and Summer fell in love with Fall. Both couples were so smitten that they forgot their responsibilities. When Summer courted Fall, one part of the Earth baked in perpetual Summer. And when Winter frolicked across the snowy landscape with Spring, another part of the Earth was locked in a miserable cold. All the creatures - great and small, winged and legged, crawlers and swimmers - and all the plants - from the tallest, oldest evergreen to the most delicate moss - were miserable.

Those who dwelt in Summer grew fat and lazy - so much so that they found it difficult to run from predators. Moreover, Summer forgot to bring replenishing rains to the thirsty Earth. Endless days of scorching sunshine and heat dried up the ponds and streams. Many creatures lost their lives.

Life fared no better when starry-eyed Winter danced with Spring. As bitter winds whipped the snow high, and the long nights shrieked with an agonizing, bone-chilling cold, the animals suffered greatly. Many could not dig themselves out of their snow-covered burrows. Those who managed to do so found it impossible to travel through the deep snow. No food could be found anywhere.

Finally the Creator, who was absorbed in shaping the constellations, heard muted cries for help from beneath the snow. Concerned, she turned her ear to the beautiful blue and green planet. What she heard - or rather what she did not hear - disturbed her greatly. Aside from the cries for help and the shrieking winds, the Earth was strangely silent. Suddenly she realized that the once gurgling, flowing, singing, watery world was as dry as a bone. The Creator returned to Earth to find much misery. Looking around, she saw the lovers mindlessly lounging in the clouds.

The Creator was furious! She hurled a bolt of lightning at the lovers, bringing them to their senses. "Look, you fools! Look upon the Earth! See how your bliss has destroyed the planet? How selfish you have been, thinking only of yourselves!"

Startled awake from their dreamy worlds, the four seasons were humbled, shamed beyond words. They immediately took up the tasks they had ignored, their efforts bringing relief to the suffering plants and creatures. The Earth sprang back to life, and gradually the seasonal rhythms returned.

The Creator punished the two couples, telling them they could no longer live together in perpetual bliss. From now on Spring and Winter would be allowed to catch brief glimpses of one another, and Summer and Fall could meet only fleetingly.

On occasion, however, the two pairs of lovers continue to sneak away to visit each other. You will know when this is happening. Each Fall, after the crisp nights have painted the trees' leaves but the grass is still vibrantly green, a warm spell settles in for a few days. At that moment, Summer is trysting with Fall in the northern hemisphere, while Winter is sneaking off to visit Spring in the southern hemisphere.

Ho!

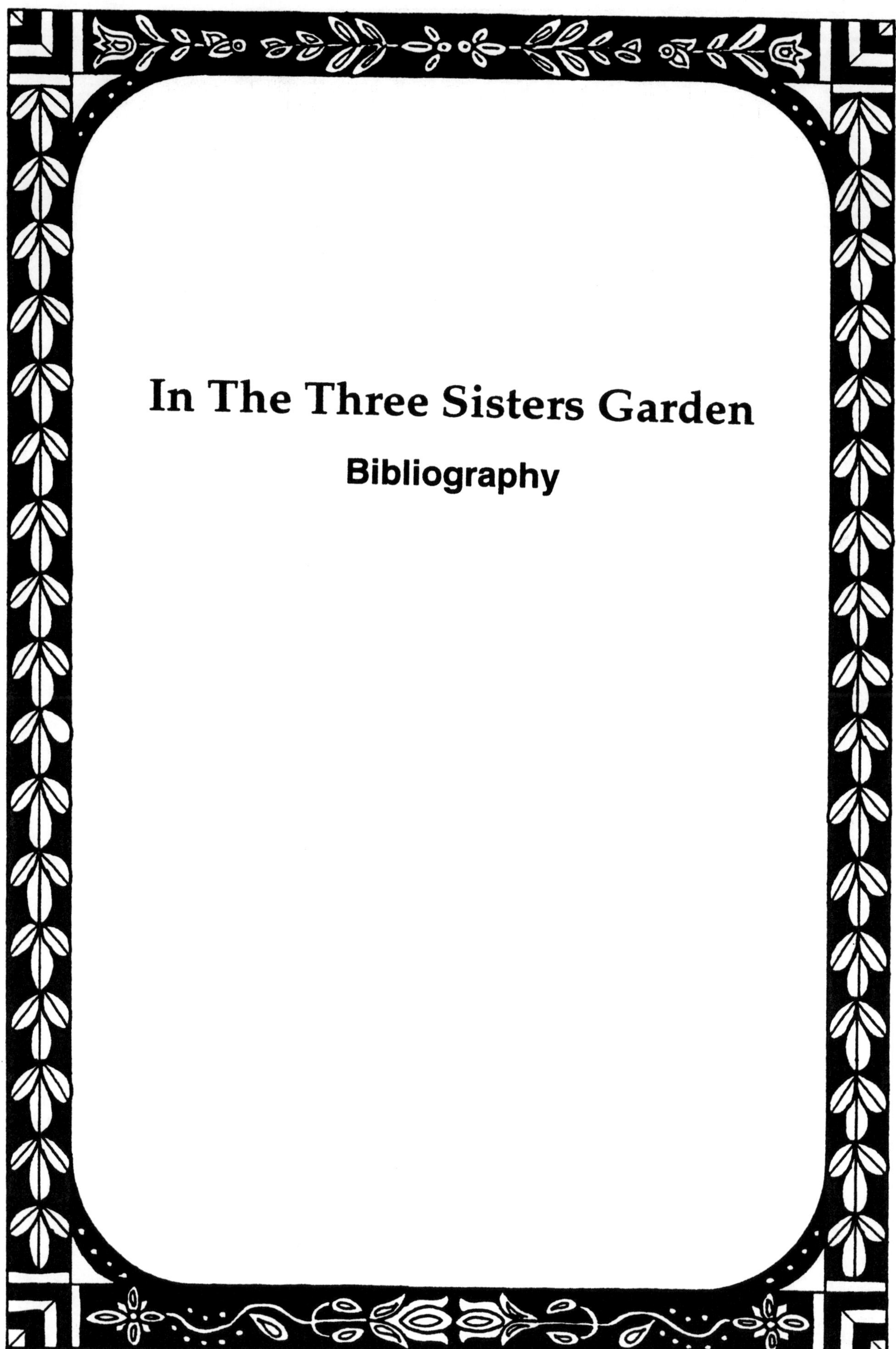

In The Three Sisters Garden

Bibliography

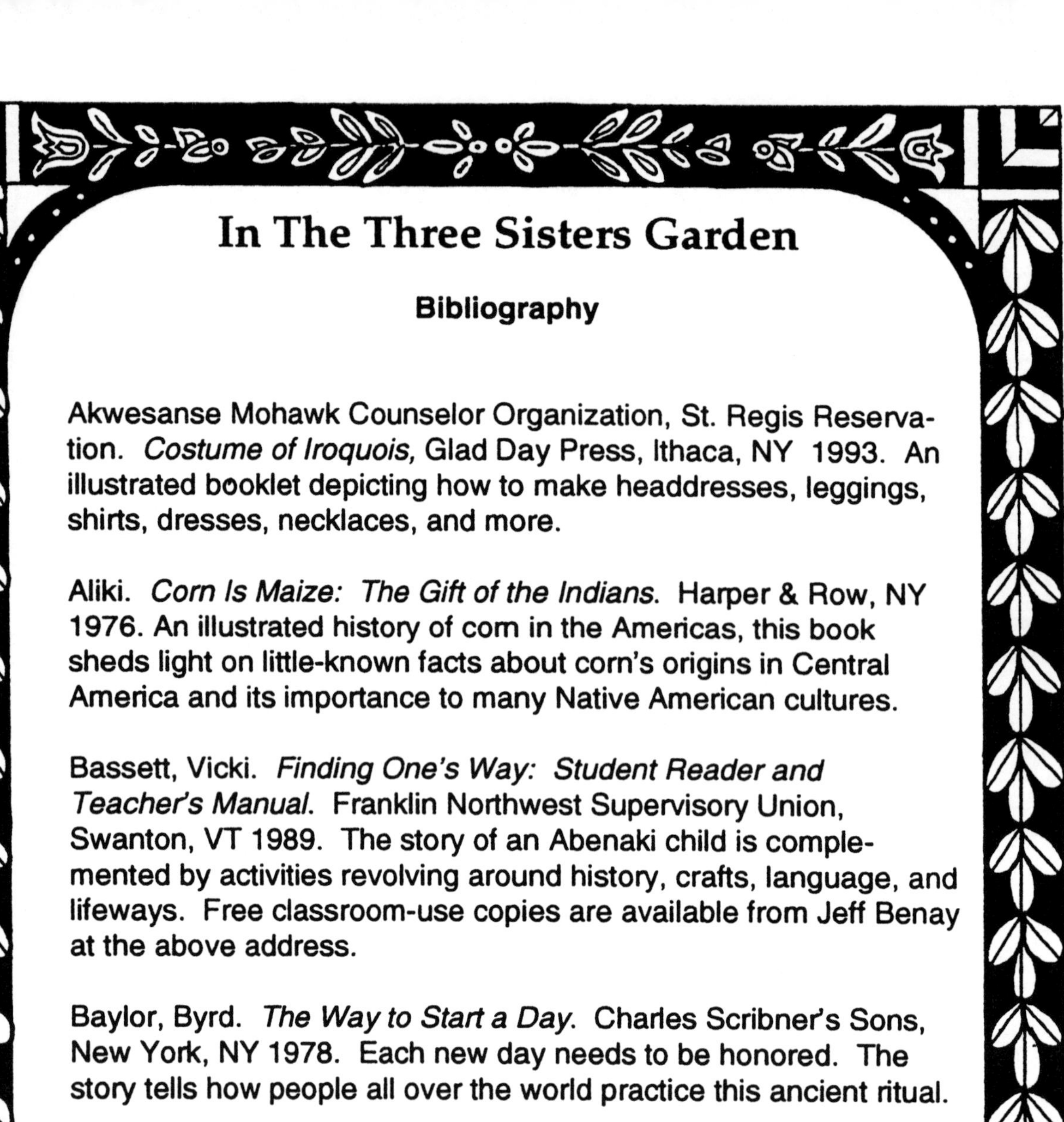

In The Three Sisters Garden

Bibliography

Akwesanse Mohawk Counselor Organization, St. Regis Reservation. *Costume of Iroquois,* Glad Day Press, Ithaca, NY 1993. An illustrated booklet depicting how to make headdresses, leggings, shirts, dresses, necklaces, and more.

Aliki. *Corn Is Maize: The Gift of the Indians.* Harper & Row, NY 1976. An illustrated history of corn in the Americas, this book sheds light on little-known facts about corn's origins in Central America and its importance to many Native American cultures.

Bassett, Vicki. *Finding One's Way: Student Reader and Teacher's Manual.* Franklin Northwest Supervisory Union, Swanton, VT 1989. The story of an Abenaki child is complemented by activities revolving around history, crafts, language, and lifeways. Free classroom-use copies are available from Jeff Benay at the above address.

Baylor, Byrd. *The Way to Start a Day.* Charles Scribner's Sons, New York, NY 1978. Each new day needs to be honored. The story tells how people all over the world practice this ancient ritual.

Bernstein, Bonnie and Leigh Blair. *Native American Crafts Workshop.* Fearon Teachers Aid Books, Belmont, CA 1982. Contains great activities and instructions for many useful crafts, foodways and ceremonial arts. These beautiful and practical ideas come from a variety of Native peoples across the Americas.

Blood, Peter and Annie Patterson. *Rise Up Singing: The Group Singing Songbook.* Sing Out Corporation, Bethlehem, PA 1992. Words, chords, and sources to 1200 songs.

Bruchac, Joseph. *The Faithful Hunter: Abenaki Stories.* Bowman Books, Greenfield Center, NY 1988. The second book by this Abenaki storyteller relates stories of the seasons, stories about family relationships and tales of the wondrous animals who walk upon the Earth with us.

Bruchac, Joseph. *The First Strawberries: A Cherokee Story.* Dial Books, NY, NY 1993

Bruchac, Joseph. *Indian Corn of the Americas: Gift to the World.* Northeast Indian Quarterly, Summer, Cornell University, Ithaca, NY 1989. This Columbus quincentenary edition is dedicated to dispelling the myths of corn in this country. It contains several articles about the importance of corn to Native cultures, including the story of "The Corn Spirit", as retold by Joseph Bruchac.

Bruchac, Joseph. *New Voices from the Longhouse: Anthology of Contemporary Iroquois Writers.* Greenfield Review Press, Greenfield, CT 1989.

Bruchac, Joseph. *The Wind Eagle and Other Abenaki Stories.* Bowman Books, Greenfield Center, NY 1988. In a collection of stories from the People of the Dawn, the Abenaki, the author relates the ancient and important teachings of Gluskabi. Through explorations, changes, and mistakes, Gluskabi learns important lessons - which the rest of the world is still discovering - about hunting, water, and wind.

Caduto, Michael. *Keepers of the Earth.* Fulcrum Publishing, Golden, CO 1988. The theme of these activities and this extensive collection of Native stories concerns learning how to be in partnership with Mother Earth. The teachings of Native peoples across the Americas help the reader to discover Earth's many wisdoms. The book includes science discoveries, which support the stories, and other teaching aids.

Calloway, Colin G. *The Abenaki.* Chelsea House Publishers, Philadelphia, PA 1989. Part of the *Indians of North America Series,* it depicts the life of the original Vermonters, the Abenaki.

Carr, Rachel. *Be A Frog, A Bird, or A Tree: Creative Yoga Exercises for Children.* Harper Books, New York, NY 1973. Black and white photographs illustrate yoga postures for children. Poems or verses guide the exercises. The exercises are designed so that children will experience, through their bodies, the ways in which they are part of nature.

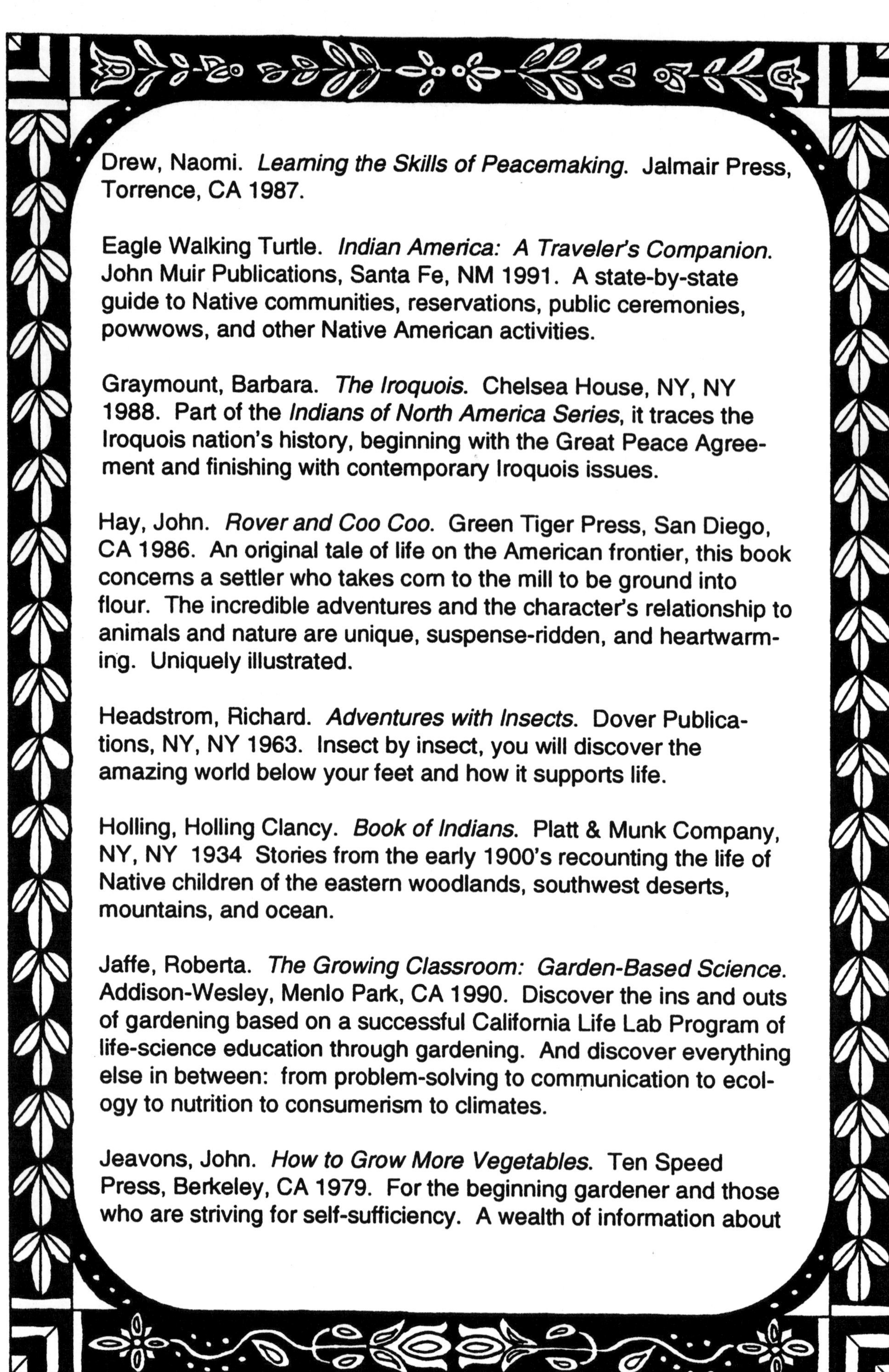

Drew, Naomi. *Learning the Skills of Peacemaking.* Jalmair Press, Torrence, CA 1987.

Eagle Walking Turtle. *Indian America: A Traveler's Companion.* John Muir Publications, Santa Fe, NM 1991. A state-by-state guide to Native communities, reservations, public ceremonies, powwows, and other Native American activities.

Graymount, Barbara. *The Iroquois.* Chelsea House, NY, NY 1988. Part of the *Indians of North America Series*, it traces the Iroquois nation's history, beginning with the Great Peace Agreement and finishing with contemporary Iroquois issues.

Hay, John. *Rover and Coo Coo.* Green Tiger Press, San Diego, CA 1986. An original tale of life on the American frontier, this book concerns a settler who takes corn to the mill to be ground into flour. The incredible adventures and the character's relationship to animals and nature are unique, suspense-ridden, and heartwarming. Uniquely illustrated.

Headstrom, Richard. *Adventures with Insects.* Dover Publications, NY, NY 1963. Insect by insect, you will discover the amazing world below your feet and how it supports life.

Holling, Holling Clancy. *Book of Indians.* Platt & Munk Company, NY, NY 1934 Stories from the early 1900's recounting the life of Native children of the eastern woodlands, southwest deserts, mountains, and ocean.

Jaffe, Roberta. *The Growing Classroom: Garden-Based Science.* Addison-Wesley, Menlo Park, CA 1990. Discover the ins and outs of gardening based on a successful California Life Lab Program of life-science education through gardening. And discover everything else in between: from problem-solving to communication to ecology to nutrition to consumerism to climates.

Jeavons, John. *How to Grow More Vegetables.* Ten Speed Press, Berkeley, CA 1979. For the beginning gardener and those who are striving for self-sufficiency. A wealth of information about companion planting in small spaces and in raised beds. Contains companion planting charts, organic insect control methods, and information about lunar planting.

Jennings, Paulla. Strawberry Thanksgiving. Modern curriculum Press, Cleveland, Ohio 1992. A Native American celebration that observes the early summer moon.

Johnson, Carol. *Might As Well Make It Love.* Noeldner Music, BMI, Grand Rapids, MI 1981. Carol Johnson's songs are not only a tremendous resource for celebrating the earth and life, but she is also available herself to give performances in schools.

Johnson, Roberta Bishop. *Whole Foods for the Whole Family.* La Leche League International, Franklin Park, IL 1987. Recipes for good nutrition, guaranteed to appeal to children's tastes, gathered from families across the country.

Kavasch, Barrie. *Native Harvests.* American Indian Archeological Institute, CT. Sources of traditional recipes and food practices of the Northeast Woodlands people.

Lame Deer, John. *Lame Deer: Seeker of Visions.* Pocketbooks, NY, NY 1989. As Lame Deer tells about his life as a Lakota Sioux in the early 1900's, the reader discovers what it meant to be a Native person at that time. His story helps to break down some of the misconceptions present day Americans have about the Native American culture.

Liestman, Vicki. *Columbus Day.* Carolrhoda Books, Minneapolis, MI 1991. This second-grade reader describes Columbus's treatment of the Native peoples. Eurocentric biases provide plenty of opportunities for discussion. It is recommended over other books addressing the topic of Columbus's visit to the New World.

Lingelbach, Jenepher. *Hands-on Nature: Information and Activities for Exploring the Environment with Children.* Vermont Institute for Natural Science, Randolph Center, VT 1989. This book contains ideas for puppet shows. It teaches ecological concepts, nature activities, science games, and has lots of background infor-

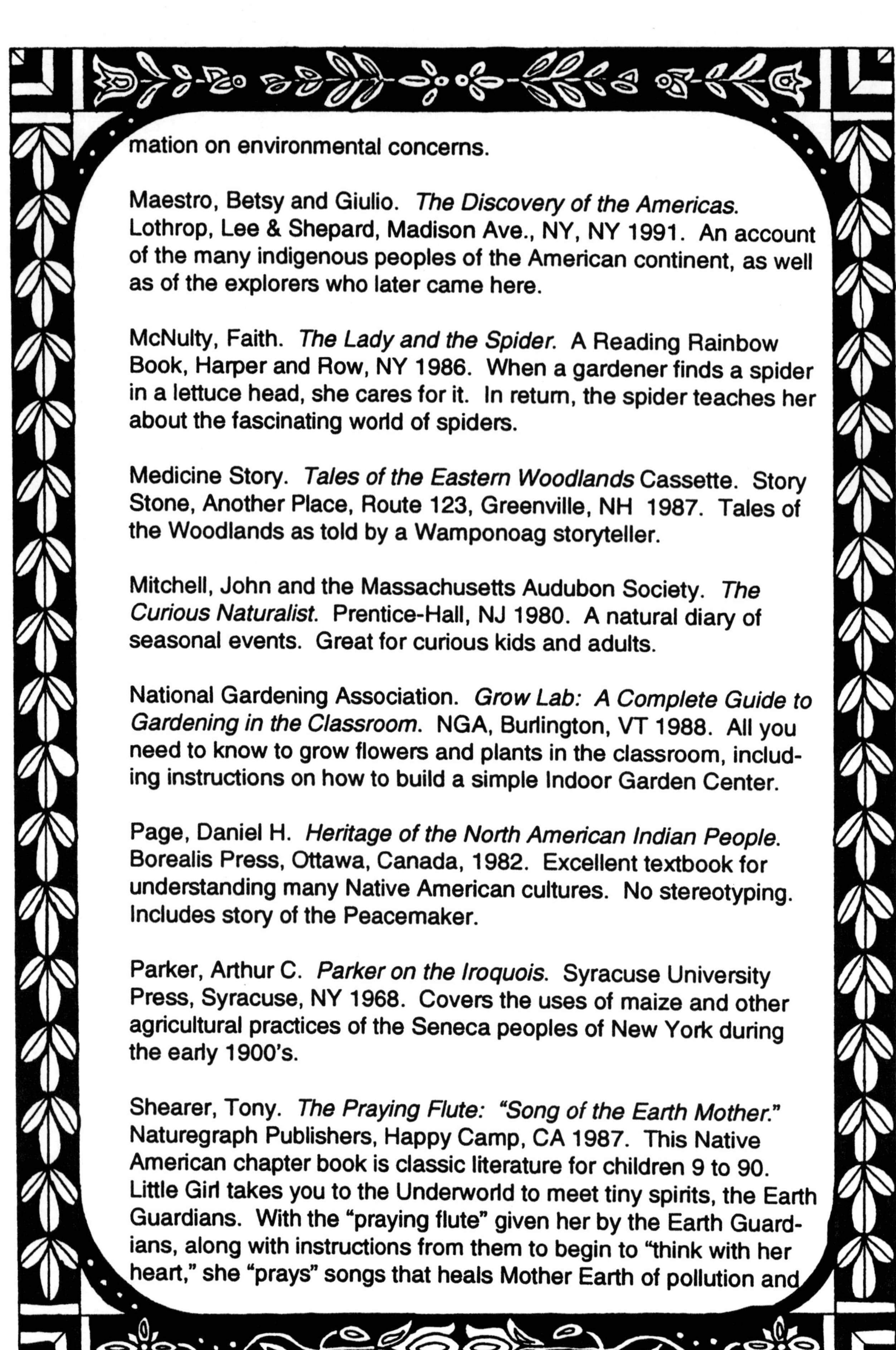

mation on environmental concerns.

Maestro, Betsy and Giulio. *The Discovery of the Americas.* Lothrop, Lee & Shepard, Madison Ave., NY, NY 1991. An account of the many indigenous peoples of the American continent, as well as of the explorers who later came here.

McNulty, Faith. *The Lady and the Spider.* A Reading Rainbow Book, Harper and Row, NY 1986. When a gardener finds a spider in a lettuce head, she cares for it. In return, the spider teaches her about the fascinating world of spiders.

Medicine Story. *Tales of the Eastern Woodlands* Cassette. Story Stone, Another Place, Route 123, Greenville, NH 1987. Tales of the Woodlands as told by a Wamponoag storyteller.

Mitchell, John and the Massachusetts Audubon Society. *The Curious Naturalist.* Prentice-Hall, NJ 1980. A natural diary of seasonal events. Great for curious kids and adults.

National Gardening Association. *Grow Lab: A Complete Guide to Gardening in the Classroom.* NGA, Burlington, VT 1988. All you need to know to grow flowers and plants in the classroom, including instructions on how to build a simple Indoor Garden Center.

Page, Daniel H. *Heritage of the North American Indian People.* Borealis Press, Ottawa, Canada, 1982. Excellent textbook for understanding many Native American cultures. No stereotyping. Includes story of the Peacemaker.

Parker, Arthur C. *Parker on the Iroquois.* Syracuse University Press, Syracuse, NY 1968. Covers the uses of maize and other agricultural practices of the Seneca peoples of New York during the early 1900's.

Shearer, Tony. *The Praying Flute: "Song of the Earth Mother."* Naturegraph Publishers, Happy Camp, CA 1987. This Native American chapter book is classic literature for children 9 to 90. Little Girl takes you to the Underworld to meet tiny spirits, the Earth Guardians. With the "praying flute" given her by the Earth Guardians, along with instructions from them to begin to "think with her heart," she "prays" songs that heals Mother Earth of pollution and

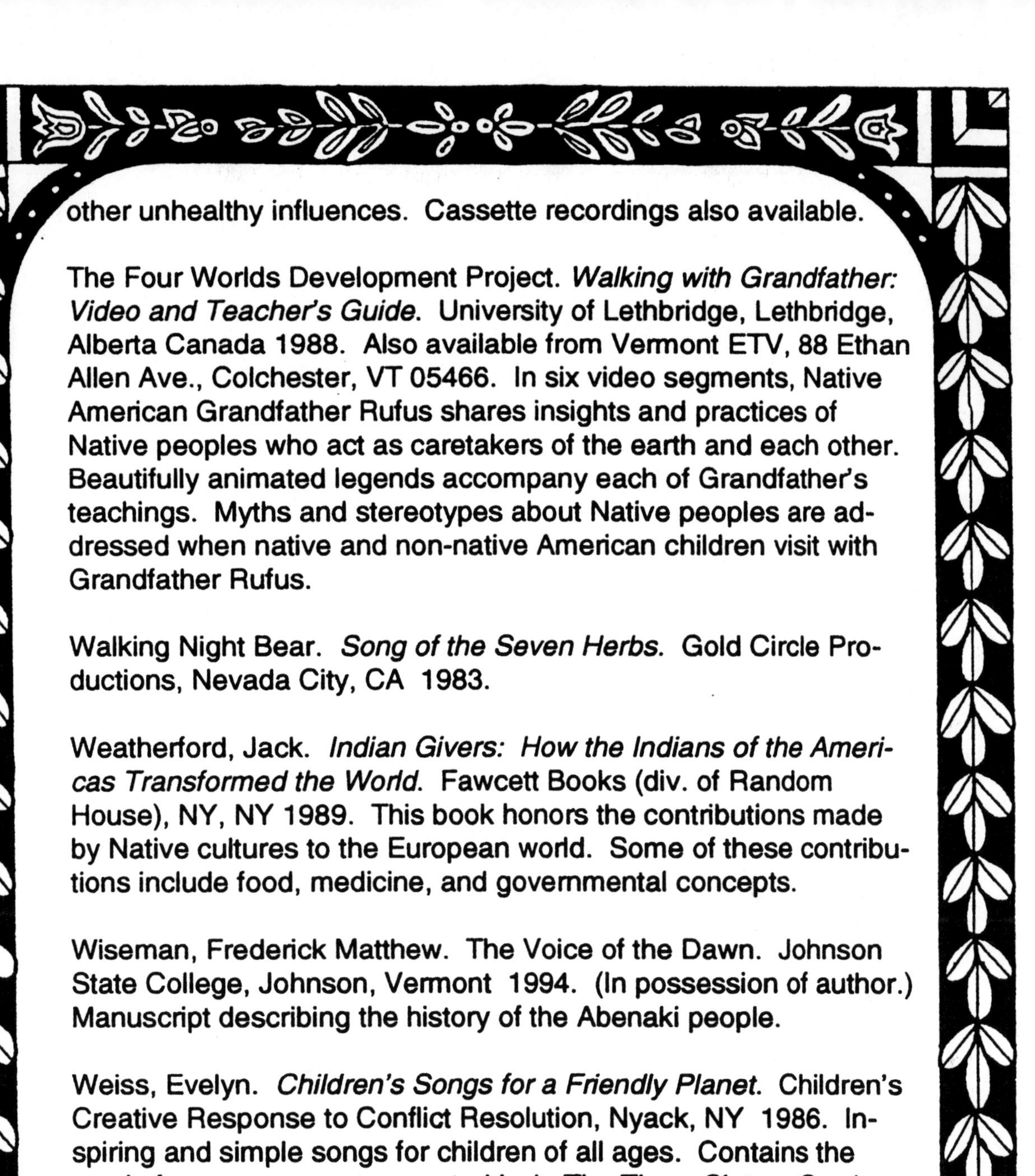

other unhealthy influences. Cassette recordings also available.

The Four Worlds Development Project. *Walking with Grandfather: Video and Teacher's Guide.* University of Lethbridge, Lethbridge, Alberta Canada 1988. Also available from Vermont ETV, 88 Ethan Allen Ave., Colchester, VT 05466. In six video segments, Native American Grandfather Rufus shares insights and practices of Native peoples who act as caretakers of the earth and each other. Beautifully animated legends accompany each of Grandfather's teachings. Myths and stereotypes about Native peoples are addressed when native and non-native American children visit with Grandfather Rufus.

Walking Night Bear. *Song of the Seven Herbs.* Gold Circle Productions, Nevada City, CA 1983.

Weatherford, Jack. *Indian Givers: How the Indians of the Americas Transformed the World.* Fawcett Books (div. of Random House), NY, NY 1989. This book honors the contributions made by Native cultures to the European world. Some of these contributions include food, medicine, and governmental concepts.

Wiseman, Frederick Matthew. The Voice of the Dawn. Johnson State College, Johnson, Vermont 1994. (In possession of author.) Manuscript describing the history of the Abenaki people.

Weiss, Evelyn. *Children's Songs for a Friendly Planet.* Children's Creative Response to Conflict Resolution, Nyack, NY 1986. Inspiring and simple songs for children of all ages. Contains the music for many songs suggested in *In The Three Sisters Garden.*

White Deer of Autumn. *Ceremony in the Circle of Life.* Raintree Publishers, Milwaukee, WI 1983. Nine-year-old Little Turtle receives a visit from the Star Spirit, who shows him the sacred healing ceremonies used to honor Mother Earth. This beautifully illustrated story represents some of the beliefs of Native peoples.

Wilbur, Keith C. *The New England Indians.* Globe Pequot Press, Chester, CT 1968. Excellent graphic reference for shelter building, gardening tools and techniques, as well as many other aspects of New England's Native cultural traditions.

In The Three Sisters Garden

Resource Guide

Michael Caduto presents "Programs for Environmental Awareness and Cultural Exchange" from the Abenaki and Iroquois traditions. Choose from a variety of programs and performances, ecology workshops, and teacher-training sessions, as well as adventures and group excursions. Write or call Michael at P.O. Box 1052, Norwich, VT 05055. (802) 649-1815.

Six Nations Museum is in Onchiota, NY, southwest of Plattsburgh near Paul Smiths College. The Fadden family, keepers of the Iroquois tradition, bring this small cabin museum alive with art and storytelling. Open Summers. Also available for $1.00 is an excellent chart that shows contributions of the American Native peoples to the world in the areas of government, language, healing, plants, scientific theory, foods, dyes, athletics, inventions, as well as more common items that we use everyday with little recognition for the Native people who developed them.

Beeswax suppliers of candlewax might be listed in your yellow pages, or ask a local orchard for information. You can also write to your local Extension Service, your State Department of Agriculture, or A.I. Root Company, P.O. Box 706, Medina, OH 44258. Beeswax for sculpting can be obtained from Hearth Song, P.O. Box B, Sebastopol, CA **94763-0601**, and from many high quality children's toy shops.

Gardening Information and Services

The U.S. Department of Agriculture Cooperative Extension Service in your area provides gardening and agricultural support, including disease and pest identification and recommendations.

Three Sisters Seed Sources

❧ Native Seed Search, 2059 N. Campbel Avenue, #325, Tucson, AZ 85719.

❧ Seeds of Change (organic seeds), 621 Old Santa Fe Trail, #10, Santa Fe, NM 87501.

❧ Ecology Action, 5798 Ridgewood Road, Willits, CA 95490 has many publications, videos, educational games, and materials about gardening, and also sells seeds.

❧ Johnny's Selected Seeds, Albion, ME 04910 sells seeds adapted for northern climates, and a few heirloom varieties.

❧ Shepherd Seeds, 6116 Highway 9, Felton, CA 95018 sells speciality seeds, including some miniature container varieties for the Indoor Garden, but not necessarily Three Sisters varieties.

Music and Songs for Children

❧ *Rise up Singing,* Sing Out Corporation, PO Box 5253, Bethlehem, PA 18015 (215) 865-5366

❧ *Sing Through the Seasons*, Plough Publishing House, RD 2, Box 446, Farmington, PA, 15437-9506 (412) 329-1100

❧ *Children's Songs for a Friendly Planet,* Children's Creative Response to Conflict Resolution, Riverside Church, 490 Riverside Dr., NYC, NY 10027

❧ *Magical Earth, Linking Up: Music for the Peaceable Classroom* and other recordings by Sarah Pirtle, Discovery Center, 63 Main Street, Shelburne Falls, MA 01370.

Common Roots Community Resource Guide
Who's Who in Your Neighborhood

Local farmers, gardeners, community gardens:

Common Roots community volunteers (parents and elders):

Local Native American community, center or resource people:

Local food shelf or soup kitchen:

Museums of natural history or Native heritage:

Audubon Centers and other environmental centers:

Local Historical Society:

Index

Community Service

Creative Arts

Gardening

Language Arts

Math

Nutrition and Health

Science and Ecology

Social Studies

The Common Roots Program

Education So Real You Can See It Growing.

The Food Works *Common Roots* program helps parents, teachers, and other educators develop an integrated curriculum that not only covers practical skills in science, social studies, nutrition, math, writing, and the arts, but also prepares children to confront social and environmental problems in their own communities.

Food Works is an educational organization founded in 1987 to help integrate the themes of food, ecology, and community into elementary school education.

- Food Works staff are available for consulting sessions and workshops with teachers, parents and community groups to help integrate the *Common Roots* program.
- Food Works staff can visit your group or classroom and present hands-on activities, slideshows, videos, or lectures on themes of food security, ecology, and community service learning.
- Food Works has developed a variety of curriculum resource materials and workshops for teachers, parents, and community members to use in the classroom. Our K-6 *Common Roots Guidebooks* are an exciting collection of hands-on, hearts-on environmental and historical activities for young learners. Now available are:

"The Wonderful World of Wigglers"
"Exploring the Forest with Grandforest Tree"
"Exploring the Secrets of the Meadow-Thicket"
"In The Three Sisters Garden"

For complete information regarding the *Common Roots* program, write or call:

FOOD WORKS
64 Main Street
Montpelier, Vermont 05602
802-223-1515

To order additional *Common Roots Guidebooks*, call Kendall/Hunt Publishing Company Customer Service at 1-800-228-0810.